George Garrett

Ten Years On The Parish

George Garrett
Ten Years On The Parish

Edited by

Mike Morris, Tony Wailey and Andrew Davies

with a Foreword by

Frank Cottrell-Boyce

Liverpool University Press

First published 2017 by
Liverpool University Press
4 Cambridge Street
Liverpool
L69 7ZU

British Library Cataloguing-in-Publication data
A British Library CIP record is available

ISBN 9781786940568 hardback
ISBN 9781786940759 paperback

Typeset by Carnegie Book Production, Lancaster
Printed and bound by CPI Group (UK) Ltd, Croydon CR0 4YY

Contents

List of Illustrations

Acknowledgements

The acknowledgements below are for those who have supported The George Garrett Archive Project since it was launched by Writing on the Wall in 2012, and to those who have played a key role in bringing this book to publication. We have received support from so many people that unfortunately there isn't the space to name everyone here. But to all those who have taken part in our education courses, produced and performed in George's plays, created our Garrett installation and short film, and the many other activities we have had the pleasure to be a part of, we thank you all.

Thanks to: The George Garrett Family, for their role in preserving George's archive, their generosity in sharing it and allowing full access, and for their ongoing support and permission to publish *Ten Years On The Parish* and George's letters. Texas University's Harry Ransom Centre for permission to publish the letters of John Lehmann. The invaluable support of Heritage Lottery, whose generous funding allowed us to launch the archive project. To Madeline Heneghan and the staff and Trustees of Writing on the Wall for their ongoing support and encouragement. For support in researching, preserving and collating George's archive: Liverpool John Moores University – particularly Val Stevenson, Emily Parson, Anne Foulkes and her team – and Stuart Borthwick; Liverpool Libraries, particularly David Stoker, Helena Smart and Sharon Oldale; Professor John Lucas and Professor Cliff Neal from Nottingham Trent University; Joseph Pridmore and Deryn Rees-Jones; The Unity Theatre; The Bluecoat, particularly Artistic Director Bryan Briggs; Wes Storey for design.

We would also like to acknowledge the important work of the late Michael Murphy who brought together for the first time in one publication George Garrett's short stories in *The Collected George Garrett*, Trent Editions (1999).

Special Thanks to 'The Garretteers' – The George Garrett Archive Project Volunteers who have worked tirelessly since 2013 to preserve George's archive and give his life and work the acknowledgement it deserves: Sean Garrett, Frank Boyce, Joan Boyce, Hannah Holmes, Ray Quarless, Rochelle Ellis, Anne McDermott, Sue Smith, Will Reid and Sheila McGowan.

You can find out further information and access George Garrett's archive at www.georgegarrettarchive.co.uk.

For information about Writing on the Wall, who launched the archive project visit: www.writingonthewall.org.uk

The George Garrett Archive is available to view and research at Liverpool Records Office, Liverpool Central Library, William Brown Street, L3 8EW.

Foreword

by Frank Cottrell-Boyce

Why should you read this book?

I first read George Garrett because my dad told me to.

My dad's dad was a stoker – just as Garrett had been. He died at sea when my father was in his teens, so when my dad read *The 'Maurie'* – Garrett's account of working in the engine room of that great Scouse ship the *Mauretania* – he was listening for some echo of his lost father's voice, hoping to glimpse the sweat and fire of his engine room. Garrett's writing allowed him to wander again the streets of 'Sailortown' – the patchwork of hectic dockside streets between Scotland Road and the docks where he had grown up. A vanished realm, comfortingly parochial but thrillingly connected to the rest of the world. I was born there and can just about remember the brilliant, improbable fauna of the tenement balconies – the monkeys and parrots brought back by sailors from far horizons – as presents for their wives, who barely ever left their native parishes.

To hear and feel the world as it was, is a decent reason to read a book.

It's why my dad read this book.

But it's not why you should read it.

It wasn't easy being a Garrett fan. The man had more pseudonyms than the Irish writer Brian O'Nolan / Flann O'Brien / Myles na gCopaleen. Until Michael Murphy brought out the Collected Writings in 1999, you had to be a bit of a detective. Dad chased down leads and found fragile scraps in the local history archive. I remember how thrilled he was when he spotted the famous mention of Garrett in *The Road to Wigan Pier*, which came with the useful information that Garrett had written under the name of Matt Low (as in Matelot – sailor). He gave a talk at the Liverpool Writing on the Wall festival in which he shared his enthusiasm and discoveries. Garrett's family came to listen and that was one of the steps on the road that lead to the publication of this book. He later helped catalogue the archive of material as part of the George Garrett Archive Project. But for the enthusiasm of his readers, Garrett's writings would be lost. The writing of working class writers is easy to lose – it's written on leaflets, in dissident newspapers, under pseudonyms and under pressure. Garrett's letters to Lehmann give us a humbling glimpse of just how much it cost him to write, to write well – to spend time getting the right word, cutting the wrong one – while enduring such poverty. In his ten years on the parish he managed to find work for just nine months. His desperation for money – and for time – quivers through every sentence. But so does his hunger for knowledge. He read voraciously and studied his way out of the siege that poverty laid to his room. He was one of the great working class autodidacts – like his fellow Scouser James Hanley and like Aneurin Bevan. All three men were born within one year of each other. Working class autodidacts are powerful because they lay claim to all culture and knowledge but they have no stake in the system. They swagger into activism like the sailors with their monkeys and parrots, with their kit bags stuffed with poetry and symphonies and political theory. Garrett laid claim to Eugene O'Neill and to Shelley as well as to Marx and to Paine. We read *The Road to Wigan Pier* to see how poverty looked to a sympathetic, intelligent, compassionate outsider. We read Garrett to find out how poverty felt. From the inside.

But that's not why you should read this book.

Garrett was writing at a time when the international economy was failing. When the official unions and the Labour Party had fallen into disarray following the failure of the general strike. He lived in a world of unemployment and casual employment. The monkeys and parrots and kitbags of 'Sailortown' may have vanished but the economics that laid siege to its people are well and truly back.

You should read Garrett because he has something to say about the times we live in now. He has lessons to teach us. Right from the very first page. The epigraph of *Ten Years On The Parish* comes from George Bernanos' masterpiece *The Diary of A Country Priest*. We live in an age when the internet allows us to pre-edit our news sources, when social media allows us – and our political parties – to create echo-chambers where we never encounter disagreement. But here Garrett dedicates his most personal work with a quotation from a French monarchist who (for a while at least) supported Franco. He read beyond himself. He challenged his own opinions. His insights were forged in the fire of debate and struggle.

This is that dedication:

> To the voice of the working woman ... which holds out
> against all the miseries of the world

Garrett saw that the fight for justice must not confine itself to demands for better pay and conditions for working men. It had to seek justice for all – male and female, black and white. His play *Two Tides* seems to be about two merchant seamen but the voices that stay with you are those of the women they leave behind – Mrs Ferry and Rose Brindon. In 1921 at a rally in Canning Square, he upbraided a fellow speaker for his racism.

When my father first encouraged me to read Garrett, it was out of historical interest and class and civic pride. But the times have changed. My children live in an age in which mainstream politicians use racism and misogyny casually as part of their campaigns, in which the casualisation of labour has been turbo-charged and rebranded as zero hours or the gig economy. Above all they live in an age in which the truth seems to have become negotiable. Even Orwell never imagined the slippery, bewildering nature of phrases like 'fake news' and 'alternative facts'. Garrett was all about truth. He worked hard to discover truth. He worked harder to express it. And most of all, he lived it.

And that's why you should read this book.

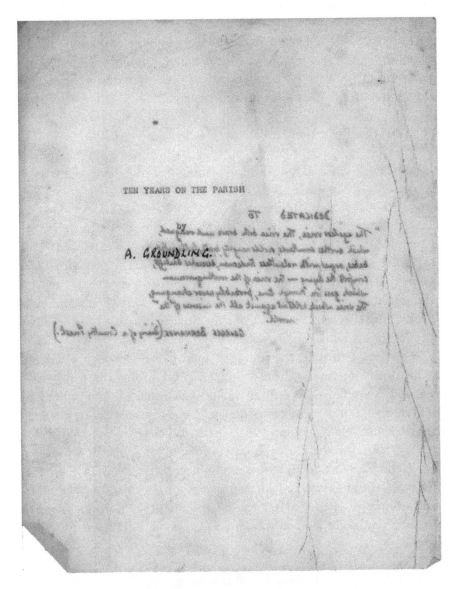

Original front cover of *Ten Years On The Parish*

Introduction

to *Ten Years On The Parish*

George Garrett (1896–1966), merchant seaman, writer, playwright and founder member of Liverpool's Unity Theatre, was a radical activist and a 'militant advocate of tolerance' who travelled the world and wrote a series of short stories, plays, documentary reports and reportage about unemployment, poverty and struggle in the 1920s and '30s. Garrett occupies a unique and significant position as the central point of a compass that links Liverpool to an international literary, cultural, social, political, theatrical and sea-going history.

Ten Years On The Parish, Garrett's autobiographical work covering the period 1926 to 1936 and written between 1936 and 1938, is published here for the first time complete. It is one of the most remarkable documentary pieces of writing written by a working-class writer, detailing poverty, unemployment and methods of resistance in Liverpool and the UK. That it was never published in Garrett's lifetime is a tragedy, the reasons for which are explored in detail later in this introduction and documented in the letters between Garrett and his editor, the poet and publisher, John Lehmann. It is a tragedy as its publication in the 1930s would no doubt have brought Garrett the respect and profile amongst his peers and the literary establishment he both craved and deserved, and one that prevented a generation from reading a milestone document that bore witness to their harsh lives and offered possibilities for resistance. We are proud (now) to be able to rectify this omission, while pointing out that *Ten Years On The Parish* represents just one aspect of Garrett's varied creative output – plays, short stories, reportage, critical essays, and more – which here we can only touch upon.

This introduction will place *Ten Years On The Parish* in the context of the times and the places Garrett lived and wrote within, but it will also explore the aspects of Garrett's life which are not detailed in the manuscript for a variety of reasons, including the desire from publishers in the 1930s to have working class writers only detail their experiences of unemployment, but which nevertheless had a major influence on him and the events he describes. This particularly means examining the time he spent in America in the 1920s. As we will see, *Ten Years On The Parish* is as interesting for what is left out of the narrative as it is for what is included. This applies most of all to the influence of American Trades Unionism through the Industrial Workers of the World (IWW), better known as the 'Wobblies', the impact of American theatre and culture upon his life and work, and how that is reflected in his radical social and political outlook and his engagement with the labour and trades union movement in Liverpool as a maritime city.

*

George Garrett was born in 1896 in Seacombe, on the opposite banks of the River Mersey to Liverpool. His Belfast-born father was a member of the Protestant Orange Lodge, his Liverpool-born mother a staunch Catholic. When Garrett was just three months old his father, most likely through drinking, lost his confectioner's business, and the family's reduced circumstances forced a move to the Park Lane area of Liverpool, within walking distance of the city's southern docks. Although poor, Garrett's family was never as badly off as those around them, and George in later life recounted tales of the children he mixed with who wore the cast-off clothes of deceased relatives and hand-me-down 'dees clothes', distributed to the poor by the local police charity. According to his son John, they reminded George of a 'children's theatre group', although they 'didn't strut and sparkle in the way that members of a theatre group would, they slunk around ... totally ashamed'. The young George was often the 'bewildered and frightened witness' to violent arguments between his parents, most often over what faith George was to be brought up in. His mother won out, and George attended St Vincent's Catholic Primary School in Norfolk Street. It was an unhappy time for George who left school at an early age and slept in stables to escape his fraught home life. He worked by day as a coal boy on the docks before he stowed away in 1913 at the age of 17, on a tramp steamer bound for Argentina.

From here on Garrett's life reads like a *Boy's Own* adventure story: he tramped around Argentina for a year working on farms and living off the land; returned to sign on as a stoker on ships at the outbreak of the First World War where he had early experience of American shipping; was torpedoed twice during the war, and was interned but escaped after one of these sinkings; married his sweetheart Grace on return from war; spent a year trying to make a life in America from 1920 to 1921; returned to Liverpool to lead the major unemployed demonstrations which closed down the city centre and culminated in police-initiated riots and his arrest in 1921; led the Liverpool contingent of the 1922 Hunger March to London; sailed again to America in 1923 where he lived for three years, writing and studying; was in touch with Eugene O'Neill's Provincetown Playhouse Theatre, roomed with future Hollywood actors, worked on the side as an 'illegal alien' in illicit breweries during prohibition and as a janitor in a police station; and witnessed the aftermath of the shooting of the boxer 'Battling Siki'.

Under threat of deportation he returned to Liverpool in 1926 as the US and the world stumbled towards the Great Crash of 1929, to endure a lengthy bout of unemployment broken by little more than five months' work in ten years. In the 1920s he wrote much reportage and three complete plays, and in the 1930s a series of highly regarded short stories which were published in literary magazines of the day (*Left Review*, *New Writing* and the *Adelphi*) alongside household names including W.H. Auden, Auberon Waugh, D.H. Lawrence, Christopher Isherwood and Stephen Spender.

In 1936 he guided George Orwell around Liverpool as part of Orwell's research for his seminal book on poverty in the UK, *The Road To Wigan Pier*. Also in 1936, while writing *Ten Years On The Parish*, he helped to found Merseyside Left Theatre in response to the outbreak of The Spanish Civil War. During this time, he wrote, acted, and toured the regions around Liverpool performing one-man shows of extracts from the work of Eugene O'Neill to capacity audiences. In 1939, following the defeat of the Spanish working class, the rise of Franco and the outbreak of the Second World War, Garrett returned to sea for a short time, but served out the rest of the war as a watchman on the Bootle docks, which at the time suffered from some of the worst bombing raids of the war, designed to cripple Liverpool's role as a key supply port. Following the war, he continued to write and perform, found a steady job on a local tanker on the

River Mersey and Manchester Ship Canal, and continued his lifelong agitation for the reform of the Seamen's Union.

George and Grace's marriage survived all their travails, and between them they brought up seven sons. Garrett's life encompassed the greatest range of political and social upheaval within which he constantly strove to find his own creative voice and use it to report on and dramatise the struggles of seamen and working class people in general. He can now be recognised as one of the most significant working class writers of his generation. To understand the scale of his achievements, it is worth placing his life in the context of Liverpool, which at the time, was one of the most important cities in the British Empire.

*

During its heyday as an Empire Port of a maritime state, Liverpool registered 44 per cent of world shipping. In 1911 alone, 177,000 seamen of all nationalities sailed out of the port. At the same time, most port employment was casual and there were constant tensions between ship owners, employers and dockers and seamen. It is no surprise then that George's 'christening' into radical politics and protest came when he attended a mass demonstration on Lime Street outside Liverpool's St George's Hall – the monumental and spectacular heart of the city – in 1911. The demonstration was called after a series of strikes by seamen, dockers and transport workers had erupted into the 1911 city-wide general strike. The Home Secretary Winston Churchill likened it to revolution, sent in police reinforcements and ordered gun boats into the River Mersey. On 13 August, which became known as 'Bloody Sunday', the police used a minor incident to charge the ranks of up to 100,000 demonstrators massed outside St George's Hall. Caught up in the melee, Garrett, a bystander on his 15th birthday, suffered a broken nose and the loss of several teeth when he was smashed in the face by a police baton.

In incidents such as this from his own life, we find many of the themes George returned to throughout his time as an activist, advocate and writer; the injustices of the state and petty authority; poverty and its effect upon the working class; the powerlessness of the poor and the defenceless, and, though sometimes violent, the need for both collective and individual action to strike back and win some sort of victory or respect. This is often accompanied by wry humour and a knowing wink towards the reader.

This can be seen in Garrett's role in the 'bully beef burial' on the 1922 Hunger March, and in his writings, such as the mocking tone of the ending of his short story, 'Swords into Ploughshares', when the Captain, out-smarted and beaten by the old sailor, Mangor, 'knew the bitter taste of defeat'.[1] It is a humour which redeems his work; no matter how crushing the circumstances there was always a joke to be had, often at his own expense; the angry, biting humour that charac-terised the system of casual labour employed in a maritime city like Liverpool.

From a young age Garrett was 'familiar with the docks and the outsides of ships';[2] he developed a fascination with the sea, and those who lived on and alongside its tempestuous highways. In *Ten Years On The Parish* he recounts how 'the seamen coming off the ships filled him with wonder as they filed down gangways holding up parrots, or monkeys, or canaries, or any souvenirs that showed a trace of a far-off country'. He 'secretly yearned to be one of them' and was 'eager to go to any part of the world.' It's no surprise then, that after he escaped Liverpool at the age of 17, stowing away and heading for Argentina, seagoing became central to George's life. Here he learned everything about comradeship, whether as a galley boy or as a member of the crew 'down below' amidst the fearsome toil of the stokers. The sea opened up his horizons, shaped his internationalism and encouraged him to jump ship in the great ports of Latin America and New York, just as it enabled him to return home, and never left him through all his bouts of unemployment in the 1920s and 1930s. The sea, and the many ports he visited, also had a profound effect on his world view. He was cosmopolitan and sympathetic to the plight and struggles of workers across the world. He maintained this outlook, even in the cramped conditions of his slum housing or warren-like tenement, which became his 'intense locale'.

It is this, the sea, Garrett's travels, particularly his relationship to New York and the American trades union movement, and the status of his hometown as a port city in a maritime empire, which dominated his life, even throughout the long years of unemployment. It informs all his work, be it drama, prose or reportage. It marks him out as unique among working class writers of his generation. In this, it is perhaps useful to read Garrett's life alongside the work of Peter Linebaugh and Marcus Rediker on the Atlantic 'world' in the seventeenth century has placed working class and radical lives at the centre of the political, economic and social struggles of the time.[3] Rather than seeing the oceans as an empty space devoid of social struggle, they argue that the lives of sailors, dockworkers, slaves, passengers, convicts and many others who experienced life at sea tell us important stories about how social struggle and radical practices were ever present. Their vision of a 'Red' Atlantic, alongside the 'Black Atlantic' of Paul Gilroy,[4] exposes the working class, radical histories which challenge the taken for granted stories of exploration and conquest which dominate our narratives of this era. These visions of an Atlantic world, whether 'black' or 'red' are also crucial in taking our perspectives beyond local or national contexts.

Read this way, the ability of sailors to move across geographical space creates an internationalist, cosmopolitan outlook, or at least, has the potential to do so. Reading Garrett's 'Atlantic' as a continuation of this trajectory involves inserting maritime labour as hugely important in keeping the empire functioning. Maritime labour was the 'Muscles of Empire', as Frank Broeze[5] terms it, but the working class solidarities that emerged from the hard labour of working on a steamship – which was no less hard than a sailing ship, but with significantly different labour and social relations aboard ship – were key to understanding Garrett's world view.

At the same time, the mobility offered by life at sea meant that Garrett embodies what the geographer Doreen Massey has termed a 'global sense of place'.[6] Travelling aboard ship meant that Garrett could recognise the various similarities that existed in working class lives in Liverpool, New York, Buenos Aires or any other Atlantic port city. He recognised that global processes had significant effects upon 'local' areas, but likewise, 'local' places have significant connections to far-flung places. To Massey, and, we suspect, to Garrett, the question then was not how local and global are distinct and separate spaces, but rather, how the specific context of a place and its role in a larger global system (in Garrett's case, the British Empire) shape society. Crucially, recognising the interconnections between local and global, and the inequalities produced through imperialism and unfettered capitalism, also opens up space to challenge and resist these practices, such as the imposition of casual labour on the dockside which was suited to the needs of the employers but was sometimes adapted and moulded by the dock workers to suit themselves.

For Garrett, this resistance was always political, but always embedded within the distinct social milieu he experienced daily. In his plays Garrett's intense settings – often the living room of a household – are connected to wider issues: the docks, maritime labour practices, wartime challenges to traditional gender roles and more. This sense of worldliness was not something that was easy to live with, especially during the long years Garrett spent out of work in Liverpool in the '30s, caught as he was between this constant paradox, between the 'far horizon' of the Atlantic and the 'intense locale' of Park Lane. Garrett's experiences away from Liverpool, particularly in New York, left their imprint upon him, even on a Thursday afternoon in a grimy 'Parish' benefits office in the Dingle discussing the changes in New York city with a Parish commissioner, or while singing 'Wobbly' songs with other Syndicalists on the Hunger March,[7] its influence stayed with him throughout his life.

This whole period of Garrett's life abroad is largely left out of *Ten Years On The Parish*. Whether this is as a result of Garrett taking his experiences for granted, or as a result of advice he received from his editor, John Lehmann, is unclear. However, to appreciate the full influence of life overseas (particularly that of New York) we must shift our focus away from Liverpool and move across the Atlantic to New York and beyond. This is an important retrospective act for a modern-day editor, as without it, a reader coming to *Ten Years...* without any prior knowledge of Garrett would be left largely unaware of the range and scope of activities he was involved in, and the huge impact it would have on his politics and his writing.

*

In *Ten Years On The Parish* Garrett's writing about his experiences of stowing away and tramping around Argentina, being torpedoed twice during the First World War, being taken prisoner of war and escaping, and living in America between 1920 and 1921, and 1923 and 1926, takes up little more than four pages of the original manuscript. Garrett first experienced America when he sailed there as a stoker during the First World War. At that time the pay on American merchant ships was almost double that of his pay on British ships, and the living accommodation and overall conditions aboard were far superior. Garrett was quickly disillusioned after the First World War, when he returned to Liverpool to find 'houses were scarce in the slums', 'rents excessive' and 'scrimmages at the hiring stands' where men's 'fists were at it' in the competition to gain a day's work.[8] Conditions on the ships were no different, and although 'size and strength pushed me to the front occasionally, and I made a few voyages on different tramps', he found 'on each arrival home getting a job became more difficult'. When their first baby arrived, with the midwife taking the whole of the thirty shillings' maternity money, Garrett and Grace's 'nerves were continually on edge' and they 'slated each other for the plight they were in'; Garrett came to the conclusion that at the age of 24 he was on the scrap-heap. Then, in 1920 he heard from friends in New York of a boom in American shipping. He opted for a 'Pier Head Jump', 'bluffed his way' on to an 'Atlantic two-funneller' and 'joined the ship as I stood, practically in rags'. Along with all the other men in the ship's forecastle, he planned to jump ship in New York and never return to England.

In the early 1920s American society was going through vast changes, personified best in the melting pot of the people, culture, political and social ideas of New York. As historian Howard Zinn notes, 'There was some truth to the standard picture of the twenties as a time of prosperity and fun – The Jazz Age, The Roaring Twenties',[9] and wages for most rose, allowing some families to buy the new mass produced goods emerging from factories. But, as Zinn also pointed out, millions lived below the poverty line and in cities across America epic battles were being fought by workers to increase pay and conditions, reduce hours, and take some share in the prosperity they had fought for in the war.

When Garrett first entered New York harbour in 1917 as a stoker aboard the *Franconia* he signed the 'aliens' (crew list) register, not as an Englishman, but Irish. This was not altogether surprising. Although born on Merseyside both his parents had Irish heritage and he was brought up in a heavily Irish neighbourhood in the middle of Liverpool's 'Sailortown'. The firemen he worked with came mostly from the North End of the city and consistently returned an Irish nationalist member of Parliament until the mid-1950s. From his notebooks, and one poem in particular, *Blanco Jack (An Epic of Easter Week 1916)*, it is clear, no doubt partly due to his mother's influence, that his sympathies were with the republican Irish. It could also be argued, with the intention of jumping ship, that he was making his first attempts to cover his identity.

That Garrett was already familiar with America is shown by the many wage-slips in his archive documenting the numerous ports he visited between 1914 and 1918, including Galveston, Houston, New Orleans and Baltimore. That Garrett had already embraced aspects of American culture can be seen in his photograph on his US visa document dated June 1918, wearing the New York fashion of the day, a 'bleacher's' shirt topped by an American-style flat cap.

The scale of the New York waterfront eclipsed even that of Liverpool, with 300,000 seamen, longshoremen, traders, shipyard workers, freight handlers, and customs men employed in the handling of waterborne commerce along its 27 miles of docks and four major rivers. Garrett soon found work on American ships, where 'wages were double those of the English ships', and he could send money home to Grace and buy himself 'a new suit of clothes'. 'Britishers were everywhere', he noted, working in all industries ashore and on the ships, signifying rising employment and wages that was to continue until the late 1920s. But his experience revealed the flip-side of F. Scott Fitzgerald's 'Jazz Age'. Not for Garrett the endless parties and pointless conversations, but rather the daily struggle to work and keep on working, while avoiding the watchful eye of the Palmer immigration raids, which in 1919 alone had led to 9000 people suspected of having radical views and affiliations being arrested and held without trial, with 500 radicals being deported to Russia.

Although Garrett experienced syndicalist ideas in Liverpool as far back as the 1911 Transport Workers' Strike, and would have come across them while at sea during the war, it was in New York that he encountered close up the radical 'One Big Union' of the Industrial Workers of the World (IWW), more commonly called 'the Wobblies'. The IWW was founded in Chicago in 1905 and led many strikes, some of immense proportions, organising the unorganised, the travellers, the unskilled and the hoboes, who didn't fit in to the craft-based unions but nonetheless were the backbone of the mills and iron towns where they often lived and worked in appalling conditions. The IWW was also important in organising the challenging of segregation and promoting inclusive notions of labour and social struggle, which worked across labour, national, class and racial divisions, as David Featherstone[10] has shown in his discussions of the formation of forms of maritime black and internationalist solidarities in this period. Following the war, the IWW came under enormous pressure during the 'Red Scares' of 1919. Their leaders were hunted down, imprisoned, executed and lynched, their members blacklisted, and even, as was the case in 32 states, victimised with laws passed making the very membership of the IWW or any other syndicalist organisations a criminal offence. As a result, in 1920 the IWW was already a shadow of its former self, and was in fact in long-term decline. However, it still had an active base of loyal supporters, and Garrett immediately joined, to become a life-long member, and, when the IWW was no more, remained a life-long supporter of Syndicalism.

In the 1920s an IWW branch was established in Liverpool by Garrett's friend and future Liverpool Labour leader, Jack Braddock, and his brother, Wilf. Bob Edwards MP, a veteran of the International Brigades who fought in the Spanish Civil War, confirmed Garrett's links to the IWW in America and his role in it in Liverpool, when he wrote in a letter sent in 1984 in reply to a query by Unity Theatre founder Jerry Dawson, who at that time was gathering some of Garrett's work for publication:

> When I was quite young I served for a short time as minutes secretary to an abortive branch of the IWW formed by George Garrett and he was the secretary. I was pleased to note that you draw attention to the fact that he was in constant touch with the world organisation with officers in America. He knew some of the great martyrs of the IWW, Jim Hill and George Everett, both of whom were murdered by the American legal system and mob rule.[11]

It was a brave move of Garrett's to have allied himself with the Wobblies, particularly considering the brutality of the attacks upon the IWW in America at that time. This connection to the American labour movement, and Garrett's active involvement and bravery is again confirmed, albeit second hand, through the writing of Millie Toole, the Salford based biographer of Liverpool Labour MP Bessie Braddock. Millie Toole was a friend of Garrett who typed up a number of his manuscripts and had long conversations with him, in person and by post, about the Liverpool and American Labour movement, the Communist Party in Byrom Street and about Bessie Braddock and her mother, the union activist Ma Bamber, who was also a great friend of Garrett. Toole's biography of Bessie Braddock carries a dedication to 'George Garrett, who told me the story', but on a much more intriguing note she writes, 'George Garrett breaking the strike-breakers in the seamen's section of the IWW in America needs a book to himself'. Although that book was never written by Garrett, or Millie Toole, it nevertheless supplies firm evidence that Garrett was actively involved in the IWW and trade union struggles while in America.

When Garrett arrived in New York there was a major strike for the Irish Republic being played out on the docks around the White Star liner, the *Baltic*, and for Dr Daniel Mannix, an Irish-born Australian Catholic Bishop known for his sympathy and support for the Irish struggles for liberation and independence. This was a movement of immense proportions – hundreds of thousands heard Mannix speak before he left the US[12] – centred around protests both in favour of and against Dr Mannix's being allowed to travel to Ireland. In New York, a walkout from the ship in favour of Mannix being allowed passage was led by the stokers, most of whom were Liverpool Irish, which for the first time saw Irish, English, and black and white American dockworkers and women coming together in what became known as the Irish Patriotic Strike. Within Garrett's archive there is further evidence of his sympathies and involvement around this movement and events linked to it. It contains two pages from a book, with the date '1920' written in Garrett's hand, about the Mayor of Cork, Alderman Terence McSwiney. McSwiney, an Irish republican, was on hunger strike, protesting against his imprisonment for his activities in the campaign for independence. It was for McSwiney's release that those who had tied up the *Baltic* in New York had also called for when they walked off the ship. It seems therefore that Garrett had more than a passing interest in this dispute. He identified as a Wobbly in the 'five and ten' Seaman's branch in New York, and it is therefore entirely possible, or even likely, as there were many attempts to break the strike, and as the IWW was heavily involved, that it is this event that Millie Toole refers to in her reference to Garrett's role in New York at that point.

One significant aspect of the dispute was the people involved, their background and what they represented in society; five out of the seven leading American women pickets were theatre actors. In New York there was the beginning of The Ghetto Pastoral; the notion that every worker, of every gender and race, has a story inside of them – the issue being how to tell that story. There developed a plethora of magazines, such as the *New Masses*, devoted to new writing, seeking out new voices – an early form, maybe, of Proletarian Culture. These were the voices of the tenements, and there is little doubt that this would have been a major inspiration to Garrett, who could easily identify with the close living and often squalid conditions. It is easy to imagine his realisation that he too had stories to tell, from tenement courts and tiny houses in Liverpool, and he would be inspired by this different way of imagining a life of protest and song.

The strike of 1920, the developments around it, and the methods used to organise the protests that led up to it, were classic indications of the 'Wobbly' form of resistance. This linking of economic and political demands with cultural protest later came to be associated with the development of the Congress for Industrial Organisation (CIO) in the 1930s; methods used to unionise the unskilled as opposed to the unions associated with the American Federation of Labour who dealt purely with industrial matters and craft meritocracy. These methods, and the ethos of merging cultural activities with protest movements, were originally perpetrated by the Wobblies.

It was the Wobbly combination of union struggles with street theatre, agitprop and other cultural interventions and activities which clearly appealed to Garrett. Many of their members and supporters went on to become household names in theatre and film, including the actor William Bendix who was in Garrett's branch of the IWW in New York in 1920, who went on to star in many films including Eugene O'Neill's *The Hairy Ape*. More generally, Wobbly members produced a massive array of theatre, songs and literature, including the famous *Little Red Songbook*, which was seen as a key part of their industrial struggle.

The second major event taking place in New York when Garrett arrived in 1920, and which was to have a significant influence upon him, was the emergence of one of America's greatest playwrights, Eugene O'Neill. Garrett was living, both physically and spiritually, at the centre of the dramatic universe. He came in at the point when the Ghetto Pastoral movement was in full swing; in 1920 Eugene O'Neill's first three-act play, *Beyond the Horizon*, had taken Broadway by storm, winning the playwright the first of his four Pulitzer Prizes for Literature. With characters whose speech was full of 'Dis, dat, dem and do's', O'Neill was the first playwright to bring the vernacular of the street to the stage; real American characters full of anger, frustration, revenge and repressed desire, made great drama within tight, confined spaces in tenements and rooming houses. It is easy to speculate, coming from the close-drawn streets and terraces where he grew up, what impact this would have had on George, and imagine the 'light-bulb' moment for him, the realisation that here was the way for him to tell his stories.

Being so close to the life of the New York theatres and living among working actors would have given him the route he was looking for to go from script to stage. The author Ralph Ellison once wrote, 'Being invisible gives you a different sense of time ... sometimes you're ahead of the beat, sometimes behind, and sometimes you're "on" it.' The bustle of New York gave Garrett, living as George Oswald James, the opportunity to sink into anonymity and immerse himself in his writing.

There is little doubt that Garrett saw O'Neill's plays (*The Emperor Jones* was also performed on Broadway at that time) and was in touch with O'Neill's Provincetown Playhouse on MacDougal Street in Greenwich Village. So powerful was the impact of O'Neill's work on George that he named one of his sons Eugene. Some of the evidence for Garrett's direct connection with O'Neill's new, raw theatre comes from his friend and founder of Merseyside Left Theatre, Jerry Dawson, who wrote:

Appropriately for one who had made contact in America with the Provincetown Players his first performance was in a WEA production of O'Neill's *The Hairy Ape*, a memorable performance which brought the smell of the sea surging over the greasepaint.[13]

Later, in response to a query from *Tribune* about the whereabouts of Garrett in the mid-1950s, Dawson said:

> His first parts in Unity were what might have been expected. He played Agate Keller in *Waiting for Lefty* and Driscoll in *Bury The Dead* – and it is unlikely that they were ever played better anywhere, for all George's experience, not only in this country, but even more in the Wobbly movement in the USA went in to them.[14]

There is further strong evidence for Garrett's contact with O'Neill's Provincetown Theatre, if not O'Neill himself, in his first play, *Two Tides*. Written sometime between 1921 and 1923, it is clear in *Two Tides* that Garrett, remarkably for an untrained playwright, quickly absorbed O'Neill's new theatre, its style and themes, and in doing so translated it into his hometown, Liverpool.

Like his American counterparts, Garrett's work deals with many progressive, challenging themes, and issues of morality are never from the surface of this or his later work. While he may have been influenced by American playwrights what is remarkable is just how far ahead of Liverpool and UK dramatists of his era he was.

Two Tides, set in 1918, just before the end of the First World War, follows the fortunes of the Ferry family, and in particular that of their sons, one at sea, one an engineer. It is an anti-war play, which carries strong female leads and strong female perspectives, and explores generational differences as well as race and power. Garrett uses social realism, and employs the close settings of O'Neill, with the drama played out in the living room of the family featuring recognisable, everyday characters who speak in their own vernacular.

There is no evidence that *Two Tides* was ever performed. However, it is hardly surprising that the young, working class, unschooled playwright, with no real connection to theatre, should fail to get his play performed in Liverpool, particularly when in the early twenties melodrama was the stock in trade of the local theatres. However, when you consider that the first performance of one of Eugene O'Neill's plays in Liverpool didn't take place until 1926 at the Playhouse, Garrett's achievement and talent stands out as all the more noteworthy, as does his confidence to firstly adapt *Two Tides* for the American stage as *Flowers and Candles*, and then write a complete American play, *Tombstones and Grass*.

*

Time ran out for Garrett's first stay in New York in 1921. When he realised Grace would not get through customs and that he too could be deported at a moment's notice, with the loss of all his savings, he jumped ship and returned home. But the Garrett that arrived back in Liverpool was a changed man to the one who had left in 1920; radicalised and inspired by his active engagement with the Wobblies and the Provincetown Playhouse, he appears to have found a new purpose in life. He threw himself into the struggle of the unemployed in Liverpool and led the Liverpool contingent of the 1922 Hunger March to London. One of George's first acts upon returning home was to publish in 1922 his first known writing, 'Marching On'; a song put to the tune of the hymn 'Hold the Fort' and handed out in Liverpool to be sung on demonstrations and to raise funds for the Hunger Marchers. Joseph Pridmore has described its origin as being inspired by Shelley's great poem, *Mask of Anarchy*, whose work Garrett would well have been aware of, and the Wobbly songbook and the words of its troubadour, Joe Hill. Throughout his life Garrett owned and kept a copy of the Wobblies' *Little Red Song Book*, and this, along with other songs is direct evidence of his engagement with the Wobbly method of using cultural forms as an integral part of the struggle itself.

Another sign of the influence of the IWW is Garrett's use of pseudonyms. He signed *Ten Years On The Parish* as 'A. Groundling', the name given to those who paid the cheapest entry fee for the standing area in the Globe Theatre in Shakespeare's time. Garrett had a love of Shakespeare's work. A critical essay he wrote on the character Prospero was published alongside essays by William Empson, a leading Shakespearian expert in the 1930s. It's no surprise that he should use a pseudonym that allied him with the poorer sections of society. Garrett used various pseudonyms throughout his life, including Matt Lowe, a play on the French word for sailor, Matelot; George Oswald James, which appears on the plays he wrote in America and G. Tarregg, on an unpublished thesis on Shakespeare's Hamlet and a number of unpublished poems. There is also a letter in the Garrett archive from a New York-based publisher, addressed to 'George Anders, Esq.', and further evidence from his son John that he also wrote for Wobbly magazines under an assumed name.

There were other reasons for Garrett's regular use of pseudonyms: an understandable and legitimate fear of being accused by the Unemployed Assistance Board of not being available for work; being paid for his writing, and therefore being denied his benefits; a fear of being further victimised or blacklisted by employers and being targeted by the state for his radical views; Garrett's own belief in emphasising the collective and the subsuming of personal identity, a practice employed by the Wobblies, and also, which in some ways helps to account for a lack of recognition for the breadth of his writing, an insecurity about his identity and place as a writer.

There is clear evidence for this in that two of his greatest and most influential admirers, the writer and novelist George Orwell and the poet and editor John Lehmann, were both, from different sides, clearly unaware of the number of short stories he had written and had published, even when, as was the case with Orwell, he had read them under the name 'Matt Low'. There is also no evidence to suggest that either of them had any knowledge whatsoever of the three plays he had completed by 1926. Garrett's use of pseudonyms presents a problem in gaining knowledge of the full scope of his writings, but also offers the tantalising prospect of further future discoveries.

Garrett's dedication of *Ten Years On The Parish*, using a quote from Georges Bernanos's *Diary of a Country Priest*, to 'The voice of the working woman ... which holds out against all the miseries of the world', reveals another key aspect of Garrett's outlook and personality. While clearly a dedication to his wife, Grace, it is also a particularly apt appreciation from someone who lived through war when women were tasked with keeping things together on the home front, but also for a seaman, who by their very nature are generally away for extended periods, which in Garrett's case, on top of all his regular sailings included, with the agreement of Grace, a total of four years living in America. It reflects Garrett's appreciation of the role women are asked to play in the family and society.

Coming from a port city in which women were often the only people providing a regular income as bag, sack and distribution workers from the factories and mills that lined the docks, while men's employment consisted of irregular pulses and movement, discord and dislocation, this writing is clearly ahead of his time; it produced in Garrett's plays dominant, modern, female characters. This is perhaps best personified in the character of Susie, a young woman in *Two Tides* (written between 1920 and 1923) who is window-cleaning while the men are at war. She wears 'blue pants', and asks, 'What about the perilous position of the women left ashore? The ship soon forgets if a man does wrong – the whole town never will if his wife slips. Down on her like a ton of bricks'. In response to the old sailor Ned's admonishment for going to dances, she replies, 'The hours I spend in a dance hall and the company I keep is my business ... I'll sample the lot – discover one passable – then hang my hat on.' This represents Garrett's progressive, modern outlook, and can be seen throughout his life in his writing and his personal role as a radical activist and social advocate.

Garrett's progressive values extended beyond gender inequalities as well. In *Ten Years...* he recounts a mock military funeral, held in Rugby during the 1922 Hunger March, which was designed to simultaneously protest and mock the meanness of the town's poor law guardians. It captures perfectly Garrett's many roles, interests and influences. Rugby's Board of Guardians, like many others in previous towns and workhouses before them, had committed the unforgivable sin of serving the ex-military men of the Liverpool contingent, who had seen action in the First World War and even in the Boer War, the detested 'Bully Beef' for their evening meal after a long day on the road to London. After the marcher's council met late into the night to agree on the protest, Garrett, dressed as a priest with a 'tall silk hat' borrowed from an undertaker's yard to complete the clergyman's outfit he had cobbled together from second-hand shops, adopted an 'ecclesiastical drawl' as he led an open air ceremony held on a 'traffic island in the centre of the town's main street', to commemorate and lay to rest 'our dearly departed comrade, B.B'. Such was the 'authenticity' of the 'funeral' both townspeople and marchers alike were fooled into thinking one of their number had died. After a sermon praising the role of B.B. who during previous wars was 'always at hand and could be rushed anywhere in an emergency', with a bugle sounding the Last Post and people weeping in the street, Garrett pulled aside a wreath and a Union Jack to reveal the *coup de grace* – a seven-pound tin of Bully Beef resting atop a pillar box. Before people could gather themselves

Garrett led the marchers out of Rugby singing a 'song against Bully Beef culture while the brass band played "Colonel Bogey"'.

Garrett's role as the 'blubbery-faced priest' at the mock funeral reveals his lifelong passion for the interconnection of performance and political activism. Here we can see the emergence of Garrett as a dramatist, using street theatre and humour to create and enact a protest within a protest, but the episode also clearly shows the deep-rooted influence of the Wobblies' integration of all manner of cultural forms, including agitprop and street theatre, into protests.

These theatrical moments on major protests were relatively rare occurrences. Like many of his contemporaries in the 1920s, Garrett's life, even when working, was harsh and precarious, populated by regular bouts of unemployment. But these experiences were put into shade by the devastation wreaked after the 1929 crash and the subsequent worldwide recession of the early 1930s. For all of their radical sentiments, those writers in the 1930s who aligned themselves with working class causes – W.H. Auden, George Orwell, Stephen Spender, and others – could never disguise the fact that, amidst the dislocation and angst the decade brought them, they never seriously had to wonder, as Garrett did on many occasions, where the next meal for themselves and their families would come from. The stark realities of daily life at that time have perhaps never been better described than in the heart-breaking yet unsentimental manner in which Garrett relates the deterioration in his family's circumstances:

> I was quickly down to pawn shop level. All my clothes went in; next the bedding. We had a spell sleeping on bare mattresses using the flock tick as a blanket. The empty table provided many a quarrel. There were sighs and snarls, and crazy thoughts of theft, murder and suicide ... One night we sat in the dark: no food, no money; not even a penny for lamp oil. Next morning the baby's clothes were gathered together for the pawnshop. As my wife placed the bundle on the table, she glared across at me. Her smothered sobs broke into hysterical abuse. Tempers burst loose. It nearly ended in murder.[15]

In the early 1930s unemployment in the UK reached three million. Garrett's description of even fathers and sons coming to blows amidst the competition for work on the Dock Road brings into sharp focus the often desperate struggle to survive which is documented throughout *Ten Years On The Parish*. Garrett, with a sharp eye for detail, in much the same way as Orwell's *The Road To Wigan Pier*, made full use of figures and official documents of the time to support his arguments. But Garrett's work also has compassion for the suffering both he and those around him were forced to endure. Unlike Orwell, Garrett was an engaged writer; an activist, who not only wrote about experiences of poverty, but set out to do something about them. In contrast, and though he later fought for the Spanish Republic in the Spanish Civil War, Orwell, at the point Garrett met him, was regarded by working class writers as a middle class dilettante, or even what would today be called a 'poverty tourist'. As a result, some of the most powerful pieces of *Ten Years On The Parish* are when Garrett humanises the individuals and brings to life events he knew intimately having played a key role in them: the mass unemployed struggles and demonstrations in Liverpool in the early 1920s and the 1922 Hunger March to London; the humorous tale of his plan to relieve a rent collector of his sack of coins, only to end up tending to him when the collector's health begins to fail him, and the desperate tale of the piano player, whose fall into unemployment and then itinerant collector of scrap iron, whose 'hands are on the wheel that is steering the Universe', precipitates a descent into madness.

Garrett was rooted in a compassionate and righteous sense of anger about the conditions he saw around him on a daily basis. His politics were embedded in his life and his surroundings. This was true in New York, but, by the time of *Ten Years On The Parish*, the continued grind of living in such a precarious state are clear to see.

*

It is no doubt true that Garrett, who initially suggested the 'unemployment book' as he first referred to it, felt enormous pressure to deliver a narrative that would have been in line with the fashion of the day; honest workers writing their own authentic accounts of unemployment and poverty, particularly in the North of England. John Lehmann even argued it was Garrett's 'social duty' to write it. However, Lehmann appears to have lacked awareness about what marked Garrett out as different from other working class writers – that of being a seaman, and how coming from a port city had given him a uniquely internationalist outlook. Lehmann displayed little interest in this aspect of his life, which could potentially have created a book unique among working class writers in the 1930s.

However, there is also a clue about Garrett's attitude given in George Orwell's diaries about when they first met in Liverpool on 25 February 1936. Orwell wrote that he was 'very greatly impressed by Garrett'. He gives a brief account of Garrett's size, 'a big hefty chap', before wrongly describing him as a Communist (Garrett briefly joined the CP in the 1920s, but left soon after). Orwell then recounts how Garrett was 'torpedoed on a ship that sank in 7 minutes', and 'worked in an illicit brewery in Chicago during prohibition, saw various hold-ups, saw Battling Siki immediately after he had been shot in a street brawl, etc.' Orwell, who also urged him to write his autobiography, then states that 'All this interests him (Garrett) much less than Communist politics'.[16]

After the Russian Revolution of 1917, many syndicalist seamen, who, like Garrett and the Wobblies, believed in the One Big Union, embraced the Communist Party, which in its early days was seen as new, radical force that could reinvigorate the movement, bringing unity and militant national purpose with the backing of a solid international organisation. For the Wobblies, who had been battered during the Red Scares in the USA, it appeared to provide a way forward. However, for most seamen their involvement and support was short-lived. Garrett recalled his friend Jimmy Breslin reporting back from a visit to Russia, that 'the poor working-class stiffs are getting it in the neck worse than here'. Garrett himself poured scorn on those in the CPGB offices in Byron Street who were more interested in debating how many hairs there were in Marx's beard rather than engaging in practical struggle. He soon left the Communist Party remarking that, 'I'd got one pope off my back, I didn't want to hump round another one'.

At the time of meeting Orwell it would have been ten years since Garrett had last visited America. Understandable then that it would not have been a pressing concern for him to write about his experiences there. However, as stated earlier, Garrett was an activist, an engaged writer who used his work, particularly his autobiographical material and reportage, to engage with and support working class struggles, expose poor conditions and hypocrisy, particularly on ships, and propagate radical ideas. His concerns more often than not were of the immediate, the pressing needs before him, for which he felt he could help effect change, either through writing, advocacy, or direct intervention. While he always carried within him the influences gained from America, and according to Bob Edwards MP, who was a friend of Garrett's, 'knew some of the great martyrs of the IWW', the struggles of America, in terms of writing about them in his work, would have been both distant in time and not of immediate relevance to the struggles he faced both on a personal level and within the workers' movement in Liverpool. It is also, given Garrett's character, highly likely that he saw an opportunity to impress upon Orwell the levels of poverty and difficulty facing working class people and the radical case for change, and hoped it would influence the book he was researching at the time. Garrett's less than favourable response to the publication of *The Road To Wigan Pier* will be discussed in the introduction to the letters he exchanged with his editor John Lehmann.

However, such was the unique nature of Garrett's experiences in his two spells in America, it is worth us turning to the second period of his life spent there to continue to explore those areas Garrett wrote little about, as in many ways they are the true context within which to understand his life and work, and the outlook and methods of struggle he employed as represented in *Ten Years On The Parish*.

*

At the end of the 1922 Hunger March, Garrett realised he was worse off than before, and that his name would be first among equals on the blacklist. With a growing family to provide for and again with Grace's blessing, he borrowed two pounds from an old woman living down the stairs and caught a train to Southampton (where he was less well known) and signed articles aboard the White Star liner, *Homeric*. He left Southampton as George Garrett and alighted in New York as George Oswald James; just one of the many pseudonyms he used throughout his life, and the one he used to sign for both of his American plays. His identity photographs taken at the time, with his hair combed to one side, a sleek pair of glasses and a suit instead of a stoker's vest, appear to suggest that, along with his name, he was also attempting to change his identity to that of a writer, one who works part time in order to gain the space to write full time.

His 1924 New York notebooks give testimony to the poets and playwrights he studied; the great modernists, Ibsen, Strindberg and O'Neill, and scrapbooks full of cuttings of poetry, from George Bernanos to Michael Gold, among them. It is a measure of how intensely he applied himself to his work that in 1925 he registered two plays, *Flowers and Candles* and *Tombstones and Grass*, with the Washington Library of Congress. Unlike *Two Tides*, these later plays were set in America, but all three show clearly just how much he had absorbed and tuned into the new age of drama he encountered in New York, using dramatic realism amidst the intense setting of the home. The plays portray ordinary working class people faced with betrayals that threaten their moral codes and rupture their understanding of what their lives represent and their hopes for the future. Garrett also, like O'Neill, is not afraid to deal with issues of race, gender and sex.

The professional binding of his dramatic works, still sturdy today 90 years later, show that they were working manuscripts designed to be read by actors, handed into theatres, and used again should the theatre reject and return them. He lived on East 42nd Street, at the heart of the burgeoning bohemian scene, and roomed with young Irish actors Barry Fitzgerald, Victor McLaglen and Jackie Gleason, future Hollywood stars then trying to make a name for themselves on the stage, two of whom later appeared in John Wayne's 1952 film, *The Quiet Man*. According to George's son John, these actors cemented within him his love of theatre. Although there is no evidence that Garrett's plays were performed in America there are in the archive two rejection letters from theatre companies in New York, the Theatre Guild and the Provincetown Playhouse, which indicate that Garrett was actively seeking to get them performed professionally. Within this milieu he was now mixing it would be natural for Garrett's plays to be seen, commented upon and subject to readings, if not full performances.

It is clear by this point that Garrett now saw himself as a writer – Irish 'tramp' writer Jim Phelan relates how, when he renewed his acquaintance with Garrett in Liverpool in 1922, whom he first met on the New Orleans waterfront, he was surprised that Garrett described himself as a writer. But for Garrett, 1923–1926 was his first period of sustained work, his 'siege in the room', testified to by the notebooks he kept full of cuttings and quotations, poems and articles on writing and performing theatre. This is Garrett's self-imposed 'University', much as it was for Maxim Gorky on the docks in Odessa. His decision to leave Liverpool relieved him of the duty he felt towards his fellow unemployed, a responsibility he took seriously. Often working at night in garages, speak-easies, illicit breweries and even as a janitor in a police station, coupled with a great literary energy to sit and write each day, suggests he used his time in America for one specific reason – to hone his craft.

However, unlike his previous experience, when Garrett returned to America in 1923 he found that 'Conditions were not as favourable as 1920–21. Wages had dropped. There was plenty of unemployment'. He 'managed to average six months' work in each of the twelve during the three years I stayed there', and so, after 'posting money home, besides keeping myself, [had] very soon used up my savings'. As the recession bit 'Americans for American jobs' became the cry, and he 'grew weary of the continual dodging about' to avoid the immigration officers, who were launching raids on rooming houses, mission halls, factories and employment agencies. Reluctantly, he made the decision to work his passage back to Liverpool, but this time with 'no savings, just two suits of clothes.'

George arrived back in Liverpool at the end of the 1926 General Strike to witness 'Strikers and Policemen playing football together'; a metaphor for everything returning 'to normal.' As George Orwell noted in *Burmese Days*, published two years later, Britain was a strongly governed country built upon a deep residue of imperialism and suspicion of organised labour. The repercussions of the failure of the general strike led to a 1927 Act of Parliament that introduced further wage cuts, and benefit cuts for those deemed to be 'not genuinely seeking work'. George managed to ship out for three months, but this and other short runs counted for no more than five months' work over the next thirteen years.

He was far from inactive; his reputation as a fighter stood the test of time during his three-year absence, but he took a role more closely aligned to advocacy and civil rights than the mass organisational work of the 1920s, although he never faltered from his work in supporting reform of the seamen's union. He was also involved with campaigners for non-violence in The Fellowship of Reconciliation, writing for their magazine and trying to minimise conflict between Catholics and Protestants.

In the early 1920s he had written for journals associated with the Unemployed Workers Movement and the Red International of Trade Unions. In the 1930s, during this long war of attrition, he maintained his wry humour and honed his skills by sticking to the pen. He left his plays behind and embarked upon a series of short stories and critical reportage that soon brought him his first publishing success, and provided much of the context for how Garrett came to write *Ten Years On The Parish*. This context is an important aspect of Garrett's life and work, and is too extensive to comment upon here. It will be discussed further in the letters between him and his editor, John Lehmann, later in this book.

The excellent work of the late Michael Murphy, who brought together Garrett's short stories for the first time in print in 1999 with *The Collected George Garrett*, situated him primarily as an artist of the short form. However, when you consider the three plays he wrote in the 1920s, his intelligent and dramatic use of street theatre within demonstrations, his touring the North West of England performing one man shows of O'Neill's work, it could be argued that he was primarily a dramatist. This is especially the case when considered during and after 1936 when he helped found, wrote for and performed in Merseyside Left Theatre, and its later incarnation Unity Theatre. However, his body of work, published and unpublished, and his remarkable ability to work across many different forms, resist him being pigeon-holed into any one category or type of writer.

In the context of the mid-1930s, the Spanish Civil War was a clear call to arms. That Garrett was actively involved in the campaign to support the Spanish working class against the fascist forces of Franco is testified to by his good friend, and mother of comedian Alexei Sayle, Molly Sayle; Garrett was the best man at her wedding and a regular visitor to their house. Molly recalled them chalking walls and pavements with the statement, 'Bombs on Madrid Today – Bombs on Merseyside Tomorrow'.[17] She admitted that at the time they hardly realised just how true this was to be.

The Spanish Civil War provided a focal point similar to the struggles Garrett had engaged in with the Wobblies on the New York Waterfront. Entering the European, and indeed global, consciousness as a struggle between fascism, communism and social democracy, the war proved ultimately both inspiration and nightmare for many on the Left. At the outset though, considering the urgency with which many working class activists and militants supported the Republican cause in Spain, it is clear that the war demanded Garrett's full attention and involvement; an elected government had been overthrown by the military, and the people, particularly in the cities, had risen up in its defence.

Merseyside Left Theatre was formed with a manifesto that declared, 'We are a political theatre involved in the struggle for socialism.' It sought out working class audiences to bring to them the 'most urgent political issue of the day – the need to rouse support for the Spanish people in their fight against international fascism'. Their first plays, which debuted at a meeting to raise funds for the International Brigades, were *Guernica* and *Spain*, and they toured the region appearing in theatres, church halls and on the streets. There was a ready response and many of their productions played to full houses.

In discussing Garrett's role in the newly formed theatre, Jerry Dawson commented that they were 'lucky' because:

They had a man who had worked with the Wobblies in America. He could set the cast firmly in Brooklyn and the Bronx. He had led the Liverpool contingent in the Hunger March of 1922. He could carry the American struggle across the Atlantic and make it British.[18]

At the same time, where George went, trouble did seem to follow, and in December 1938 he again found himself under arrest, along with 11 other cast and crew members, after the curtain was brought down upon the Left Theatre's performance of Clifford Odett's *Waiting for Lefty*, which they were presenting in Chester as part of a pre-Christmas Drama festival. Bishop Norman Tubbs, The Dean of Chester, along with a number of other 'prominent patrons' walked out at a perceived blasphemy in the play. It appears that this was an excuse to put a halt to a radical drama being performed in a theatre that, because of the trades-unions and Labour party branches being circulated, had an audience with a distinctly working class tinge to it. The director, a young Jerry Dawson, was summonsed to court; this on a day when he was starting work in a new school and had to tell the headmaster he needed a day off to attend the court for putting on a 'blasphemous' play. Due to not complying with the demands of the Lord Chamberlain's office, the defendants were bound over for 12 months with costs. The case made national publicity and was even discussed in the House of Commons.[19]

But Garrett's role, as so often in his life, encompassed more than the art. As Dawson said, 'In these years, too, it was not only G.G's ability as an actor that was invaluable to such a theatre group but even more what he was as a man. Many of us learned much more about the meaning of Socialism from our contact with him than we did from *Left Book Club Choices, Left Review*, or *New Writing*.'

Though on a personal level the 1930s for Garrett again became a struggle to survive, they also brought him his greatest creative success, with 13 of his short stories being published in literary magazines between 1934 and 1937. At this point too he was labouring away, with interest from a number of influential editors and major publishers, writing and trying to complete *Ten Years On The Parish*. However, due to his living conditions and the difficulties he faced trying to complete the manuscript, Garrett suffered a minor breakdown, and felt he could no longer continue working on *Ten Years On The Parish*. Except for *The 'Maurie'*, a short story based on his experience of his time below decks on the Cunard ship the *Mauretania*, written just after the war and never published in his lifetime, he didn't write any further short stories. He appeared from afar to those who had published him to have disappeared from the writer's movement.

But Garrett was ahead of the game. He formed part of the classic 'meteque', looking both to home and away, and inhabited the same in-between world of other port city writers. His work has been discussed in the context of a loose 'school' of port city writers, alongside that of Liverpool born James Hanley and Irish tramp writer, Jim Phelan. Like them he was defining himself by what he felt culturally as opposed to an identity foisted upon him by the imposition of state borders. Garrett was organically part of, as argued by Tony Lane in *Liverpool: City of the Sea*, a 'port that bundled everything together that was to do with ships, solidarity and seafaring'. Garrett adopted the same attitude, which like the city, 'looked outward, not over its shoulder'.[20] To understand Garrett is to understand his life in the context of the journey of a port city writer from a place that has always been out of line, out of space in many ways to its own nation state.

Garrett's involvement with the Unity Theatre up to the war and into the late 1940s, contradicts the idea that his writing career was at an end after his last short story was published in 1937. Alan O'Toole makes the point that the Unity Theatre was 'an enterprise which took both literature and "the message" straight to the people on the streets', and George no doubt felt this to be a 'more worthwhile project on which to devote his time'. Alongside acting he devoted many hours to writing and contributing scenes and dialogue to new plays, and is credited as the co-writer of *Man with a Plan* and *One Hundred Years Hard*, two plays that were highly successful across the North-West region in the early 1940s. However, his letters reveal his anguish and ultimately his despair at financial and contractual wrangling with his publishers. As further evidence for the reasons why Garrett threw himself into his work with Merseyside Left and Unity Theatres, O'Toole cites Garrett's dissatisfaction with the literary clique surrounding the magazines he was published in. He argues that it may have been that 'George realised that the average member of the working class did not read *Left Review*, much less *The Adelphi* and other such self-consciously 'arty' magazines.' He goes on to note that 'It is always rather disillusioning for a working class writer to realise that he has an almost exclusively middle class audience.' After attending one weekend school of the *Adelphi* magazine Garrett suggested, due to their sycophantic attitude towards its editor, John Middleton Murry, that the delegates should line up outside the toilet for the privilege of passing him his toilet paper![21]

His decision to abandon his efforts in prose at almost the same time that he wandered in off the street and offered his services at one of the first sessions of Jerry Dawson's newly established Left Theatre, is no coincidence. In many respects this was Garrett through and through; older now, suffering some ill-health, and with too many family responsibilities for him to be able to volunteer in Spain, it's clear that he saw his chance to contribute to a living struggle through theatre, a medium he loved and understood. At a time when the torpor that fell over the Labour movement following the defeat of the 1926 General Strike and the decimation wreaked by the '30s depression seemed to be lifting, 'the leisurely art of short story writing must have seemed somewhat irrelevant'.

The efforts of the Unity players, of those who died in Spain and all the other activists, were in vain. The Spanish working class suffered a terrible defeat at the hands of Franco, and soon, when the Second World War broke out, as predicted, the bombs that dropped on Madrid really did begin to rain down on Merseyside. For Garrett, in an irony he would surely have appreciated, the Second World War offered him his first opportunity for employment in ten years, albeit one in which he was now asked to risk his life for a country that had blighted his own for so long. He sailed on the *Nagara* to Argentina in 1939 and 1940. These appear to have been his last voyages. At the age of 44 it would have been some task to work again in the brutal intensity of the engine rooms again after so many years unemployed. In mid-1940 Garrett left the sea and served out the rest of the war as a night watchmen on the Bootle Docks, a posting that left him exposed to the regular night-time air raids of the Luftwaffe.

Following the end of the war Garrett was again active with Unity Theatre, taking part in street shows in support of Labour who were brought to power by a population who wanted an end to war deprivations and were spurred on by a mood for social decency that swept the country. George, regardless of his Wobbly sympathies, not only supported the campaigns for Labour to be elected but also took part in writing and performing in *Man With a Plan*, a play which aimed to maintain support for Labour as its popularity waned when the reality fell short of the population's expectations. This was particularly true when Stafford Cripps' (Chancellor of the Exchequer from 1947 to 1950) austerity programme began to bite. The play, in which Garrett wrote at least two key scenes, and performed the role of a Liverpool-Irish Docker who vows never to return to the deference shown to the bosses before the war, was a huge success.

Even with the disappointment of seeing seamen's leaders jailed by the Labour Government and witnessing the rapid right-wing lurch of two of his closest political friends, Jack and Bessie Braddock (which no doubt confirmed within him his suspicion and distaste for politics and politicians), Garrett continued to play his part in the labour movement by writing scenes for the Unity's *One Hundred Years Hard*, commissioned by the Trades Council to celebrate its centenary in 1948. It is perhaps fitting that in this play, the last he helped to write, he reprised his own role as that of his younger self during the 1922 Hunger March.

By the mid-1950s, according to Jerry Dawson, it seemed that time was passing George by. To those who argued that he had lost his heart for the fight O'Toole explained that Garrett kept up his activity in the local community and in the Seamen's Union, but 'was disillusioned, not by the class struggle, but with politics.' The proof of this is that he again threw himself into the campaign to reform the Seamen's Union and reinvigorated the old Seamen's Vigilance Committee, George's persistence in campaigning against the endemic corruption in the NUS, at a time when its General Secretary 'was philosophically disposed to the view that Liverpool was full of militants', eventually paid off. The National Seaman's Reform Movement, in a campaign that paralysed British shipping in 1960, won the 'Seamen's Charter', which paved the way for reductions in hours and increases in pay, as well as a series of democratic changes to the union, including the men's right to select their own delegates.

Speaking at his final meetings six years later in 1966 at the time of the first official seaman's strike since 1911, George's heart would have been warmed by the placards calling for the workers to 'Remember 1911', but by this stage, to many of the younger strikers at least, George was but a token presence. Who by then would have been aware of his incredible life story and commitment to the movement; the older ones maybe, but the younger strikers by that time had more pressing concerns. This would not have mattered to Garrett, who throughout his life had always followed the Wobbly example and done his best to remove himself from the limelight.

He lived his life 'below the radar', always interested more in the power of the collective over the elevation of the individual. In his short story *The 'Maurie'* Garrett describes the scene on board as the down-below crew 'swarmed below decks' as like a 'Subterranean Theatre letting in'. It is also an apt description for George himself, the ultimate subterranean, who laboured 'below decks' to create a body of literary and propagandist work about the life and conditions of the working class. Alongside Garrett's internationalist outlook, it is possible here to think of him as a 'subaltern cosmopolitan'. 'Subaltern', a term drawn from the work of the Italian Marxist Antonio Gramsci, who whilst imprisoned by Mussolini used the term as a cover to escape the prison censors who were monitoring his writings. Gramsci uses the term 'subaltern' to denote the working classes who are excluded from and dominated by society's established structures, and this aptly denotes the work 'from below', challenging established hierarchies and orders, that occupied Garrett for most of his life. He was also clearly 'Cosmopolitan' because of his inherently internationalist outlook from his time as a sailor and in the USA. Garrett forms part of a wider maritime and trades union network of radicalism and solidarity which, as outlined throughout this introduction, shaped his worldview and beliefs. That such a figure emerged from a transatlantic port city life such as Garrett's is not surprising – the port environment has always been noted as cosmopolitan and dynamic. What marks out Garrett was the range and scope of his writing and his underlying belief in solidarity and socialism across entrenched barriers of class, gender and race.

*

Ten Years On The Parish is flawed; partially fragmented, with a narrative that doesn't always flow. The depth and breadth demanded by the life of the hand that wrote it is often to be found wanting, and its sudden conclusion mirrors that of its author's decision to move on to pastures new, where he felt his creative energies would be put to better use. Yet, for all that, it is a vitally important piece of work, created by a working-class writer from a city whose experience he was able to record and disseminate through a range of publications and activities with the sole aim of working to improve the conditions of his class. And in this way, therefore, the flaws become an essential part of the text, just as his own flaws – he was no 'plaster saint' as his sons were keen to point out when they talked about the language he could use and the times they would be on the receiving end of his often short temper – were a part of his make-up. In essence they are the scars he collected in the struggle to find his voice against almost overwhelming odds.

One thing that was never in question was Garrett's integrity. For Alan O'Toole it is this integrity that is the reason for his historical and political obscurity; 'George Garrett served socialism well by his actions, by his words and by his example. It may well be that he served it best by helping to preserve a more warm and humane vision of socialism which too many of us rejected too hastily after 1917'.[22]

A speech delivered by Garrett in 1921 to a mass rally of the Seamen's Vigilance Committee in Canning Place in Liverpool, preserved, ironically, by Sergeant Seaton, an undercover CiD officer attending and recording the protest, perhaps sums up best his bravery, integrity and his internationalism. Brave because on the platform, including the chairperson, were two openly racist speakers arguing for white seafarer's jobs and the expulsion of 'aliens'; this just a short time after the race riots of 1919 during which one black seaman, Charles Wotten, was murdered by a white mob at the Queen's dock, an area less than half a mile away from where Garrett was speaking.

In this volatile atmosphere there was no guarantee that Garrett's words would be well received, but that didn't cause him to shy away from the principles he innately believed in. It is a speech, which in its breadth and knowledge of international movements, could only have been delivered by someone with the personal experience of protest movements across the world, and one who understood the true value of solidarity. It is also a speech that is particularly relevant today; another reason why Garrett's life and work can still move and inspire us to also be 'militant advocates of tolerance'.[23]

Fellow workers, it is all very well criticising the alien as one of your speakers has been doing, and telling you he is the cause of your unemployment. It is not so. The present rotten system is the cause. These speeches by my friend here are only storing up racial hatred ... We must stick together or we will not get anywhere. All workers are slaves to the capitalists, no matter what their race, colour or creed is, and there is more slavery under the Union Jack than under any other flag ... You Britishers, you sometimes give me a pain. I don't tell people I'm a Britisher. I had no choice being where I was when I was born. How many of you have the guts of the Indians who are following Gandhi in India today, or following Michael Collins in Ireland? These people are only trying what we should be doing, breaking the bonds of their serfdom ... In every country in the world the children [are] taught that their particular country [is] the best ... That kind of education which plays into the hands of the capitalists must be eliminated, and they must fight for the emancipation of all workers, no matter what country, colour or creed.[24]

Here we see clearly Garrett's internationalism at work; not for him the divisive and negative politics of blame, instead, a brave call for those listening to recognise wider systemic injustices that lay at the heart of the imperialistic and capitalist world which he inhabited.

After delivering his final public speech during the 1966 seamen's strike, Garrett threw his own bus fare into the collection and walked home. He died later that year, on 28 May 1966, of throat cancer, after a life given over to creativity, art and struggle. He went out the way he had lived, supporting the underdog, the restless and the poor, leaving behind a body of work to be proud of, and a legacy, still growing, as one of the most significant working class writers of his generation.

Notes

For notes and additional information on names, places and events that appear in the text please refer to pages 274–287.

1 George Garrett, 'Swords into Ploughshares' in Michael Murphy (ed.), *The Collected George Garrett* (Nottingham: Trent Editions, 1999), p. 169.

2 George Garrett, *Ten Years On The Parish*, original manuscript.

3 Peter Linebaugh and Marcus Rediker, *The Many Headed Hydra: The Hidden history of the Revolutionary Atlantic* (Boston, MA: Beacon Press, 2000).

4 Paul Gilroy's *The Black Atlantic: Modernity and Double Consciousness* (Cambridge, MA: Harvard University Press, 1993) challenges some of the nation-centric accounts of history, and instead argues for a diasporic 'black Atlantic' that refuses traditional categorisations of nationality and ethnicity. Despite being over two decades old, it remains one of the most important books about the Atlantic World and its continuing impact on contemporary culture.

5 Broeze is referring in particular to lascar, or South Asian, maritime labour, but the overall point of the British Empire being held together through maritime labour holds true. F. Broeze, 'The Muscles of Empire – Indian Seamen and the Raj 1919–1939', *Indian Economic & Social History Review*, January 18.1 (1981): 43–67.

6 D. Massey, 'A global sense of place', *Marxism Today*, 38 (1991): 24–29.

7 The references here come from the original manuscript of George Garrett's *Ten Years On The Parish*.

8 George Garrett, *Ten Years On The Parish*, original manuscript.

9 Howard Zinn. *A People's History of The United States* (London and New York: Longman, 1980), p. 373.

10 David Featherstone, *Solidarity: Hidden Histories and Geographies of Internationalism* (London: Zed Books, 2012).

11 Letter from Bob Edwards MP to Jerry Dawson, 17 January 1984. Edwards was unfortunately mistaken in the names. For Jim Hill read Joe Hill, and

for George Everett, Wesley Everest, both of whom were killed (Everest was lynched in the town of Everett), the first undoubtedly a political execution based on still disputed charges, and the second lynched by a right-wing mob. He is also most likely mistaken about Garrett knowing Joe Hill, who died in 1915, and Everest who was killed in 1919. There is no doubt he at least knew *of* them both, and was, based on Bob Edward's reference to Jerry Dawson, in touch with various members of the IWW in America whom he would have met while living there. A letter from the IWW written in 1922 to Garrett agreeing to him writing a pamphlet for them about the situation of seamen in Britain also confirms his ongoing relationship with IWW. Their influence upon him was such that Garrett named one of his sons 'Wesley' in honour of Wesley Everest.

12 Joe Doyle, 'Striking for the Irish on the New York Docks' in Ronald Bayor and Timothy Meagher (eds.), *The New York Irish* (London: Johns Hopkins University Press, 1996), pp. 357–373.

13 From the preface by Jerry Dawson to Garrett's *Liverpool 1921–1922* (Liverpool: Unity Theatre, 1984).

14 Merseyside Unity Theatre Archive, held at Liverpool Central Records Office.

15 George Garrett, *Ten Years On The Parish*, original manuscript.

16 George Orwell, 'The Road to Wigan Pier Diary', in Angus and Sonia Orwell (eds), *George Orwell, the Collected essays, Journalism and Letters, Vol.1. An Age Like This, 1920–1940* (London: Secker & Warburg, 1968), p. 187.

17 Alan O'Toole, 'A Personal Conversation with Garrett's friend, Molly Sayle', unpublished monograph, p. 28. Available in the George Garrett Archive, Central Records Office, Liverpool.

18 From Left Theatre, Merseyside Unity Theatre, a documentary record, Jerry Dawson, 1995.

19 Alan O'Toole, 'A Personal Conversation with Jerry Dawson', unpublished monograph, p. 28. Available in the George Garrett Archive, Central Records Office, Liverpool.

20 Tony Lane. *Liverpool: City of the Sea* (Liverpool: Liverpool University Press, 1997), p. x.

21 Alan O'Toole, 'George Garrett: Seaman, Syndicalist and Writer', unpublished monograph, p. 69. Available in the George Garrett Archive, Central Records Office, Liverpool.

22 Alan O'Toole, 'George Garrett: Seaman, Syndicalist and Writer', unpublished monograph.

23 Michael Murphy (ed.), *The Collected George Garrett* (Nottingham: Trent Editions, 1999), p. xxiii.

23 Michael Murphy (ed.), *The Collected George Garrett* (Nottingham: Trent Editions, 1999), p. xxv.

Notes on the Text

The manuscript of *Ten Years On The Parish* is a complete document, although still a partially fragmented text. For George Garrett it was still a working document; though the large majority of its 165 pages are in type, there are some sections that had to be transcribed from Garrett's handwritten text where he had made additions, amendments and footnotes to the typed document. Garrett's handwriting was incredibly small, something which in the 1950s led his friend Millie Toole, who typed up some of his earlier stories, and possibly the manuscript of *Ten Years...* to complain, and presented ourselves with difficulties in interpreting some of his writing for this publication. Overall, we feel we have been successful, but have highlighted in the text itself, or in endnotes, where there is still uncertainty over particular words or sentences.

There is some mystery over the original introduction to *Ten Years....* Michael Murphy, in *The Collected George Garrett* (Trent Editions, 1999) published under 'Autobiography', a piece titled '*from* Ten Years On The Parish'. In this account, Garrett writes in some detail about stowing away at the age of 17 on a tramp-steamer bound for Argentina, yet it doesn't appear as part of the original manuscript, within which Garrett devotes barely two lines to these events. It seems most likely that the piece published by Murphy was written some time later than the original manuscript, possibly even after the Second World War. Based on the available, although admittedly limited evidence, it appears that this represents the beginning of an attempt by Garrett to write his complete life story rather than the one that mainly detailed his experiences of being out of work during the late 1920s and 1930s. In the 1950s the writer and journalist Millie Toole was in regular correspondence with Garrett. In a surviving letter, she urges him to keep writing to her, particularly about his experiences during the strikes on the New York Waterfront and his memories of the

Communist Party when it was based in Byrom Street in Liverpool. This correspondence and encouragement, from a writer who publicly acknowledged him in her own work, may well have been the catalyst for George to return to the manuscript he laid down in the late 1930s. It is a tantalising glimpse into the potential of what George might have been able to tell us of his life if he had completed the project. It is published here as it also bears the title, *Ten Years On The Parish*, and therefore belongs with the substantive manuscript, and to give the reader as complete an account as possible, in his own words, of Garrett's life both prior to and during the 1930s.

Two sections of *Ten Years...* have previously been published as stand-alone reportage. In 1937 'The First Hunger March', Garrett's account of the 1922 march to London, for which he led the Liverpool contingent, appeared in John Lehmann's *New Writing* magazine. In 1980 a section of *Ten Years...* was published as 'Liverpool 1921–22' by Liverpool's Unity Theatre, and again later by Unity Theatre founder, Jerry Dawson. This included a short additional introduction that doesn't appear in the original manuscript of *Ten Years...*, which indicates that this too was prepared by Garrett to appear specifically as a stand-alone piece.

Garrett also used his experiences detailed in *Ten Years...* to create short stories. Two of these were published: 'The Parish', which recounts a scene of men waiting to find out whether they will be granted relief and their treatment by the officers in charge, was published in the magazine *Left Review* in October 1937; 'The Pianist', a heart-wrenching fictionalisation of Garrett's encounters with a classical pianist driven to a mental breakdown though his experience of long-term unemployment, appeared in Jerry Dawson's *Out of Liverpool: Stories of Land and Sea* in 1980.

In the manuscript of *Ten Years On The Parish*, although an autobio-graphical work, Garrett rarely refers to himself directly, describing himself at times, amongst other things, as 'The Young Seaman', 'The Syndicalist', and 'The Blubbery-Faced Priest', and continues this pattern by disguising both the main characters and place names.

In the typed manuscript Garrett has crossed out 'Liverpool' and replaced it with 'Sprayport'. 'Exchange Flags' becomes 'Bourse Square' and 'Lord Street' becomes 'Emporium Street'. Again, it is difficult to decipher exactly why Garrett continued to hide and distance himself so extensively both within and from his work, except to note the reasons given above for his use of pseudonyms; fear of losing benefits, fear of the blacklist (although Garrett was well-known in Liverpool for his radical activities, as recounted in *Ten Years...* when he readily admits the accusation of one of the Parish Commissioners that he is constantly agitating on street corners), adhering to the Wobbly tradition of subjugating the individual to the collective, or even simple modesty.

Regardless of the reasons, we have chosen to be faithful to the manuscript and include the place-names as indicated by Garrett's latest edits. Where necessary, names of the main characters are given in endnotes. Other than correcting any obvious misspelling, we have by and large left the manuscript as it was originally written. Any minor changes or amendments are highlighted in endnotes.

Although, as stated earlier, *Ten Years On The Parish* is a complete document, there is, unfortunately, one complete page missing, which is highlighted in the text. However, it is a tribute to George's family that the document, and the fairly extensive archive we have collected, exists at all; that they have carried it down the generations is testament once again to the esteem in which George was held, and their instinctive understanding of the importance of his work.

This publication is dedicated to them, to all of George's family, and to all those who have supported the George Garrett Archive project and made this publication possible.

Autobiography

from *Ten Years On The Parish*

A stowaway has to begin somewhere and the best place is at the docks. Mine was the Liverpool Docks. Liverpool in 1913, with its seven-mile dock road running parallel to the River Mersey, and its elevated street-railway overlooking both. The road itself, straight but not very wide, which flanked the line of docks at that time stretching from the Herculaneum to the Hornby was, except on Sundays, daily congested by two long streams of horse-drawn traffic, two slow-moving processions moving in opposite directions at a set pace, and carrying merchandise of every description as piled-up evidence of the din and activity aboard the ships in dock, ships whose ports of call touched every part of the seven seas.

To and from them, lumbering along, past warehouses, railway depots ship repair-yards, and the many gaudy public-houses wedged in between, crawled these two continuous lines of vehicles: wagons and carts of different lengths and shapes; two-wheeled floats, heavy drays and high springcarts; four-wheeled timber-drags, pony wagons, one-horse wagons, and team-horse wagons; loaded with everything from wet hides to new boots, chocolates to deadly poisons, feathers to marble slabs, and gold ingots to scrap iron.

Harnessed in the shafts were horses of varying breeds and hues: brown horses, black horses, white horses, speckled horses; all pictures of unrestraining strength and cleanliness, with their coats glossed, their gears shining, their shoes polished, their sleek manes be-ribboned. Knowing horses, too, heeding the words of the carters sauntering leisurely at their sides, who spoke to them intimately, endearingly, or reprovingly as the mood demanded. And all for the purpose of regulating the pace of the long slow-moving procession, interrupted occasionally when one or more of the vehicles reached as breaking-off point either a side-street or dock gateway. This alone was the recognised reason for leaving the main body abruptly. 'No rushing out of your turn,' seemed to be its unwritten law. Exemption was only copper-bordered fire-engines, whose galloping steeds were convincing proof of the desperate hurry that usually brought them down to the docks. Apart from these, and considered in a special class, were the masters' prancing pony traps that went dashing by, their cocky drivers almost proclaiming to everybody within range: 'We run this show, don't forget. All the orders come from us.' The commanding sweep of their eye was a reminding link between the horses and the deck-crowded ships in dock.

Dock after dock, and rushing bare-armed about the sheds and quays, swarms of go-ahead truckmen entirely dependent on the ships. Everywhere, ships; more steam than sail, charging the air with smoke and noise. Coal barges, trawlers, small coasters, ocean liners, and cargo boats. Tramps of all nationalities, represented by the flags that flew at every stern, but all outnumbered by the red ensign which, fluttering from more of the flagstaffs, indicated Britain's far-flung trade.

Yet, despite this fact, it was extremely difficult for a boy from the slum streets of dockland to obtain a job on one of the ships as a member of the crew. The unhidden preferences of many shipowners for coloured seamen and alien seamen so limited his possibilities, that the only openings left were through the sea-training ships used as reformatories; or by being introduced to a ship's officer by somebody with influence who could be a clerk from the company's office, a fee-grabbing boarding-house keeper, or a member of the existing crew with long enough service to recommend a new hand.

A poor boy minus any of these contacts had little chance of going away on the ships. True, he could work by them or on them in port, as a steamlad at the cargo winches, or a rivet-lad with the repairers, or as a scaler chipping the insides of boilers; and even these jobs, dirty as they were, required introductions and at the very least an exchange of winks with the shore foreman. But going to sea in the ships was something entirely different; to do that, in dock parlance, necessitated a reference from the Holy Ghost.

There remained a final and most risky alternative, that of stowing away; risky because of the likelihood of being immediately discovered and roughly handed over to the police, or a worse likelihood of later being found dead through starvation or suffocation long after the ship had sailed.

Though luck can play a part in the stowaway's survival, knowledge of a ship's structure is a decided advantage in determining the conditions of discovery or surrender. Yes, surrender eventually, because there comes the moment when a hungry stomach and parched lips compels the stowaway to crawl out from his hiding place and give himself up. It was under such conditions that I made my first deep-water voyage.

Long before leaving school at the age of thirteen I was familiar with the docks and the outsides of ships. It was a necessary part of my daily noon-hour errands to meet my mother outside the slum school and from her receive my father's dinner which usually consisted of cheese or meat sandwiches, and fivepence, the price of two pints of beer. Off I would dash then to whatever part of the docks my father happened to be working as a stevedore. He was a tall, powerfully-built man. For him, and the exceptionally strong men engaged in his class of work, beer and sandwiches constituted a staple diet. On it they would often labour through thirty hours or more without a break.

On Saturday mornings it was a more urgent part of my task to search the dock road for my father and collect that portion of his wages he felt like handing over, for during the next few days he lived mainly without the sandwiches.

Most of the shipping companies paid their stevedores at hut-offices situated inside the dock sheds. It was through being directed towards these that I became accustomed to finding my own way across many of the traffic bridges that separated one from another.

Added to these regular romps were the frequent sailing-day visits to the Princes Landing Stage, but first stopping to have a gaze at the withered woman centenarian, bent and grumpy, who lived in a shack at the top of the Floating Bridge and sold toffee-apples. Muttering continually to herself, she would turn a half-penny over in her hand dawdled so long over serving that it was sometimes necessary for me to snatch the apple from the window-box, and bolt, leaving her still muttering over the coin in her hand. Then a quick dash down to the Landing Stage where the Atlantic liners were embarking their passengers. There, merged in the police-controlled crowds, I would stand and stare, join in the hand-waving farewells and parting shouts, until the liners siren blared a deep warning note, harbourmen rushed to cast off the mooring ropes, and the tug's tightening hawsers pulled the big ship into midstream as the sensitive crowd on the Stage quietened gradually to the drag and widening distance between, for many of the passengers were emigrants who would probably never return.

On leaving the slum elementary school, down to the docks I went to work as a steam-lad at the cargo-winches. As a result I soon became familiar with the insides of ships, and more curious regarding the men who took them away to sea and brought them back to port again. I wanted so much to know some of these men, to get on speaking terms with them if possible. They filled me with wonder as they filed down the gangways holding up parrots, or monkeys, or canaries, or any souvenirs that showed trace of a far-off country. These men were to me somehow a race apart with a gait of their own. Secretly I yearned to be one of them, yearned so intensely that often I was thrashed at home for staying out all night with the youthful driver of a baggage cart whose job it was to collect the sailor's bulky canvas bags from their respective homes and deliver them aboard the ship just prior to sailing time which varied with the changing tides.

Frequently I helped to hump these long canvas bags into the men's forecastle. To me, there was something mysterious about the bunks where each bag was dumped. They seemed hardly big enough to hold the body of a normal sized man. Except for the men, everything else about me in the forecastle was on a small scale. And in that cramped space I formed an opinion that men brought thus close together often become pally. Anyhow, it seemed like that as they handed me the last of their quart bottles of beer from mouth to mouth without the least concern for hygienic 'Don'ts'. In this outward congeniality they were to all appearances comrades. Desiring as I did to become one of them, I would linger to the last moment in their company in the hope of being asked 'Did I want a job?'; and never daring to suggest the need myself. Yet my eyes were constantly on the lookout for a likely place in which to stow away.

I was eager to go to any part of the world. I had heard, for instance, that it was possible to work a passage to Australia by signing on a ship's articles for a nominal wage of one shilling per month. I was more interested in the passage than the shilling and used to spend days at a time loitering about the wharf where any ship, either steam or sail, was loading cargo for Australia. But nobody ever invited me aboard to sign, even for a shilling a month, and I never would ask; first because I did not relish the idea of disclosing my secret; and secondly because I dreaded a taunting refusal.

Nevertheless, every opportunity found me at a different wharf. Ships loading for the United States of America always appeared to be well guarded against boys of my type. Forbidding quartermasters stationed at the ship's rail seemed to sense that I was waiting to steal up the gangway. Just a twitch of their eyebrows was sufficient to scare me. The moment I felt this way it was sheer waste of time dodging around any longer. So off I would miserably trudge to another ship where a similar disappointment was repeated.

But I was determined to make a voyage in a ship, somewhere. My first actual attempt at stowing away was in the 'tween-deck of an Elder-Dempster loading for the West Coast of Africa. I had heard that the cargo-men were going to work throughout the night in order that the ship could leave the dock in the morning tide at five o clock.

At nine-thirty that night, under cover of darkness, I approached the dock gates a bit timidly. The excuse already in my mind in the event of being challenged by a policeman was that I was on a message with my father's supper. I had fivepence savings in my top pocket, and a couple of cheese sandwiches intended for my own use, but ostensibly for my father. The mere showing of these would support my story. The important thing to know was exactly the name of the ship I was going to, the dock she was in, and why the cargo-men were working late. These details I had in readiness. They had been gathered in the ordinary way earlier in the day while listening to the job-talk of the men who had presented themselves at the dock-stand for hiring, but had not been selected for the working gangs.

Being night-time, the dock-road was almost deserted. Near the gate handiest for me to enter I hesitated, and looked cautiously around for the policeman on duty. He was in his hut, his back towards me. Ducking past his window I hurried on in the dark, footsure of every stone for the ground was familiar. On I went and in my haste nearly bumping head-first against the unusually low ball and hook hanging from one of the jib-cranes now at a standstill. All about were rows of white-topped barrels arranged for trans-shipment into the silent black-tarred barges below hardly distinguishable from the water surrounding them.

Crossing a bridge, I carefully picked my way along a dimly-lit quayside, chary of tripping over the mooring ropes because of my inability to swim, and also because of two previous daytime experiences of being fished out of water; once when I slipped off the edge of the quay into the dock and quickly had half-a-dozen would-be rescuers splashing about me; and again, when I was swept over the side of a ship by a rebounding sling of bag oil-cake.

On reaching a convenient place where I could see and not be seen, I stood with my body pressed against the she-wall, watching until the dockers at the far end of the quay had gone away for their supper. This hour, ten o'clock to eleven, was usually spent in the nearest public-house where beer, cheese and bread and maybe a pilfered onion dipped in salt made up the customary meal.

Across the darkness of the dock there was neither sound nor movement. Here and there streaks of reflected gas-light shimmered on the water's surface. Satisfied it was now safe for me to move on I did so, keeping close in to the shed-wall. I neared the ship. Nobody was about. Quickly I sneaked up a cargo-plank on to the deck, glanced nervously around me, then flew aft. By the light of an electric cluster I descended the hatchway ladder, and stepped sideways into the 'tween deck amongst the cargo. It did not take me long to spot a stack of boxes and gummy bales high enough to obscure me from view. Behind there I lay down, stretching my body out full length, and waited, almost afraid at first to breathe for fear of being discovered. But within ten minutes I was munching one of the cheese sandwiches, and after a slight indecision started on the other.

I knew when eleven o'clock had arrived by the talk of the men returning down the ladder, the drumming racket of the steam winches on the deck overhead, the warning roars of the hatch-boss as he bawled 'Stand clear, below!', the banding of the heavily packed slings as they swung hard against the [manuscript illegible] and were lowered down the hatch for the convenience of the men already lifting boxes into place within an arm's-length of me. Thus the hours passed.

Later on, from the men's conversation, I figured it was nearly four-o'clock. Then I heard a loud voice telling them that the last sling was being sent down, and when this was stowed all the hands were to come up on deck.

The talk near me ceased. The men were evidently ascending the ladder. The iron cross-beams were next dropped into the deep sockets. While the hatch-covers were being laid on, one of the stevedores must have remembered a coat he had left behind. He came down the hatch to search for it. And there he found me, asleep as he thought. Perhaps it was as well he did so, because as he said at the time and I fully believed him, that in a few more minutes, once the hatches were fastened down, I would have been suffocated and chewed by rats.

He was rather sympathetic. 'You've come to the wrong ship, son,' he told me. 'Your father's not in any of our gangs.' Walking ashore with him was no trouble. I mingled with the rest of the men and strode boldly out of the dock gate.

The streets were still in darkness. Sneaking into the house at half-past five meant an immediate bashing for me. The maternal coaxer was a sawn-off blindpole. My makeshift lie of helping the baggage-lad in the stable and falling asleep there, no more saved me than might have done the straightforward admission of my intention to run away to sea. What happened only strengthened it.

A few weeks afterwards, I made another attempt at stowing away, again on an Elder Dempster boat. Actually I had been working on this ship, so to some extent I could move about more freely without feeling I was under suspicion. This time, because of my fortunate escape down the hatch, I chose a covered-in recess near the funnel. It was a dark corner of the gratings on the steamy boiler-tops. From where I was, I could peep down at the negro fireman stoking their furnaces while they jabbered away in their own native lingo. The sweltering heat and thickening fumes soon drove me, soaked through and coughing, out of my hiding place. I became fainthearted too, fearing a collapse and perhaps being roasted alive. That was why I dodged ashore as fast as I was able, before a doubting ship's officer began some awkward quizzing.

I was blackened from head to toe with coal-dust and soot. The policeman at the dock gate thought I had been working overtime. So did a group of jealous steamlads further along the road for they yelled something about greasing the foreman's hand. Even to escape this stigma I would not tell them the real truth. I was not for telling anybody.

Some days later, when a sea-going chum of mine returned home from a voyage to the West Coast of Africa shivering with malaria, he looked so jaundiced and thin, speaking scarcely in a whisper, that I decided not to board any more ships likely to take me where that might happen. Yet somewhere I had to go.

I deliberately sought the company of other sea-going youths I knew, listening attentively for any word that might suggest how they had started on the ships. One had been placed by his uncle; another sent direct from reformatory. This fellow had not long since been rescued from a South-American bound ship that had sunk in the Bay of Biscay. But this did not deter me. His was only one ship; there were thousands on the ocean. Besides, he was looking for a job in another ship himself. But of greatest importance to me was his statement of having been in two ships where stowaways were found at sea and put to work. 'They were cute fellows, too,' he added. 'They didn't show up until long after we'd dropped our pilot.' I learned something from that and also that it was easier to stow away to Argentina than any other part of the world.

Consequently, I widened my knowledge and search of the docks. It was a simple matter to borrow the daily shipping paper from the nearest corner public-house, for that was a habit of sailors' wives in the neighbourhood who had sent me in to ask the barman. Secretly I would scan the reported movements of ships, and then tramp the whole seven-mile length of the docks to make sure the paper was correct; that a certain ship about to leave was at the wharf mentioned. For hours maybe, I would survey it from the quayside, thinking out the safest place to hide myself; and when.

That was how I came to stow away under the poop of a cargo boat, the S/S – on a Saturday afternoon. I had already been aboard on the Friday, loitered about as if seeking a job, sauntered on to the after-deck, and saw that cattle-pews had been rigged up on which the joiners were then noisily hammering down the wooden roofs. It was a practice for ships in the South American trade to carry a small number of prize pedigree cattle to be used for breeding purposes on the ranches of Argentina.

I walked along to the poop which was almost blocked-up with trusses of hay. Stopping casually at the door, I had a quick peep inside. My mind was made up. The top of the stacked-up hay would serve me as a comfortable bed. I estimated there would be sufficient space between that and the deck-hand in which to squeeze my body along the top, and so settled on a place to hide. Then making sure of the exact tide-time for the following day, I trudged the seven-mile journey home without telling anyone of my plans.

The next day, shortly after noon, I strolled leisurely along the quayside. There was nothing about my appearance to excite suspicion. I had no parcel of food; no extra clothing. I was just as I stood in my shabby dungarees. But my eyes were continually on the alert. The ship's hatches were battened down ready for sailing. It being dinner time, nobody was about the deck. I glanced up and down the quay and, satisfied all was clear, nimbly vaulted over the ships bulwark and darted aft. A massive-headed bull filled each of the four cattle-pens. With a slow twist of the head they turned their muzzles towards me. I could not resist starting back at them. The way they seemed to glare in return made me dither all over. I hurried straight to the poop and stepped inside.

Immediately I noticed that some of the hay had been shifted. With the opportunity of a better look around I saw also that my previous intention of lying on the top would have to be dismissed. A number of the trusses had obviously been taken away; others had been restacked so as to leave a passage in the centre, wide enough for one person to easily pass in and out of the poop, presumably to oil the chains of the steering-gear. Whoever entered would only have to raise their eyes to spot me. There was no time to ponder. Scrambling up the hay and over the top, I moved as far away from the passage as possible, until I found a place where I could drop down to the floor between some trusses and the side of the ship.

I don't know how long I stood there jammed in that position. My predicament was such that I was tempted to work my way out again and scamper ashore. But I did not. I was too afraid to move one way or the other. Besides, I realised it would be just as bad for me to be caught rushing off the ship now, as it would be to be caught aboard it. Also, I had done so much scheming for weeks past that I could not afford to spoil my chances now.

As there was yet no sound of anybody moving about, I risked making myself a little more comfortable. Narrow space had been left between the bales of hay to allow for ventilation. With a struggle I was able to manoeuvre the bales around until I could fit crouched in between two on the bottom, while the three top tiers remained built in over me. Through an interstice beyond I would be able to glimpse the legs of anybody passing in and out of the poop even if I could not see their body or face.

Soon there was a commotion and running about on deck. I sat very still. Overhead, the sailors were hauling in the mooring ropes. Shortly afterwards, the steering chains scraping close by me began to squeak and rattle as they were jerked horizontally through the floor-sheaves from port to starboard, and back. Then the startling chush, chush, chush, chush of the propeller beneath shook the whole stern so much that I dreaded any minute the top bales of hay would fall in on me. This spasmodic shaking continued for a while, then they settled down to a steady, quivering rhythm. I was inwardly excited as the floor jounced under me. The ship was on her way.

It may have been a couple of hours later when I heard the clatter of footsteps coming towards the poop. A man seemed to shuffle up the passage, muttering and swearing to himself. I could not understand a word he was saying. In my imagination it had some reference to me and what was sure to happen once he laid his fingers on me. I was all tensed up and too terrified to budge, especially when his trousered legs were right against my peephole. My trembling did not stop until several minutes after he had gone out. I murmured: 'Oh God.'

The next arrival, obviously a livelier type of man, almost bounced into the poop. 'Now, Joe,' he called to somebody else on the outside. There were more quickened footsteps and another man entered.

'Where is it?' this one asked in a cautious undertone.

'Here,' answered the first man. 'Stand in out of sight,' he advised. 'I thought old bothered balls was never coming out again. I wouldn't give him water.' He used some swear names, then paused. 'Good luck,' he said. There was a sound a guzzling and a heave of satisfaction. 'Here; it tastes good. Take a good swig. Finish it off if you can.'

'Whose is it, though?'

'Never you mind. Sup it up. Dump the bottle overboard.' They finished the beer and left the poop together.

It was nearly dusk when the propellers slowed down and stopped. The poop went deadly still. Against the ship's side I could hear the gurgling lap of the water. What worried me most now was that the crew might come along on a final hunt. I had disturbing thoughts of pitchforks being prodded into the hay. Before that was carried too far I would surrender myself. But nobody came. Then the propeller restarted again. The reason for the short stoppage dawned on me. The pilot was being dropped.

Darkness came on. The squeaking strain and rattle of the steering chains was less jumpy. The deadened rustling of the hay vibrated in time to the steady chush-chush of the propeller below.

I could hear the occasional snorts of the bulls on the deck and the stamping and scraping of their hoofs. But none of the crew were about; had they been so they could not have missed my unrestrained wearisome yawning. Though my head nodded for a doze I dare not go asleep. I was too frightened and uncomfortable. Besides being terribly cramped I had an annoying crick in my neck that made me grunt. Worse still were the tortuous gripping pains that forced me to at last ease myself against the hay. I was panicky of any flow and its consequences.

Because of the dark, I could not wriggle out of my place to stand up for fear of blunderingly upsetting any trusses into the passage; I would not have been able to see to replace them. Occasionally I did manage to twist my body from one crouching position to another, but it was impossible to stretch my legs.

The night wore on. I was feeling hungry but by no means sea-sick. Only the stale smell and stuffy warmth of the hay made me a bit feverish. I chewed stalks of it to keep my lips moist. I listened for footsteps, but nobody else entered the poop and for this I was thankful. There was of course the ever-present suspense of expectancy, but apart from this and the night-nervousness I was not really unhappy nor had any regrets. At least I was actually at sea.

Daylight crept around again. I sat for a long time wondering if the ship was far down the Welsh coast, or near to Ireland, or past Land's End; and what Land's End looked like, and whether somebody would be standing on top of a cliff shaking a white handkerchief as the ship went steaming by. This and a desire to return the greeting were among the curious ideas that passed through my mind.

They were interrupted by the approach of clattering footsteps again. I fixed my eyes on the peephole and fervently hoped there was no trace of a pool in the passage to betray my whereabouts. A pair of legs passed and repassed. Once more it was the muttering man. I could not understand a single word he was saying though my ears were strained for the five minutes or so he was in the poop.

There would be others after him I survived. I remained quite still. Exactly what hour of the day it was I did not know. I did know I was becoming hungrier and hungrier and felt a sickening weakness with it. My body was aching all over. Eventually I was compelled to shoulder my way out the ship's side and stand up to stretch my arms and legs. As I did so, a top bale of hay was pushed aside, and a man's fat round face rose above me and stared straight in on me. Too bewildered to duck down again I silently met his stare.

He had a brown drooping moustache the same as my father's; tobacco juice trickled down one side of his chin. This, and the face of him wearing a new dungaree jacket convinced me he was not an officer. Easy-going from his expression, he showed no surprise at seeing me; nor did I feel very frightened of him. He seemed to have found me at the exact moment I wanted to be found.

His head and shoulders raised a shade higher. 'Come up out of that,' he ordered me in a tolerably gruff voice. 'I just thought there was somebody in behind there all the time.'

I clambered over the bales of hay and jumped down in the passage about a yard from where he stood wiping his chin with the back of his hand.

'Anybody with you?' he asked.

'No, sir,' I answered timidly, for I half-expected a cuff on the ear or a formal reprimand; nothing more. I had no real dread of this man.

'How long have you been in there?'

'Since Saturday dinner-time, sir.'

'Hmm-m.' Spit. 'Twenty-four hours, eh? I hope you've left no bloody bread crumbs about.'

'I had no bread, sir.'

He stared hard at me for a moment. 'See any rats at all?'

The question made me clammy all over. 'No, sir,' I stammered.

He eyed me up and down as if in doubt. 'Alright. Stand there a moment,' he ordered. 'I better make properly sure there's nobody else in there.' His fat stumpy body bellied over the top tiers of hay, right across to where I had been hidden. He searched as far as space permitted in between the trusses.

'Anybody else there?' he shouted, but received no answer. I was afraid for a while that another stowaway might pop up and make a liar of me. I was much relieved when this did not happen.

The little fat man backed slowly out again and dropped on his feet alongside me, puffing from the exertion. He flicked some chaff from off his coarse serge pants.

'Alright,' he said. 'Come in.'

On following him out I noticed his brown canvas shoes. These accounted for me not having heard him enter the poop. Trailing after him along the deck, I was more interested in what I saw around me than in any punishment that might be due. There was no land anywhere. The ship was completely encircled by green water, miles and miles of it. Except for the white curling ripple caused by the ship's bow, the sea was as smooth as glass. From a clear sky the sun shone warmly. Everything seemed different to what I had expected. The absence of land puzzled me most. I kept staring around and around. Repeatedly I glanced over my shoulder in case a promontory or a cape might suddenly break through on the horizon as proof that the land was actually back there somewhere. Hovering over the ship's stern were dozens of shrieking seagulls that went swooping downwards in relays to float a while on the water. Behind them was the faint frothy scrawl of the propeller.

As my escort and I drew near to the cattle pens, I promptly sidled away towards the hatch. Those bulls appeared too fierce for my liking.

Yet I could not resist looking back to see if they were attempting to follow. Their big protruding eyes were, and that was sufficient to quicken my step.

Past the pens, the little man turned to me. 'Half-a-mo,' he said as he halted. 'There's no hurry. You'll get me in a row time enough.' From his mouth then he gathered a large blackish quid of tobacco and dropped it into his coat pocket. Then he wiped his chin with the back of his hand. 'Is my face clean?' he asked.

'Yes, sir,' I answered. I was tempted to tell him he needed a shave, but dare not take the liberty.

'Alright.' Spit. 'Come on. Up here,' he said.

I followed him up a ladder and on to another deck where a few open doors were hooked back on the outside. Out of one popped a young man's bare head.

'A capture, Boce?' he asked as he nodded towards me.

'Aye,' answered my escort offhandedly. 'I just found him under the poop.'

'Ummmmm,' grimaced the other as we passed on.

I was taken up another and much cleaner ladder that lead on to the bridge. There, a middle-aged watch-officer pacing back and forth halted to stare across at me, then resumed his pacing. My escort stopped outside a cabin door, told me to wait, and disappeared to the far side of the bridge.

Left alone, I could not refrain from staring about me. I was dazed and in a dream. I did not feel I was an object to be stared at. Instead, I felt that everything existed for me to stare at in wonderment. Everything around me was so clean. The bridge parts were painted white. The brass portholes glittered. The boards under my feet had been scrubbed spotless.

The little fat man came back to where I was and rapped on the cabin door. From inside, a voice shouted: 'Who's there?'

'It's me, captain,' replied my escort. 'I've got a stowaway out here.' In the next breath he whispered to me: 'Take your cap off.'

I did so. Hands by my side I stood, dreading the next moment. For I was fully prepared to see a scowling martinet strut out of the cabin.

The door opened. Another little tubby man confronted me. He was wearing only a woollen singlet and a pair of fine serge pants. One side of his braces were unfastened. The nearest suggestion to a uniform was the well-worn peaked cap on his head. His hair was white, also his clipped moustache. His prolonged scrutinizing unnerved me.

'Well,' he began abruptly. 'What have you got to say for yourself?' I hung my head but did not answer.

'Speak up,' he prompted. I was trembling. My cap dropped from my fingers to the deck and had to lay there.

The captain bawled again. 'Will you speak up when you're told.' I raised my eyes appealingly towards the other little fat man who had brought me up to the bridge. Somehow I was depending on him to smooth matters over for me. But he never opened his mouth.

When the captain stepped out over the threshold, I drew back a pace. 'Hold your head up,' he ordered. Automatically I obeyed. I was absolutely terrified. There was no escape. I was in a trap with miles and miles of water around me, water that seemed to have changed from green to deep blue in those few minutes. I glanced around in despair. The distance to the horizon was considerable. Inwardly I prayed for seven-league boots.

The captain roared again: 'What's your name?' I told him in a whisper.

'Does your father know where you are?'

'No, sir.' I mumbled.

'Does your mother know?'

'No, sir.'

'What put this idea into your head?'

I was near to tears. My lips were quivering. 'I don't know, sir.'

'You don't know! Eye-wash,' he barked. He turned to my escort. 'Whereabouts did you find him, Boce?'

'Under the poop, sir.' The boatswain was describing how he had gone under the poop to see if any hay had fouled the steering gear, when the captain broke in impatiently.

'Why the hell don't you have the poops thoroughly rooted out before we set sail? Isn't there enough bloody messing over these fellows each trip? I'm tired of telling you—' He seemed too exasperated for words, then suddenly snapped out: 'Go on! Take him forward and give him something to eat.'

I picked my cap up, and was glad to follow the boatswain down the ladder. At the bottom we both stopped short on hearing the captain call out. His tone was milder.

'Listen, Boce. Give him a good scrub down too. He looks as if he needs it.'

'Aye, aye, sir,' answered the boatswain. We continued on our way to the forecastle. Round the bend of the saloon and out of sight of the bridge, the boatswain poked the tobacco quid back into his mouth.

'There you go,' he declared with the uncomplaining shrug of a prophet. 'What did I tell yer. Getting me into a bloody row. That always happens.'

'I'm very sorry, sir,' I said. 'Honestly I am.' Had it been in my power I would have bought him all the best chewing tobacco in the world. I thought I could impress him by using a big word learnt by me before coming aboard. 'I hope nothing detrimental happens to you, sir,' I said.

His forehead wrinkled in astonishment. 'Eh? What's that?' Spit. His face relaxed once more.

'Oh, aye.' Spit. 'Never mind. It can't be helped. You've got to start somewhere. Come on.'

We walked along the foredeck. At the entrance to the forecastle alleyway, a few members of the crew were lounging about in shirt sleeves, and regarding me with curiosity. I kept close on the heels of the boatswain.

'Come on,' he said, directing me up the alleyway and into the sailors' pokey forecastle. It was almost dark inside, although the time was midday. The little daylight showing through the portholes was scatteringly reflected on the glaze of the oil-skins hanging on the hawse-pipe corner. I could count six men's faces. Their features were not too clear. They were seated on the wooden forms skirting the low bunks and stopped speaking as I edged inside the doorway. The boatswain was staring down at some food dixies on the floor, for there was no table.

He addressed the men. 'Have you fellers all had your dinner?' he asked.

'Aye. We're finished,' came the reply.

My hunger returned as the boatswain stooped down to examine the dixies. 'Any of these been slopped?' he wanted to know.

One of the men pointed to a dixie in which cotton waste, potato peelings, soup, and half-bitten slices of putting were thrown in together. The boatswain shoved this dixie aside, then drew the others closer.

'Alright,' he said. 'There's plenty here. Lend him a plate, one of you.'

Spontaneously, four tin plates were offered to me. I stepped across to the man nearest, who also supplied me with a knife, fork, and spoon. On the knife's yellow handle, the initials T.E. were deeply cut, evidently the owner's private marking.

I stood, hesitant. Despite my hunger I was loath to help myself to food on the floor without a direct invitation to do so. Even when the boatswain remarked, 'Nobody's going to wait on you,' I knelt down half-heartedly by the dixies. One contained potatoes, another soup, another meat, and another, thick slices of plum pudding into which I would have dived immediately had no one else been present. Under the eyes of the men I was too embarrassed to do anything but kneel there gawping. I glanced slyly around from one to the other, coming back oftenest to the one I considered the fiercest-looking individual I had ever seen.

He was broadly-built and had a close-cropped bullet-head from which two ears stuck out like oval-shaped handles. His swollen bruised lip appeared to have been hit by a drunken brawl. It flashed through my mind that he was an ex-convict recently released from prison. In comparison all the other men seemed harmless weaklings. I felt he could have easily murdered them all without much effort. The way his two hands gripped the side of the form seemed as if he was about to pounce as he caught me glancing up at him. His lips were twitching to speak. I was powerless to move. His hand stretched outwards. 'Give me that plate here,' he demanded in a coarse voice. I immediately passed the plate across. 'Do you want any soup?' he asked. 'It's thick barley. It'll put a back on yer like an elephant.'

'Yes, please,' I murmured.

'Hand the dixie over.'

The soup was nearly cold. One helping was sufficient. Besides, I was eager to start on the pudding as soon as I reasonably could. The bullet-headed man lightly kicked the other dixie towards me.

'Go on,' he urged. 'Take no notice of anyone. Get it all down yer. It's probably the last decent meal you'll see in this packet until we reach Montevideo.' He moved along the form and made room for me to sit beside him. Thus encouraged, I sorted out my meat and potatoes, finished eating one plateful, and was soon filling another, regardless of the men absorbed in conversation.

Meantime, the boatswain though still in the forecastle was no longer concerned about me. Though indulging in some cross-talk from where he stood, he kept screwing his eyes across to the bunks. Then he walked over to a narrow wooden cupboard and began rummaging the shelves. All the men ceased their conversation and stared in surprise. One of them jumped up in resentment.

'What's the idea, Boce?' he asked. 'You've no right to meddle in there. What do you want?'

'Want?' emphasized the Bosun. 'Want, eh? I planted a quart of ale in the poop and some dirty bastard's gone and swiped it.' His eyes seemed to rest on the bullet-headed man as if he were the culprit.

The latter recognised this and shook his head in a chortling denial. 'It's no use looking at me, Boce,' he said. 'I know nothing about it.'

The boatswain for once seemed to be vexed. 'I don't care who it is,' he declared. 'I'll jollop the next bloody lot. I'm in earnest, too.'

While the remainder of the men became serious in their denials, the bullet-headed man kept smiling throughout as if the whole incident was a joke. His behaviour provoked the boatswain's direct accusation.

The bullet-headed man's definite 'No. Not me!' was not accepted.

I was afraid of a wrangling match that might develop into a fight. Though I was grateful to the boatswain for his kindness towards me, I had also taken a liking to the bullet-headed man who in his own rough way had made short shift of my shyness. I felt it was unfair for him to be blamed in the wrong. His voice bore no resemblance to the voices I had distinctly heard in the poop. I decided to tell what I knew about the beer and Joe.

Try as I did, it seemed impossible for me to get a word through the men's cross-talk of inferences and contradictions. I was deliberately ignored. While deferentially awaiting permission to speak, I considered it wiser not to mention anything about the poop. To do so might cause mischief on myself and others, and worse still condemn me as a clat tale. I went on eating.

While the rest of the men were still serious about the missing beer the bullet-headed man assured of his physical power treated the accusation lightly.

'Aye,' he said. 'I know what happened. One of them bulls aft drank it. I was along there last night, one of them was singing "The Rose of Tralee" at the top of his voice. Aye. Ask any of the lads.'

This provoked the boatswain to open hostility. 'Whose bleedin' leg are you trying to pull,' he said, preparing to leave the forecastle. He turned to me and in a lowered voice promised to bring me some soap. He added sarcastically, 'One of these generous fellows might give you an old towel.'

I said, 'Thanks very much,' and he left the forecastle.

TEN YEARS ON THE PARISH

By

A. Groundling.

I suppose I am officially listed as a bad case. Aged forty, able-bodied; two weeks work in the last five years, and barely ten months between 1926 and '37. From '23 to '26 I was in America and prior to that was unemployed for two years; making my English working record less than one year's work in twelve.

It was not my first sample. That began as a boy of fourteen after leaving a slum school in Sprayport's [sic] dockland. Straight to the ships I had to go as a casual boy-labourer to barrow coal, and was picked occasionally from the other poor boys who hung around the cargo-sheds for a job. Some had run away from their homes, and in the dinner hours begged bread from the dockers; a currant scone being a luxury they all rushed to grab. At night they slept in empty houses, warehouse doors, and smelly urinals, until the police bundled them off to a reformatory for five years, and jailed their fathers for not paying their maintenance.

I had some of this sleeping-out, mostly in an old stable near the docks that was rented by a man who carried seamen's baggage. He took me to the ships at all hours of the night, and I helped him hump the bags into the forecastles. Many a time I sat on a form, hoping one of the men would not turn up, but was always baulked when the boarding-house keepers brought their supply of substitutes aboard.

At last I had to do what many boys were doing, stow away to sea; and hid myself in the poop of a tramp bound for Buenos Aires. Two days out, the bosun found me and yanked me up to the skipper. After a lecture and a meal, I was put into the bunker to shovel coal, and bullied into shifting a man's share. This continued for a week. Then they sent me down the hot stokehold. It was not work; it was torture. Secretly I cried. My hands were like raw meat. My body was racked with pain. Off watch, I lay in a wooden bunk without bed or bedding. The crew had only brought sufficient covering for themselves. The ship was hard for them, so there was little sympathy for me. I dare not lay up. As a stowaway I had no rights. Often in the tropics I staggered along the deck too exhausted to speak. It was a month before the ship touched land again. Though ragged and penniless I was glad when night came to sneak down the gangway ashore. The captain bawled to me not to come back. I didn't mean to.

Buenos Aires was a progressively busy city. There was a demand for labour in factories, on the docks, or aboard other ships. Passports were not necessary. I could not make a job contact at first. But I never went short of food. There was always the certainty of a meal in one of the forecastles. Near the docks were stretches of long grass. The weather was warm. I slept out without fear, or sometimes under a ship's awning. An Englishwoman who managed a sailors' drink-shop got me a job on the docks humping two hundred pound sacks of grain. They nearly bent me in two. I was just turned sixteen. When an opportunity came I dropped this job and straightened my back up properly. Three Britishers [sic] in their twenties who knew the country well coaxed me to go on the tramp. We wandered through miles of ranch-land, living principally on stolen fresh-killed meat. Our worst enemies were the mosquitoes; our main discomfort the nightly dewfalls.

In 1914 war broke out. I was back in Buenos Aires. Jobs were plentiful in ships. I sailed for England, and in the four years that followed experienced lots of frights and excitement. Prisoner of war; escape. Back to sea again. Submarine dodging; torpedoed. More escapes. And luckily surviving all the dangers that were part of the daily life.

Immediately after the armistice I married. Empty homes were scarce in the slums; rents were excessive. An ordinary four-roomed cottage jumped in price from eight shillings a week to twelve and six. In larger houses many poor people were paying that much for one or two rooms. Amongst those who had a bit of money there was keen competition to slip any rent collector a couple of pounds for advance information of a house becoming vacant. There was no house for us. We moved into a large sized room of a sub-let house, confident of the future. The war had been fought and won. There would be jobs for everybody, and proper homes too. The politicians said so and returned soldiers re-echoed it.

Within a few months, prewar experiences were repeated in the daily search for work. Along the docks, young men recently demobbed competed with their fathers. There were scrimmages at the hiring stands. Men nudged and glared and shoved and swore. Then their fists were at it.

It was the same aboard ships. Complaints to the union delegates to control it went unheeded. There was always a jostling crowd. My size and strength pushed me to the front occasionally, and I made a few voyages in different tramps. But on arrival home, getting a job became more difficult. Lots of men displaced by women in factories and offices now swarmed the dockside, where hydraulic cranes and electric trucks were ousting the regular dockers. Ships starting to burn oil engaged smaller crews. Trade was leaving the port. Wages were being slashed, except for the trade union officials. Food prices were high.

At the Labour Exchange, ex-munitions workers and some returned soldiers were drawing twenty-nine shillings a week from the government, while others managed on their gratuity. But unemployment benefit proper of only seven shillings was limited to a few selected trades, including boiler-makers. Many of these former gold-watched week-enders were already tramping around as aimlessly as casual dockers. For the unskilled; no work, no income.

I was quickly down to the pawnshop level. All my clothes went in; next the bedding. We had a spell of sleeping on the bare mattresses and using the flock tick as a blanket. The empty table provoked many a quarrel. There were sighs and snarls; and crazy thoughts of theft, murder and suicide.

Around the docks men became degraded in their anxiety for work. Bribery was rampant, direct and indirect. One example was that of a woman in the slums whose husband was a stevedore's foreman. He hired the men for shipwork [*sic*]. Their wives in need of immediate cash had to borrow money from the foreman's wife. Her weekly interest of a penny in the shilling was always assured. In three months the amount paid back was higher than the original loan which was still owing and had to be renewed to prolong the men's employment.

Even had I been willing to fit in to such a scheme, the chance had passed by. I had forfeited my docker's tally by going away to sea. Ashore it was impossible to find a job, nor could I easily get a ship. To walk six miles to one of the docks and see a ship's deck swarming with men was almost a daily experience. Walking was compulsory; there was little money for food; there was none at all for fares.

Whatever went short, the rent had to be paid. To miss it meant a squabble with the other sub-tenants who were too hard pressed to carry someone else's burden. One was an old labourer who every morning tramped the docks, yet rarely worked two days a week; his wife hawked fish. Another was a deserted wife who went out charring to feed her children. The third was a consumptive widow whose three orphans were dependant on a small pension. All of these dreaded eviction; all knew that other people close by were waiting to move in at the first opportunity; so all paid the rent out of fear.

But the worst bugbear was the municipal night-inspector who came hammering at the door after midnight. His surprise visits upset everyone, particularly children. His job was to catch those of opposite sexes sleeping in the same room, then summons the parents for breaking the bye-laws. Only married couples were allowed to sleep together. Two adults of the same sex could occupy the one bedroom. Four children below the age of ten counted as two adults. Once a boy or girl turned ten they were reckoned as adults.

In the house where I lived, the orphan boy of ten was forbidden by law to sleep with his widowed mother. For warmth and sentiment they did sleep together except when the night-inspector was about due. Then night after night, the boy was carried upstairs to a dark attic, and left there to scream, while his mother waited below in the cellar kitchen for the inspector's ratta-tat-tat [sic]. With a family of mixed children, conditions were worse. As there were no spare rooms to put them in, brothers and sisters had to sleep in the one room, though not necessarily together. It was usually past midnight before they risked going to bed. Always the last question was: 'Where will we run to if the night-man comes?'

A court fine shortened the interval to the next visit. Meantime, parents would be pestered by the day-inspector with: 'Have you found another house yet? Are you looking for one? You're long winded about it'. It was no use replying that apartments were scarce, that rents were high and that most landlords objected to children. These were gruffly dismissed as excuses. 'They all say that,' was the usual comment.

Soon the night-inspector was back again; banging at the front door, being admitted, rushing up the stairs, pushing into dark bedrooms, flashing his torch across the bed, into faces, under the bed, and taking a peep into cupboards as he reeled off the stock questions: 'How many sleep in this room? Sure there's no more? Where's so and so? Next room? Righto. Goodnight.' Then off down the stairs again, slamming the front door behind him. A few minutes later he would be hammering at a house opposite. Young married women whose husbands were on night work, or at sea, or still in the army, dreaded leaving their bedroom doors unlocked. But they had to; there was no escaping the law.

Children never knew what midnight they might be dragged from their sleep. As soon as it was rumoured that the nightmen [*sic*] were in the neighbourhood, parents dashed upstairs to the bedrooms. There was never time to dress. Boys and girls, bare-footed and blubbering, were hurried out of the backdoor to be hidden in a tumble-down W.C. that was mildewed and stinking from long and constant use. Here they huddled together, trembling at the bark of a dog or an approaching footstep, until word was brought, maybe around two o'clock, that the nightmen were gone or that it was only a false alarm. But false alarm or not, the children still had to be in school at nine that morning.

Our own baby arrived. The midwife took the whole of the thirty shillings maternity money. Food was still very dear. There was less of it now for three of us in the second year of peace than was allowable to one person under the war rations scheme. Early each morning I left the house, and stayed out all day without anything to eat in the company of other men doing the same. At night I would find that my wife had not eaten because I was out. I had stayed out so that she could eat. The result was a quarrel.

Our nerves were continually on edge. Over a meal she had foraged we seldom spoke. One misunderstood word would start a flare-up and a flood of tears. We slated each other for the plight we were in. Our making-up would be shattered the next day; again no job; again a pawn-ticket more on the mantel piece. There came the all-night lie-awake until the following morning.

The workless were everywhere; at the street corners, on the docks, in emergency labour exchanges, outside newspaper buildings, crowding the shipping offices; any place they thought they might hear or read of a job. Standing about in groups, they grumbled and spat, as they criticized the government for breaking its promises. Many of them still boasted of their share in winning the war, and argued about the value of their medals. These were something to fall back upon. Later, the pawnshop windows were piled up with them. They had changed hands for a few pence. Mutterings of disillusionment followed. Men spoke bitterly as dupes. They used the term 'scrap-heap'. Its meaning became clear to me. At the early age of twenty-four I was on it.

In the middle of 1920 there was a boom in American shipping. I was eager to get to the other side. There were friends of mine working in New York. That was the place for me. My wife was game to eke out somehow until I could post her some money. If I landed a good job I would also send the fare for her passage and the baby's.

Nightly I haunted the docks for the chance of a pierhead jump. But every time the boarding-house men were brought along. Shipped in this fashion they signed their future earnings away. The shipping-master of at least one big company ran a boarding-house as a side-line. So between types like him and others who exploited men's anxiety, the possibility of a job without greasing some-one's palm almost disappeared.

One morning I bluffed my way into one. I had gone aboard an Atlantic two funneller [*sic*] to become part of the surging crowd shouting for a job. An officer standing on a chair was calling names out from a list. As each man answered 'Here, sir,' or 'Coming,' he squeezed through to the doctor's room to be examined, then went to the saloon to sign the ship's articles. As the men in their excitement pressed forward I was gradually worked to the back. Knowing there was another way to the doctor's room, I hurried off to find it. Three men were waiting their turn to go in. I stood behind them, listened for the order 'NEXT!', walked straight in, dropped my pants for a rupture test, buttoned up again, got my stamped chit, and went across to the saloon to sign the ship's articles. This done, I queued up at another table for my allotment note.

The shipping-master was writing them out. He stared hard at me, then looked down his duplicate list.

'Have you signed?' he asked.

'Yes,' I said. 'Just now, over there.'

'You're pretty smart, aren't you,' he sneered. 'How did you get the job? You've never been in this ship before.'

'No,' I answered. 'It's my first trip here.'

'And it'll be your last,' he grunted, 'I'll see to that.' He passed me the allotment note. As I turned away, he called me back and threw down a shilling. 'Here! Get yourself a drink,' he said. 'You're worth that for your bloody impudence.' It paid for a packet of cigarettes and my tram fare home.

I joined the ship as I stood, practically in rags. The pawnbroker could keep the clothes he had belonging to me. All I required was a stoke-hold singlet and a secondhand [*sic*] pair of dungaree pants. In a week I would be in New York. Once my body was out of England it was not going back. Most of the men in the forecastle were saying the same thing.

In New York, work was plentiful. Britishers were everywhere. On the trolley cars, in the restaurants, in office buildings, in factories on the docks, and in the ships.

I joined an American ship. Wages were double those of English ships. Within a few months, besides sending sufficient money home, I could buy myself changes of underwear and a new suit of clothes.

Tidy in appearance, I found work ashore. Out of my wages, a weekly remittance went home regularly, also occasional parcels of baby clothing. I was keeping myself without stint and saving towards my wife's fare. The idea of her coming to New York had to be abandoned. The Emigration officers were stopping women on the landing pier, and deporting their husbands who had gone down to claim them. I too, as a ship's deserter, was likely to be arrested on sight. Afraid of having my savings confiscated, I returned to England after a twelve months' absence in 1921.

Domestic happiness was re-established. Though rents were high and houses still scarce, we decided to look for one as soon as I got a job. Optimistically we rented two rooms, bought some new furniture, and ate satisfying meals. For breakfast we could afford eggs and bacon, and a bit of best butter. Butter was a luxury at two and two pence a pound. Once a week we enjoyed a theatre and sometimes invited friends. We had money to spare.

I felt independent. There was no immediate hurry to look for work. When I took a morning jaunt along the docks, the first rebuffs did not upset me, though the scrambling for jobs seemed worse than before. Men of fifty had dyed their hair and shaved off their moustaches. Young men resenting the move were loud in their abuse. 'Go and wash the blacking off your head,' they would shout as the old men slunk away, mumbling. But jobs came no quicker to any of them. They appealed to their trades union for advice and help. The officials bluffed them. Wanting contributions, not complaints, they cancelled all branch meetings. The men were staggered. Thousands of them threw away their membership books. They didn't know where to turn next.

The government opened more Labour Exchanges. Unemployment benefit embraced a wider number of men. It included seamen. The weekly grant was fifteen shillings. At first I would not humiliate myself for such an amount but was soon glad to. The fifteen shillings was payable for six weeks then suspended for six weeks, its continuance being determined by a Labour Exchange official. What happened in the meantime was no concern of his. If an applicant had no private resources, he starved or stole. Very few would go near the poor-law guardians. The workhouse was detested. Men preferred jail. Some committed suicide.

My savings soon dwindled despite economising [*sic*]. The breakfast stopped and the theatre. Gradually all our clothes went into the pawnshop, then the pawnable [*sic*] shoes. My wife would not venture into the street in daylight. She was too self-conscious of what the neighbours might think. Her shabby appearance became worse. Tearfully she parted with her wedding ring; next, her engagement ring. They were to be redeemed the moment I found a job.

Daily searchings [*sic*] produced none. Open competition on the docks became an exasperating waste of time and boot leather. Most vacancies were filled by 'overnight selections' pushed in because of influence. It was happening everywhere, and making the unwanted more despondent.

We had to sell the furniture. This was a hard blow to our pride. The clothes and the rings had been sneaked to the pawnshop without the neighbours knowing. They were bound to see the furniture go. I had not the nerve to wheel it myself to the auction-room. Another chap hired a handcart and took it for me. When the auctioneer told me the low price it fetched I did not believe him. When I handed the money to my wife, she did not believe me. Shortly afterwards we stripped the oil-cloth off the floor; that raised a few shillings.

We were now down on a starvation level of one meal a day. My wife's face went yellow and haggard. I became thin and more raggedy. We both soured. Friction was unavoidable. Everything seemed to provoke it; no work, lack of money, our rags. Luckily the baby's stock of clothes provided him with a clean change.

The price of food remained excessively high; bread at sixpence a two-pound loaf; margarine at a shilling a pound, and milk at five-pence a pint. A quarter-pound of bacon and four eggs cost a shilling. Meat like butter, was prohibitive at ten shillings a pound. Once a week we tasted a little; a kindly neighbour used to send in our Sunday dinner. Apart from that we were limited to bread, tea, and margarine, obtained on credit at a small cellar grocery store, where an extra halfpenny or penny was added to each article. It was a form of usury we could not escape.

One night we sat in the dark: no food, no money; not even a penny for the lamp oil. Next morning the baby's clothes were gathered together for the pawnshop. As my wife placed the bundle on the table, she glared across at me. Her smothered sobs broke into hysterical abuse. Tempers burst loose. It nearly ended in murder.

It was useless telling a distracted woman that thousands of men were tramping the streets. She did not see them, so she did not know. She only knew the man next door was always in work. The man next door! Though I never saw him, I often wished he would fall down a ship's hatch and break his neck. There was trouble each time he was mentioned.

I was desperate. Money, money, money, was the daily cry. The rent-collector who came to our house was a temptation. He was a fat tubby man, and wore pebbled spectacles. On his stomach hung a gaping satchel into which he dropped his takings. I made up my mind to have some. If I could coax him into the lobby and accidentally tip the satchel, he would lose more from it than he would ever pick up. He could not stoop, he was short-winded, and his spectacles suggested he was half blind too.

My chance came on a warm afternoon when the other sub-tenants were out. My wife not knowing what I intended was upstairs nursing the baby. Through the window I spotted the collector on the opposite side of the street. He had finished his rounds. I beckoned him across. He did not seem to heed me. I went out the front door and called him. He turned around and started back. The money satchel bulged on his fat stomach. My pretence for asking him indoors would be repairs. He had never refused a reasonable request.

He wobbled across the street, mopping his forehead with a white handkerchief. I now felt that the warm day might be an excuse for his not coming in. That would not hinder me. Once his foot reached the top step, I would drag him indoors if necessary. As he stepped onto the pavement I was wondering how to begin the conversation. He came towards me. He seemed all stomach down to his knees.

I had to say something. 'Can you spare a couple of minutes,' I asked him.

He clutched at the railings, then sat down on the bottom step with a grunt. 'Christ! I'm all in,' he gasped. 'Whaddyer [*sic*] want? Hurry up. I mustn't stay too long.'

I was staring down at his satchel. It was full of silver; half-crowns and two shilling pieces. It must have weighed heavy. I was eager for him to stand on his feet and come up the steps. He still sat wiping his forehead.

This annoyed me. I had fully expected him to walk straight up. Then I was going to tell him about the broken bannisters, and invite him in to look at them. He seemed in no hurry to move. This aggravated me. But for the people passing by I would have grabbed him under the armpits and dragged him up the steps.

I swore under my breath, 'You fat bastard,' I muttered, 'I could strangle you for making me wait like this.' I raised my voice. 'You'd better come in and have a look at these banisters,' I said, 'before somebody falls downstairs and breaks their neck.'

He gripped the railings and slowly pulled himself to his feet. The sweat was pouring down his face. 'I've no – I've no time to bother with banisters now,' he gasped. 'It'll be all right though, I'll – I'll send a man in the morning.'

I lost my temper. 'The morning,' I roared. 'This is the time to look at them, never mind the morning.'

He stopped wiping his face to stare at me. I felt my over-eagerness had made him suspicious. I toned down a bit. The idea of tipping his satchel then was given up. I would catch him some other time. But now I must clear myself.

'It won't take you a minute,' I said. 'You can pop right out again.'

'Oh, I don't feel much like popping in anywhere,' he answered. 'I'll see to it all right. You needn't worry. There'll be a man here first thing in the morning.'

I dare not press him after that. 'All right,' I agreed, 'so long as you don't forget.'

He was still wiping his face. 'Christ, it's hot,' he grunted. 'Phew!'

As he went to walk away, he staggered backwards against the railings, and gripped them with both hands. He twisted his head about, to work his neck free from his collar. His eyes rolled towards me. 'Get me a drink,' he murmured.

It dawned on me that he was ill. I could not leave him to stand unattended in case he pitched forward on his face. Leaping down the steps I took his arm, led him back to sit down, and quickly unloosened his collar. Then I dashed into the house for a cup of cold water. I soaked his handkerchief too, and bringing it out, sat down beside him on the step. He was puffing and blowing.

'This job's got me down,' he complained. 'I wish I could pack it up.'

'Why don't you,' I asked.

'Oh, it's, it's not as easy as you think,' he answered. 'I couldn't get another. Not with, not with my health. I wish, I only wish I had yours.'

He commenced to fasten his tie. Then standing up, he shifted the heavy satchel around off his stomach to his side. But for my earlier intention, I would have volunteered to carry it for him. I did not want to arouse his suspicions any more.

He stuffed his handkerchief into his pocket.

'I feel a bit better now,' he said. 'I must get a move on. Thanks very much. I won't forget those banisters. I'll report it, soon as I get in the office.'

He didn't seem too steady on his feet to me. 'I'll walk to the top of the street,' I offered, 'and put you on the tram.'

'I don't think it's necessary,' he said. 'I'll manage now.'

I thought it best to walk part of the way with him for fear he collapsed or somebody grabbed at his satchel. I knew he would not have gone far in some parts of New York without that happening to him.

'Aren't you afraid,' I asked him, 'of carrying so much money around?'

He looked at me in surprise. 'Christ, no,' he said. 'That never worries me. I've been doing this for years.'

I helped him on the tramcar. Two weeks later he was dead.

Around the Labour Exchanges I heard men speak of worst temptations. They said that starvation would drive any man to crime.

In discussing a chap who had stolen two hundred pounds, they hoped he would never be caught.

'That fellow has guts,' one of them remarked. 'That's more than can be said for some of us.'

Patriotism as a topic was sneered at. Men regretted ever joining the army. Some said that conditions would be no worse if Germany had won the war. They praised Russia and Ireland, where men were fighting for their rights. In England, they would not move.

I was ready to move. There were others of the same mind. The majority seemed to be waiting.

September 1921, saw a surprising change. Newspapers reported unemployed disturbances all over the country. In the London area, Boards of Guardians were besieged by thousands of desperate men, and forced to grant outdoor relief in cash instead of workhouse tickets. This inspired a Sprayport cartoonist to picture the unemployed as pot-bellied plutes [sic] receiving cheques from an official while a distracted ratepayer looked on. Underneath was printed: 'Why Work?'

Thousands went wild over that at an unemployed meeting in Sprayport that had been specially [sic] called to follow London's lead and demand 'Work or Maintenance'. The Poplar guardians had gone to prison for giving high scales of relief; no one on the platform had hopes of those in Sprayport doing the same.

The chief speaker was an ex-police sergeant, who, after twenty-four years in the force had brought his men on strike for the recognition of their union. In a few more months he would have retired on a pension of £3.19.0 a week. Though his sacrifices had left him in rags, some of the unemployed saw a flaw in it; the man had been a policeman and no enthusiast could overlook that.

It's a common saying in working-class circles; once a policeman, always a policeman; his previous training makes him he cannot help but twist. So from the first unemployed meeting, the ex-police sergeant was a suspect, particularly in the minds of the younger men wondering how a cracked voice like his could draw big crowds.

He was virtually a grey old man. In his youth he had been a miner. The blue scars on his face were marks of accidents in the pits. He called eggs 'HEGGS'; his speeches had no go in them, being too moderate for most of the younger men who expected action instead. All of London's unemployed were receiving outdoor relief in cash; Sprayport had not advanced a crumb beyond its bread and treacle.*

Yet here was this shabbily dressed old fogy, each night on an open-air rostrum, saying he wanted no trouble with the authorities and that violence does not pay. In the opinion of the young men listeners, he was deliberately keeping the crowd in order, and confirming their suspicions about him; once a policeman, always a policeman.

One Sunday evening, his changed tone made thousands of them stare. 'The City Council,' he declared, 'won't do anything for any of you, unless you go to them in a body to show them how you're fixed. Next Wednesday is Council day. They'll be at the town hall in force. I want the unemployed to come there with me. We'll hold a meeting on Bourse Square.'

---

* 'Relief in Sprayport. In Sprayport the principle of paying out of work relief varies. In some districts the guardians pay the dole in money; in others payment is made in kind. The Sprayport Union, for instance, adopts the latter method. Each case is judged separately so that there is no really fixed scale: there is only a minimum, and this is a food order to the value of 7s.10d, but as the union purchases by contract, the order is equivalent to 10s. if the goods were purchased from the shops. (Relief for man, wife, and three children 13s. 2d)

The minimum order for man, wife, and one child comprises:–

6 oz. Cocoa	1 lb. Soap
16 lb Bread[†]	1 lb. Margarine
1 lb Syrup	1 lb Sugar
2 lb rice	4 ozs. Tea

The parish of Sprayport, on the other hand, gives money relief. On the clerk to the union being asked what the scale was, for public use, he replied that he did not think it a matter for publication.'

Sprayport Weekly Press 3-9-21

[†]Made up of two eight-pound starvers, as big as harvest festival loaves, which advertised that the poor persons carrying them were low and on the parish. Various dodges were used to sneak them past the neighbours. The favourite one was to stow them in an old bassinette and cover these with coarse sacking as if they were a bundle of washing. Then the bassinette was wheeled through the back street and passages until there was a chance to whip out the loaves and get them into the house.

The crowd broke into a murmuring. 'Bourse Square,' some of them exclaimed. 'Why the man must be going potty.' And the suspicious ones muttered: 'It's another of his moves.'

Bourse Square, a closed-in quad with its venerable-looking buildings, had always been forbidden ground to the city's workingmen. Here the well-dressed merchants and brokers met daily in the centre, around a squat Trafalgar memorial to transact their business deals. The wide-domed Town Hall backed on to one side, its high windows uncurtained [sic], while those of the buildings opposite bore the gilded names of century-old firms. Arched passage-ways served as short-cuts to the busy streets roundabout, but were never used by workmen except when they had a repair job on the square.

To suggest the crowd meet there was sacrilegious; it was doubtful whether a dozen men were likely to take the risk. Police hidden on the office stairways could swoop down on them without warning, and baton them to the ground before there was a chance to turn.

The crowd was apprehensive, and the old police-striker sensed it. 'If no one else goes,' he said, 'I'll have to go alone.' His hands shot out in a challenge. 'Djer think I don't know what I'm doin',' he asked. Did I serve twenty five years in the force for nothing? Am I likely to play the fool now?'

The crowd was impressed. His long police-service counted. He was bound to know more about the law than they did.

Wednesday afternoon arrived. Bourse Square was invaded; ten thousand men swarmed around the memorial, now in use as a speakers stand. There had been no organized march on to the Square, except for a contingent of seamen and dockers, who at the beginning had formed a nucleus for the old police-striker to address his remarks. Then the crowd collected quickly through parties of twos and threes darting across from nearby streets and waving to others to follow. Very few police could be seen, which led some of the unemployed to believe that the authorities would not start a riot for fear of damage to the quad and its buildings.

The crowd had already made progress by breaking the traditional awe of the Square, and ragged men proud of the achievement lolled contentedly against the Town Hall railings. Others less at ease dodged around at the back all the time, their eyes fixed on the office stairways from where the police might suddenly charge.

All were waiting for a lead from the platform. The old ex-police sergeant strengthened his influence. With him on the platform, stood a young bareheaded minister. His fuzzy hair heightened his stature. His appearance had increased the confidence of the crowd. 'We're safe enough where there's a clergyman,' lots of them were saying.

This vigorous Baptist preacher was giving the old biblical tags a new interpretation. 'I believe,' he declared, 'that when Christ said: 'Feed my lambs, feed my sheep' he meant it literally.'

A few of the men on the platform had bitterly reached the stage where they despised all clergymen. But this fellow was different to the types who disgusted them with organised religion. There was no sign of hypocrisy or unctuousness in his make-up. More important, he was winning the crowd with the same statements that others had roared at them with loud enthusiasm but less effect.

'You must compel the Lord Mayor to meet a deputation,' he wound up. 'You're fully within your rights as citizens.'

Some squabbling as to whom should constitute the deputation was settled by a stocky built man in a black Stetson hat. Stepping forward, he nominated the now popular police-striker and clergyman, and while the crowd were still suggestible recommended other men he considered reliable, then counted them over. 'Ten. That's plenty,' he shouted. 'We don't want too many.' Disappointed aspirants protested in vain. The crowd cried them down.

A worried-looking Labour councillor elbowed his way to the foot of the platform. Some of the deputation bent down to listen. He whispered that the police-chiefs were inside the town hall waiting for orders to clear the square. The crowd would be trapped unless they were immediately coaxed around to the main street fronting the town hall, where there was a chance of escaping between tramcars and through the side-streets. If they could be peacefully marched away there would be no batoning.

The deputation could not agree to the immediate marching away, being committed to meet the Lord Mayor by the personal pressure of ten thousand men. The councillor, seeing their difficulty, looked very disappointed as he squeezed back towards the town hall.

Another Labour man pushed through to the monument, and asked permission to make a statement. On promising to keep it short, he was lifted above the heads of the crowd, and placed on the edge of the plinth. Bawling out there was going to be trouble, he advised that all the ex-servicemen present to go quickly to their homes before they were led astray by the scum on the platform. One of the deputation instantly hit him on the chin, knocking him back on the men beneath. Some of those struck at him until the old police-striker begged them to let him go. He was sat on his feet and allowed to pick his way out without further mention of the scum.

The term seemed appropriate enough. Apart from the clergyman and one or two others, the men on the platform were a shabbily dressed bunch. The bare elbows of one stuck out of his torn coat sleeves, while another's clean linen collar showed up the frayed patches on his shirtband, yet these two appeared respectable alongside the fellows wearing army grey-shirts, whose black mufflers and threadbare dungaree pants made them ruffian-looking enough for any crime.

Before jumping down off the monument, they urged the crowd to move around into the wide street fronting the town hall. 'Get along, everybody,' was the order. 'We'll make the Lord Mayor come out on the balcony.'

The huge crowd pressed forward, and lined up facing the town-hall entrance.

The deputation, after an irritating delay, was admitted past the big glass doors; two phlegmatic flunkeys pointing the way. They bounced inside, and then hesitated. There stood the missing policemen, hundreds of them, jammed side by side in the main hall and along the corridors. Though they made a passage-way it was difficult to squeeze through them. The touch of their uniforms was almost sufficient to cause a riot. Yet they appeared more uneasy than the over-confident crowd waiting on the outside, craning their necks and whispering to each other as the deputation passed into the ante-room.

The Lord Mayor, accompanied by the Chief Constable, agreed to go upstairs to the balcony and show himself to the unemployed. His gracious smile was the formal greeting for any public occasion. The clergyman mistaking it for sneering complacency flew into a rage. Grabbing the Lord Mayor's chain, he threatened to 'pull the dog collar off him.'

The Chief Constable instantly dragged his hand away. 'Now then,' he said, 'None of that.'

The clergymen flared back. 'We came here for work for these unfortunate men below,' he roared, 'and all he can offer is a grin.'

That's all the Lord Mayor could offer just then. He was too bewildered for anything else. He walked to the balcony to show himself to the unemployed. The deputation filed out after him.

Even they were amazed at the scene below. The crowd, greatly increased, had formed into one deep solid mass, packing the wide street and both pavements to the walls, and completely hiding the shops from view. Behind them, lines of tramcars were at a standstill. Drivers clanged their bells, and kept shouting to the men lined up in front. They answered back with good-natured chaff, but as part of that mass of flesh they were immoveable. Every man had pinned his yellow Labour Exchange card in the lapel of his coat and was smiling up at the balcony. They were showing themselves to the Lord Mayor.

His beaming smile was a fixture. If the seriousness of the situation had now entered his mind, there was no sign of it. Apart from the stock promise, 'We'll do what we can,' the deputation had gained nothing of value from meeting him. But they had learned plenty through looking down from that balcony. The crowd, arms linked together, and standing stock still, had stopped all shopping and traffic in one of the busiest thoroughfares in the city. This stoppage had not been planned beforehand. It had happened out of the circumstances that had brought the unemployed together. Distinctions of craft and creed had disappeared. The badge of unity was a yellow Labour Exchange card.

They were a merry crowd. Perhaps that made them more dangerous. An overbearing police-officer or an impulsively drawn baton might have led to a wreckage of shops that would have spread throughout the city.

The deputation fearing this, and knowing the crowd were unprepared for any organised police attack, withdrew from the balcony. If the police intended to provoke a riot, the responsibility would be theirs, no matter how much they denied it afterwards. Another fear was the likely presence on the pavements of shady types waiting for a private smash and grab haul. The crowd itself had not come to smash windows and scatter their contents. They wanted work.

When the deputation reached the bottom of the staircase, the police were still jammed in the corridors. There was a relief in seeing them there, and the consoling thought that they dare not precipitate trouble where so much damage could be done. Despite this, the deputation decided to first manoeuvre the crowd out of the way of possible attack, before giving the unsatisfactory result of their interview with the Lord Mayor. Then they stepped through the big doorway.

The crowd burst out cheering. A suggestion that they form four deep was laughed at. They preferred to stay as they were, blocking the full width of the street and sidewalks. The deputation had to walk a few feet in front as the huge mass began moving at a crawl towards the town-hall entrance. Arms locked together they wheeled slowly around, broad-side on, into another busy street. Tramcars could not pass. All other traffic was turned back and diverted. An advance party of a dozen anxious men hurried ahead to quietly warn chauffeurs whose cars were parked by the kerb, to run them around the nearest corner and leave the roadway clear. The chauffeurs gaped for a while at the massed thousands moving slowly towards them, then jumped quickly into their cars and drove off.

The crowd poured on to a wide open square, and halted. From a house close by, a chair was borrowed for the old police-striker to stand on. Giving the report of the interview with the Lord Mayor, he said it was only a beginning.

The crowd were not disappointed. They seemed in too good a humour to be vexed. Many of them had started out that afternoon as individuals, curious, and half-afraid; and had ended the day linked together, more determined than ever. Some asked eagerly for the next meeting. The old police-striker was allowed to fix the date. Against others of the deputation who were not as satisfied as himself, he said that things took time to develop.

'We've done well for the first day's outing, I think,' he added. 'Much better than I expected.'

Facing the crowd, he held up his hand for silence. 'With your help,' he began, 'we'll continue these slow walks through the main streets. Shoppers won't believe there is so much poverty in the city unless you show them. You will simply walk past the shops because you have no money to go inside. Goodness knows, you badly need it; we all do. As times are, we can't help being a great nuisance. The big firms will lose thousands of pounds by our walking. But we must do something. It will be cheaper in the long run for the authorities to give us 'Work or Maintenance'. And they cannot give us work or we wouldn't be here like this. So, next week, bring more of your friends along and we'll look at a few more shops.'

The crowd peacefully dispersed. There was one chief topic of conversation, the size of the next demonstration. 'We'll bring twice as many next time,' some were saying, 'And we'll roust all those hangers-back at the Labour Exchange. They'll have to walk the same as anybody else.'

The deputation now became the organising committee, the young parson offering them a small room at the back of his church. The following evening they met there to discuss future activities, and to consider the scales of relief to be demanded from the Guardians of the Poor. Except for the Parson all were unemployed and mostly in rags; a few of them casually mentioning they had sold most of their furniture for a tittle [*sic*] of its cost. Sitting around a long board-table, they elected the old police-striker as chairman. And then the hullabaloo commenced.

There was three overnight Communists, a Politician-loathing syndicalist, a zealous young clergyman, an ex-naval petty-officer, a demobbed army sergeant, a released conscientious objector, and an assertive Roman Catholic, there specially, he said, to watch the Communists game.

Each speaker stressed his own particular cure-all; speeches wandered from parish relief to conquest of empires, and each differing opinion was loaded with the uncertainty of what motive was prompting the rest.

One long flow of jargon was abruptly ended when the demobbed army sergeant stood up glaring, and thumped the table for attention. His bull-neck twisted aggressively beneath his knotted black scarf.

'We've had enough of that stuff for one night,' he declared. 'In fact, quite a lot of the talk here has been double-dutch to me. It seems we are trying to swallow a pumpkin whole with a mouth only big enough for grapes. I don't know whether my circumstances are worse than anybody's else's, and I'm not saying this for talk's sake. But my wife hasn't got a boot on her foot, and my kids are a bundle of rags. I served three years in France. That's one reason why I'm not going inside the workhouse. I'll do a burst somewhere, and go to jail first. There must be thousands like me. Oughtn't we to concentrate on our agitation for work?'

He sat down as the stocky man in the Stetson hat rose. 'Yesterday's demonstration settled that question,' he said. 'There's about sixty thousand unemployed in this city. The authorities cannot provide work for them at a minute's notice. What they might do is offer jobs to some of us. If we accept, the unemployed will lose confidence. It will be a form of betrayal. We must hold out and press for a decent standard of maintenance first. The only things the Guardians give plenty of is abuse. We can alter all that. And if we can't do it by peaceful walking through the streets, there are other methods.'

The old police-striker looked up quickly. 'I'll not be a party to any violence,' he said.

'Nor me,' exclaimed the parson. 'I'm a pacifist, definitely.'

The ex-navy man sneered across the table. 'A few whacks of a bobby's pogo-stick will knock all that out of your nut,' he asserted. 'And that mop of hair won't save you.'

The man in the Stetson smiled. 'He didn't seem much of a pacifist yesterday when he grabbed the Lord Mayor's chain,' he said.

'That's different,' answered the clergyman. 'That man's face annoyed me.'

No agreement could be reached on the scales of relief. It was decided to write for information to other parts of the country, and use it as a guide for the next committee meeting.

On the following Wednesday morning, the Labour Exchange queues buzzed with instructions. The unemployed were asked to muster in Emporium Street that afternoon. Emporium Street is a wide shopping centre, bearing the bulk of the city's tram services, along which the trams go crawling as close together as railway carriages.

At half past two, shabbily dressed men and women swarmed into it from all directions. There was at least twenty thousand of them. They lined up into the mass formation of the week before, and linking arms together spread themselves across the street from sidewalk to sidewalk. Yellow unemployment cards were pinned to all their lapels. Most of the men wore war medals too, or pawntickets [sic] to prove they had recently possessed them. The committee took their place in front, looked behind at the cheery mass, then shouted 'Ready!'

Off they all stepped at a crawling pace. Traffic was again stopped. Tram bells clanged in vain. A couple of drivers who persisted in trying to force a way through were dragged off their cars and warned.

Policemen hemmed in by the huge crowd were helplessly carried along at its measured pace. The weather was fine and the general atmosphere cheerful. Occasionally a ranting committee man would dash up the stairs of a stopped tramcar and roar his opinions from the top. But few of the crowd were interested in speeches. They were too jovial in the warmth of a new and hopeful fellowship. Walking leisurely through the streets this way was preferable to brooding in their miserable back-street hovels. For two hours they slowly moved along past the big shops, then they peacefully dispersed.

That night the full committee met in the church room to deal with the letters that had come from all parts of the country. Those from the London boroughs where 'Work or maintenance' was being applied helped them very quickly to agree on scales of relief. With these they could meet the local Board of Guardians as soon as that body cared to send for them. Until then, the demonstrations would go on.

The old police-striker asked for other business. Reluctantly he had to listen to most of the committee men expressing their uneasiness over the conduct of the police. It was very suspicious. They seemed to be acting too quiet; acting as if they were waiting for the first opportunity to run amok and baton down as many of the unemployed as possible.

The old police-striker fidgeted until he at last lost his temper. He said that all this talk was nonsense. There was no reason why there should be any batoning. The crowd themselves were too orderly.

'I hope you have not forgotten,' he went on, 'that today twenty thousand of our people paraded past all the big shops without as much as a pane of glass being broken. That doesn't look as if they were out to cause trouble. The police authorities are not blind to that. Lots of the policemen that walk alongside us are quite decent chaps. I know most of them. They're with us if anything. We don't want to do something that will set them against us.'

A young man in patched dungarees was on his feet immediately. 'That's all right for you,' he snapped, 'but we don't trust them like you do.' He turned to the others. 'I suggest we take no more risks,' he said. 'We've been lucky so far. Let's alter our walking day, and advise the crowd that in the event of any baton charge they must dive into the first big shop nearest their hand. They can escape through the side-doors. I don't want to see hungry men being deliberately knocked about.'

Up jumped the parson. 'Nobody else does,' he said, 'but you're not leading me into mischief. I'll resign first.'

The man in dungarees glared across the table, and muttered under his breath. There was an awkward silence. The old police-striker broke it gently.

'Look here, man.' He began. 'Don't you understand what would happen with this shop idea of yours. We'd play right into the authorities hands. They'd hold us accountable for every little petty theft that was reported that day. They'd say that the unemployed were an organised band of thieves. And they're not. They're all decent, law-abiding citizens.'

The young man was implacable. 'I know all that,' he declared. 'And that's why their heads will get bashed in all the sooner. It's worrying me. I don't want to see it happen, see.'

The old police-striker smiled encouragingly. 'It won't happen,' he said. 'You take my word.'

On the following Monday afternoon, droves of unemployed hurried along Sprayport's widest street to Sprayport's large Hall plateau. The oblong-shaped hall is like a huge Greek Temple with its Corinthian columns standing sixty feet high. Several rows of stone raise the Hall itself above the street level. In front is the city's largest open public space. Across the wide busy street on the left are a group of other big impressive buildings: the Museum; the Sprayport Reference Library; the well filled Sprayport Art Gallery and the Sessions court.

This was the setting for the largest meeting yet held. Men and women kept crossing the surrounding tramlines from all sides to join the mass of people already assembled on the plateau. These in turn attracted the interest of casual passers-by who dawdled awhile before coming across to increase the numbers further.

This large crowd already lacked the cohesion of the two previous ones. Unemployed cards were not in evidence. No arms were being linked together. There were plenty of gaps. It might have been because of the plateau's reputation for batonings, and the advisability of being free enough to run if necessary. Very few uniformed police were to be seen, although there were plenty of plainclothes detectives moving about in pairs.

From the top of the stone steps, the committee stared over the heads of the vast crowd, and then at each other. They were in a difficult position. This was the third demonstration. No offer of work schemes had been made by the City Council, and no offer of sustainable relief had come from the Board of Guardians. There was nothing fresh to tell the crowd excepting what most of them already knew, that prominent members of both ruling bodies and of all political shades were using the newspapers and party platforms to discredit the unemployed leaders. The stories included the dollops of gold supposed to be coming from Moscow.

Some of the committee had to dash away early to sign on at the Labour Exchange. Those remaining co-opted a woman trades-union organiser just back in town from the Labour Party's annual conference, and disgusted with its dilatory treatment of the unemployment problem. She was now surveying the restive crowd below. So was the old police-striker and the others. All were undecided on what to do next; none of their improvised speeches had sounded very satisfactory, being merely a repetition of old and familiar phrases.

The young man in the dungarees, ever suspicious of the old police-striker, suddenly blurted out: 'Come on. We're wasting time standing here like bunch of dummies. Let's take them around the shops again.'

The clergyman swung on him immediately. 'Oh damn the shops,' he yelled.

The police-striker's glance conveyed the same. To prevent further argument, he again stepped forward to address the crowd, too vast to hear much of what he was saying.

'I think we'll go for a walk,' he suggested. 'A short walk. It's too late for anything else. We'll all be art critics this afternoon. We'll go across and have a look at the pictures in the Art Gallery. These places are as much for us as anybody else. They belong to the public.'

He moved off down the steps, leaving the rest of the committee free to follow if they chose. Only the clergyman and woman organiser went after him. The remainder stood fuming as sections of the crowd flooded across the tram-lines.

The suspicious young man turned to the others. 'Well,' he said 'Isn't that proof enough? What did I tell you, that old bastard's leading them into a trap; him and that bloody devil-dodging parson.'

The others kept staring across the gradually emptying plateau to the crowded street beyond, their eyes fixed on the short flight of steps fronting the Art Gallery entrance. The clergyman and the old police-striker were slowly ascending, surrounded by a pack of followers.

The clergyman's fuzzy head disappeared through the doorway. Impatient men and women streamed in behind. The gallery steps, the sidewalk and the wide roadway was a mass of eager pushing people.

Suddenly hundreds of foot-police rushed out of the sessions court and adjacent buildings, batoning heads right and left. The frightening confusion of the crowd was worsened as the mounted police galloped up and rode full charge into them, trampling and scattering in all directions. Many of the unemployed lay stretched out in the roadway. Others were led away to hospital to have their wounds dressed.

From the plateau, the few remaining committee men ran across the street to try and rally the crowd together. But the police attack had been too well planned. Unlike the half-nourished unemployed they were privileged to carry truncheons and sticks and were cracking everybody they could lay their hands on.

Inside the Art Gallery, more police caused pandemonium. Men yelled aloud as they were batoned down. Others dashed around panic-stricken. A few desperate ones dropped from an open window into the side-street and got away. Those attempting to follow were struck from behind. The police closed all windows and doors. There were no further escapes. Batons split skull after skull. Men fell where they were hit. The floor streamed with blood. Those laying in it were trampled on by others who were soon flattened out alongside them. Gallery workmen were battered too. The police had gone wild. The old police-striker, appealing to their decency, had his arm broken and his head smashed. The young parson, protesting, was knocked bleeding to the floor, and as he lay unconscious his head was batoned again. An ambulance took them both to hospital. Fourteen of those most seriously injured followed later. Others were bandaged on the spot. The hundred and forty who remained, including the woman organiser, were bundled into black marias and driven to the lock-up.

Four of the committee-men who escaped met a few hours later in a backstreet clubroom over a small tobacconist's shop. Crossing to a corner bench they just nodded to the men playing cards and those around the billiard table, then sat down. They were so miserable that the bartender offered them a cup of tea apiece on tick. For a long time they sat worrying over the others now in gaol, imagining them being punched and blood-spattered by brute-policemen abusing an advantage. They cursed the old police-striker for his obstinacy, and were bitter about the parson being batoned on the floor. They swore if it ever happened to them, they would revenge themselves if they waited for years.

Heavy footsteps on the stairs silenced them. They glanced uneasily towards the door. The bartender too was listening. He hissed a warning 'Shush' to everybody. Two men playing billiards stared a moment then went on fluking their shots.

A burly detective sauntered into the room. Others crowded in behind them, enough to double-bank everybody on the premises. They stood gazing around them, waiting for instructions.

The inspector-in charge quickly eyed all the faces present, spotted the unemployed committee-men in the corner, beckoned them with his finger, and invitingly said: 'Come on, you lads.' As they seemed uncertain of whether he actually meant them, he crossed to where they were sitting and touched each on the shoulder in turn. 'Come on, you,' he said. 'And you. And you. And yes, you as well.'

They stood up reluctantly, not knowing what to think. They had done nothing yet to be charged with; had never been in the Art Gallery, had quarrelled over the idea of going near it. Yet here they were under arrest and already picturing the brutality of the cells with themselves as victims. They looked consolingly at each other; their day would come.

One of them turned to the Inspector. 'Can't we have a cup of tea before we go,' he asked. 'I haven't broken my fast since this morning. Margarine toast; that's all there is in our houses.'

The inspector allowed them to gulp a cup of tea before they were escorted downstairs to the street. As they walked along there was no ordering about, or dragging or twisting of arms that is commonly employed by uniformed policemen. Nor was there a howling mob following. Very few passers-by troubled to notice them. The detectives in their conversations were as amiable as old friends. The prisoners looked on this as part of the game to blind passers-by to what would happen inside.

They passed through the prison-gateway of the main bridewell into a small receiving room where the detectives left them to be searched by two surly-looking policemen. These promptly ordered them to drop their pants and drawers down over their ankles. While doing so, the Roman Catholic was brought in to be booked. Seeing the others almost naked he commenced to unfasten his braces.

Two communists were first to be searched. Their pockets were turned out, and the lining of their clothes patted and squeezed. They hid no weapons and money. The police searchers felt over them again. They were puzzled. Still no weapons and no money.

The policemen gazed at each other, then the surliest one in exasperation bawled out: 'Where is it?'

'Where's what,' asked the young Communist.

'You know what.'

'I don't. Really.'

'You don't, eh. We've heard that yarn before. COME ON. OUT WITH IT. Where's all this money you're getting from abroad.'

The young Communist smiled. 'Aw chuck it,' he said. 'Somebody's been pulling your leg.'

'Eh! What's that,' roared the police-searcher. 'Now less! We want none of your blasted lip in here. UNDERSTAND. Get over there the pair of you.' They were shoved to one side.

The Roman Catholic seemed as puzzled and disappointed as the police-searchers because the Communist had no money. Neither did the others. When his own turn came, he did; two-pence half-penny, and a finger ring made out of a penny while soldiering in France. These and his three cigarettes were taken from him.

The policeman who had done most of the shouting unhooked a bunch of keys from the wall and grunted: 'Through here, all of yer.'

Halfway along a darkened passage the first four were locked in one cell. Stone-flagged, cramping and stuffy, its only furniture was a short wooden plank on which three could sit. The fourth immediately crept back to the door and pressed his ear to the peephole.

He motioned the others to be silent. They turned their eyes from the barred window and anxiously awaited his advice. He had been jailed previously in America and deported during one of the Emigration Department's periodical raids on unnaturalised labourers. Without budging from the door he whispered to them not to say a word regarding their defence of anything connected with the street demonstrations.

'Talk about any old thing but that,' he said. 'This is a middle cell.

We've been deliberately bunged in here to talk. It's an old dodge. Those smart-boy detectives will be planted on either side to take down all that's said. So give them something to think about.'

As his mates sat rigidly over-cautious he stepped across and loudly asked: 'Are any of youse young fellers interested in spiritualism?'

One of them brightened up instantly. He had dabbled in spiritualism and believed in mental telepathy. He promised to give a demonstration before the night was over. It was merely a matter of getting into the right mood, he explained. This required time. He begged them not to disturb him while he tried to concentrate.

They edged away from the seat to watch. Though sceptical they were half-afraid of him going off in a trance or working himself into a mad fit. But they were also curious to see what exactly he would do. Body bent over he kept staring at the floor. The remainder slyly nudged each other and winked. Then they grew more attentive. A change <u>was</u> happening to him.

His hands began to tremble 'til they shook from head to foot. With an effort he raised his body and fell back against the wall. His eyes seemed considerably wider. His face was flushed and contorted. Veins bulged out on his forehead and the sweat was pouring from him. After a while his features relaxed and he breathed easier again. His eyelids flickered. Then stared around and recollected where he was.

'I've been speaking to the wife,' he said. 'I've told her here we are and not to worry.'

The others thought it wise to humour him. 'Whereabouts is she,' asked one.

'In the Isle of Man. She's gone to a season job at an hotel. Her sister's minding the kids 'till she comes back.'

The deportee from America looked at him curiously. 'The Isle of Man did yer say?'

'Yes. The Isle of Man.'

'Well listen. If you can send a message all that distance, try one a little nearer. Get in touch with some of the lads locally and ask them to smuggle a few packets of ciggys [*sic*] in here. I'm dying for a smoke.'

The cell door swung open. The surly police-searcher shuffled in. He sniffed the air several times.

'Who's smoking here?' he demanded.

'Smoking,' queried the man from America.

'You heard what I said.'

'There's no one smoking in here.'

'I-DON'T-LIKE-THE-WAY-YOU-SAY-THAT.'

'I'll bet there's a lot of things you don't like.'

'SHURRUP!'

He glowered at them, lingered a while, then walked slowly to the door. 'Don't have me to come back again' he warned. The key turned in the lock.

The deportee whipped across to the peephole and listened. 'He's gone,' he said 'I know what I'd like to do with that snotty bastard.' The others knew too but they kept it to themselves.

(It may be pertinent to ask here why men arrested in the afternoon as these five were, were detained in a cell all night without proper food. A cup of unsweetened slush and a hunk of dry coarse bread handed in about six in the morning could not be stomached. None of them had any sleep for no bedding had been provided. The night was one of prolonged suspense. Not one of them knew the nature of the charge against them. Nor did they know if their families had any idea of their whereabouts. They were harassed by the prowling jail-keeper, and because of their distrust of the whole police-machine were compelled to sustain each other with faked conversations. It was either that, or sit moping and making their misery worse. To lay on the stone floor meant a dose of rheumatics. Sitting too long in the same position cramped them. Only one at a time could stretch his legs in pacing up and down the ten foot cell. Yet in the next morning, weary, hunger-sick, and unshaven, they were hustled into court to be picked at by men who had slept well, ate well, looked well, and were paid well.

The prisoners were at a disadvantage before a single word was uttered. Their appearance was against them. Dirty, tired and unshaven, they looked like a gang of cut-throats. Of the five who stood in the dock, only one had a presentable suit of clothes. The others were in rags. Any magistrate prejudging them might easily have been excused. Luckily the deputy-stipendiary seemed a gentle-mannered old fellow. He formally remanded them.)

The following week, the hundred and sixty defendants filled the court. The committee were held back on major charges. The minor cases were disposed of straightaway by fines or being bound over. Many of those men had bandaged heads.

Of the full committee itself only the old police-striker and the parson showed signs of injury. The old police-striker seemed the worst. His head was thickly bandaged and his broken arm was in a sling. But he bore no animosity towards the police. He said they were too excited to know what they were doing. The younger prisoners were more puzzled than ever by this peculiar attitude.

The parson was too wrought up to be so forgiving. Trouble in the church over these outside activities had resulted in the deacons who failed to secure his resignation, resigning themselves. Meanwhile, the stopping of the parson's salary added to his other injuries. There were enough bandages around his head to make a turban for a Rajah. When he unwrapped them to reveal four ugly scalp wounds, his hair was shaved close like a low caste coolie. His mop of curls had disappeared, also his pacifism. He was bursting to fight every policeman who entered the witness box. He could hardly believe his own ears. He stared at each man giving evidence and winced repeatedly. 'That's awful,' he muttered. 'Awful.'

'My God,' he exclaimed at last, 'I must get out of this place. It's horrible having to stand here listening to those men perjuring their souls.' He made a bee-line for the door. Burly policemen blocked the exit. He turned back dejectedly.

The old magistrate peered over his spectacles. 'You can't leave the court you know,' he said.

'Oh but it's, it's unbearable having to listen to men lying like that after they've nearly half-killed us. I really can't control myself.'

'You must try.'

The old magistrate throughout was extremely tolerant. He displayed none of the arrogance of his subordinates. At one point he made the police-solicitor quickly withdraw a sneering reference to this 'so-called minister of religion'.

The case lasted for several days. The police had applied for a committal to the Assizes. The old magistrate ruled that if evidence could be taken in time there was no reason why the case should not go to the Sessions. As the police did not want the Sessions, the prisoners considered it best to be tried there. To save time they refrained from cross-examining a succession of boring police-witnesses. Every minute was valuable.

Despite this, on two consecutive mornings, one particular prisoner arrived in court fifteen or twenty minutes late. He had to walk five miles, having no money for tram fares. The magistrate appealed to him to make a special effort to come early, and suggested he leave the house half-an-hour before his usual time. 'You are delaying the case' he reminded him.

Next morning there was no sign of him again. Fifteen minutes passed; no appearance. Twenty minutes; still no appearance. The court ushers could be heard bawling his name up and down the corridor. There was no response.

In court, everybody was fidgety. The other prisoners keen for the case to proceed kept turning round to glance at the clock. Twenty-five minutes went by; the finger soon reached the half-hour. The prisoners were feeling annoyed. The old magistrate must be too, they thought. Then it suddenly occurred to them that perhaps their missing colleague had been knocked down in the street by a motor car. Thirty-five minutes! They whispered anxiously to each other and considered the advisability of asking permission to phone the hospitals. Some persons in court were tittering. The usher roared 'Silence!' The old magistrate gazed solemnly towards the door.

In strolled the missing one as repentant as a schoolboy who has lost a prized mark. 'I'm very sorry sir,' he burst out, 'for breaking my word this way. But it couldn't be helped. We were in a dreadful fix for the time this morning. There was no clock. We had to pawn it last night for something to eat.'

The old magistrate stared a moment, adjusted his spectacles, then put his hand over his face. His shoulders shook as he smiled to himself. It was the cue for everyone else. A current of merriment spread through the court. The usher's forced 'Silence!' ended in a chuckle. His hand flew to his mouth.

The magistrate frowned at him. The usher's face became stern again. 'SILENCE!' he roared, and scanned the court. The hubbub instantly ceased.

The magistrate looked down at the police-solicitor's bench. 'You may call the next witness, now,' he said.

A young chubby faced detective took the oath and began his evidence. The deportee from America could not resist twitting him.

'You said you heard me talking about scabs?'

'Yes.'

'And I qualified what a scab was?'

'Yes.'

'Do you know what a scab is?'

'I understand it is a person who takes another man's job during a dispute.'

'That's right. How long have you been in the force?'

'Two years.'

'You joined in 1919?'

'Yes.'

'Was there a dispute on?'

'Yes.'

'And you took another man's job.'

'Yes.'

'So you are what is inelegantly known as a scab?'

'Er – yes.'

Nobody else bothered to ask any questions.

The old magistrate committed all the prisoners to the Sessions. They were released in heavy bail on condition they took no part meantime in the street demonstrations. The parson and police-striker being so ill went straight home to bed. The women organiser left town at once to resume her trades-union work. The remainder met together in the back street clubroom to discuss the formation of an alternative committee. They were determined the organisation would go on.

Ten picked men were called into conference the next evening, including a demobbed army lieutenant, an ex-sergeant major, and an ex-naval warrant officer. They agreed to take over immediately. If they were arrested then a third committee would replace them.

Their methods were entirely different. The Art Gallery blunder had taught a lesson. Massing across the street had to stop now, they said, or else more unrestrained batonings would follow. A small body of disciplined policemen could always scatter an unwieldy crowd. On this occasion more than twenty thousand had been scattered in a few minutes. The same twenty thousand in a processional order of fours extending over a long distance would weaken police co-ordination. If one end of the formation was suddenly broken by a charge, the other end could retreat or retaliate according to the circumstances of attack. This was only possible with discipline. Much of the unemployed had recently served in the army. They would respond readily to orders again. The problem was to find out how many could be relied upon. A registration scheme was suggested. Suitable premises would be necessary. There was no money to pay rent. The new committee pondered over this. Though aware of the parson's private difficulties they sent an appeal to him for help. He arranged for the church basement to be placed at their disposal.

The lieutenant, ex-sergeant major, and ex-navy man were put in charge. They recruited a bunch of clerical workers, obtained some second hand entry books, and had the church basement prepared for the enrolling. Word was passed around all the Labour Exchanges. Groups of unemployed trooped along from every part of the city. From ten in the morning 'till ten at night the volunteer clerks were kept occupied. It was hard to convince some of their wives who brought them cans of tea and sandwiches that the writing was not being paid for.

Nearly eighty thousand unemployed were registered within a week. Artisans, labourers of all sorts, and men whose apprenticeship had been interrupted by the war. The principal information sought was their war record, time served, rating, and description of medals. This was to counterpart the statement being made that the unemployed were not bona-fide ex-servicemen.

Ex-officers (a few) and N.C.O.'s (hundreds) were ticked off for early reference. All were regrouped under district headings, then sub-divided into neighbourhood units of twelve, under the control of an ex N.C.O. who now ranked as street captain. The men by knowing each other would sneak up on strangers. They had in mind the possibility of plain-clothes detectives joining the organisation for disruptive purposes. A double-check against this was the grudge the unemployed police-strikers bore towards those who had taken their jobs.

A list of duties was agreed upon. Street captains were to be responsible for unit discipline and conduct. From amongst themselves they would elect a leader for their own district. All district leaders would be answerable to the disciplinary section of the second committee.

The most dominant figure in this committee was the ex-sergeant major. Still under forty years of age, he had been an all round athlete, heavy-weight boxer, and physical instructor. The privations of two years unemployment had left him almost a wreck. His face was white and drawn. His clothes were buggy and threadbare.

But enthusiasm soon revived the barrack square voice and army mannerisms. Once again he became a crisp tongued fanatic for obedience, expecting so much of his own way that the committee were divided as to how far he should be trusted. The men he drilled had more confidence in him. They were as eager to do each movement as smartly as he was to see it done. Those inclined to be too frivolous or too slow were ordered to 'jump to it or clear out'. In back streets, shuttered cellars, and on waste lots, the units were put through their paces. Before mustering on the streets in processional order they were instructed not to antagonise the police in any way but to be prepared to close in and disarm them if any attempt was made to use batons.

The parson came along to see them. His head was still heavily bandaged. 'I cannot go with you yet,' he said. 'But one thing I do ask you. Make no insulting remarks to the police. I have met many decent fellows in the force since Monday, and they have told me privately what they think about things.'

When the unemployed next mustered in the streets the police fell in single file alongside them. A yard behind each policeman walked a watchful street captain. Led by the second committee they all marched to the Board of Guardians offices.

It was the first day the first committee were being tried at the sessions. They were now represented by counsel. A fund had been raised by sympathisers to help meet the expenses. The trial opened before the recorder. The proceedings were almost a repetition of those in the magistrate's court.

Police witnesses followed each other in monotonous succession. The defending counsel's cross-examination centred on two main points: Had the parson or the police-striker advocated violence? No! Then who gave the order to baton them and their followers?

Nobody knew. From the latest rookie constable to the about-to-be-pensioned superintendent, all were ignorant.

The superintendent swore he did not give the order. 'All he remembered,' he said, 'was seeing the unemployed running with their heads down.'

Defending counsel was on him immediately: 'Ah, that solves it,' he declared. 'Now I know what happened. Your policemen were standing with the batons drawn, and the unemployed were so fascinated that they could not resist the temptation of banging their heads against them.' He paused for a moment. 'Did any of your men receive so much as a scratch?'

'I don't know,' was the answer.

As Moscow was being blamed daily for every social disturbance, it was not surprising to have a feeler thrown out during the trial by the prosecuting counsel. He picked on me. Our exchanges throughout had not been friendly. He was annoyed because I was amused by his attempts to discredit me in the eyes of the jury. Then came his question to definitively prove the type of blackguard I really was.

'Do you receive any money from a certain government,' he rapped out.

I looked straight at him. 'Yes,' I answered softly.

He seemed flabbergasted. He never imagined I would 'bite' so easily. 'What is the name of that government?' he asked.

'The English government,' I answered. 'I'm on the dole.'

All the other defendants smiled. Counsel was fuming. He ordered me to leave the box. There was twopence [sic] in my pocket at the time. I had handed my wife the fifteen shillings dole the day before. Most of it went immediately to pay the bill in the small grocery shop. This had to be settled before another loaf could be asked for on credit. When my wife and I left home in the morning for the sessions court we had fivepence [sic] between us. This was to buy a cup of tea apiece during the lunch adjournment. The woman organiser took my wife to a restaurant. I went around to a cheaper place and spent threepence [sic]. The twopence left was to pay the wife's carfare if I was sent to gaol. Through the mix-up I missed her. She was back in court before me. I was stopped at the door by a very officious police-sergeant, stationed there to keep the public out. I looked such a ragamuffin that he pushed me down the steps. I told him I was entitled to go in.

'I'll entitle you with this,' he roared as he raised his stick and rushed at me.

I walked away smiling, which annoyed him more so. He chased me around the corner then went back to the door. I strolled off and met a detective who recognised me instantly. He asked me where I was going and I explained what had happened.

'Come on back with me,' he said 'I'll get you in.'

We reached the doorway. After chaffing the officious sergeant I hurried into court ten minutes late.

The other defendants went into the witness box. The woman organiser explained that when arrested she had only been back in town an hour. Art Gallery officials gave evidence against the police. This did not stop the jury from finding the defendants guilty of unlawful assembly.

The Recorder sentenced them to one day's imprisonment, which meant their immediate release. His own comments on the case were reserved for the next day, and printed in the local newspapers.

'I have sat for more than twelve years in this court,' he said, 'and during all that time I have done my best as far as possible to support the police and to compliment them when I think that they have been right. I am bound to say there are features in this case that are, to my mind, profoundly disquieting. There is nothing in the police evidence to suggest that there should be any violence. I think most unnecessary violence was used to these men in the Art Gallery. One reason why I did not send the defendants in this case yesterday to prison was that two of them had been cruelly punished already, and, in my opinion most improperly punished by the police.'

The two committees merged into one, the ex-sergeant major and his assistants being left in full charge of the street processions. Almost daily, eight to ten thousand disciplined men marched four deep around the principal shopping centre. A single file of police walked alongside. The pavements were packed with followers. Mingling with them were plainclothes detectives shadowed by unemployed men specially picked by the sergeant-major. 'My inner gang' he called them.

The procession was nearly a mile long. As it wheeled slowly around the busy corners all cross traffic was jammed. No vehicle but an ambulance was allowed to break the ranks. The sergeant major would risk no separation from the main body.

One afternoon, a blustering police official brandished his stick to forge a passage for more tramcars. 'Out of the way,' he barked, 'or I'll smash you to smithereens.'

The nearest street-captain skipped aside, waved his arms wildly to those in front and yelled 'Halt!' The order was relayed the length of the procession. All the men stood still, most of them wondering what had happened.

The sergeant-major rushed back along the ranks, 'Stand easy!' He hurried on to where the police-official had dragged a couple of the unemployed to one side. 'Get back into line, you men,' he ordered.

The riled police official swung his stick up. The ex-sergeant major raised his eyes but never flinched. He shook his finger warningly. 'If you're looking for trouble let us know,' he said. 'You'll get more than you bargain for this time.' Gazing back along the ranks he roared 'Atten-shun!' The men's feet clacked together. On the command 'Quick march!' the procession moved off again. The sergeant major stood by until the last line drew level, then fell in behind leaving the police-official to vent his temper on sniggering tram drivers.

On the daily walks that followed there was no further friction between the unemployed and the police alongside. Instead there was many a laugh.

A very fat police-sergeant usually headed the procession. He had a couple of chins, a walrus moustache, and weighed about twenty stones. The unemployed nicknamed him 'Adequate maintenance'. This was soon contracted to 'Old Adequate'. Within a week it became 'Comrade Addy'.

'Comrade Addy always walked out in front, stick in hand, waving parked cars out of the way. On a level street he could regulate his pace, but downhill, once started, he could rarely stop himself. The weight of his body would rush him forward.

A few times he was caught unawares when the sergeant-major to test the men's discipline, suddenly roared out: 'On the double. Pick 'em up.'

As the procession and its escort broke into a run, 'Comrade Addy', swearing under his breath would shoot ahead as if the unemployed were chasing him. What those close behind saw most were the rolls of fat hanging over the neck of his tunic, and the cheeks of his backside jogging up and down.

After a couple of minutes the 'As you were!' slowed the procession to ordinary marching time. 'Comrade Addy' unable to stop at once, would pull up further down the street, panting for breath, and waiting for the front ranks to reach him.

'Oh, you bunch of rascals,' he would gasp, his face streaming with perspiration. Then came his appeal 'No more of that running lads,' he'd say. 'No more. It isn't fair. Once is enough for today. Phew!'

It required three weeks of this marching around to drag relief from the local Board of Guardians. There seemed to be no excuse for this delay. They knew that distress was widespread. They had their eyes, they could read the newspapers, and had been notified by the Ministry of Health of the continuance of exceptional unemployment. There was also the published evidence of their own officials (1), and sufficient proof that poor families were selling up their homes. (2)

(1) 'Sprayport poor-law officials say that distress in the city is worse than any period since 1907, when it was found necessary to open labour yards, and well on a thousand people were on the starvation line.' Sprayport Weekly Press. 3-9-21

(2) 'There were many excellent ex-servicemen and general citizens whose needs were extremely urgent, who were reduced in many instances to selling up their little household goods and chattels to keep body and soul together, but were strongly opposed to taking advantage of anything that partook of the nature of poor-law-relief. I say all honour to these men, but I would also say to them that going to the guardians for the purpose of getting on this relief work in no way creates the stigma of poor-law relief as hitherto understood'. Chairman of the Sprayport Finance Committee. Sprayport Daily Press, 24-9-21

Neighbouring towns had granted the new relief scales, but not Sprayport. The individual dread of the workhouse atmosphere was still so much of a deterrent, that though the city council had arranged for five hundred men to be employed through the parish relief depots, very few applied. Those ugly, dilapidated branding holes were the last places any poor person wished to enter.

The purpose of these mass demonstrations to the guardians was to destroy this individual fear. The men's deputation harped on it. The traditional pre-war attitude to unemployment had to cease, they said. There must be no more dependence on charity soup-lines. The demand now was 'Work or Maintenance'.

Though the deputation pressed for the London scales of relief, they had to compromise on a lower amount. One point they were resolute on: no relief on loan. To accept otherwise might place some recipients forever in debt to the poor-law authorities. The guardians said it was a Ministry of Health ruling. The deputation remained firm. The guardians gave way.

The new scales were a big improvement on the old bread and syrup standards. Man, Wife, and one child were increased from a plain food voucher valued at seven and tenpence [*sic*], to a split cash and food allowance totalling twenty-six shillings. The cash half was intended for rent and coal, the other half consisting of food vouchers. For larger families, proportionate rises up to fifty shillings far exceed the fifteen of the Labour Exchanges which allowed nothing for the family at all.

The food vouchers could only be exchanged at a few grocers listed by the guardians. Walking into one of these shops tested any poor recipient's self-respect. A married man would seldom go. Treating the relief as an alternative to wages, he expected his wife to dispose of the food voucher. Against his grain he had applied for it; it was now her job to exchange it.

Shawl over her head, she had to trudge along to one of the listed shops, and if it was crowded, loiter outside until the women with the purses had moved from the counter. Then she ventured inside to be greeted by a boyish assistant.

Rubbing his hands he'd politely ask: 'What can I do for you, Madam?'

Glancing around the shop first, she would produce the food voucher, then whisper across the counter: 'Do you take theses here, please?'

The assistant, impatiently, would blurt out, 'A parish coupon? Yes. Why didn't you say so at first?' As the woman stood tongue-tied he became more annoyed. 'Hurry up, missus. There are other people waiting,' he'd say. 'Shout out. What do you want?'

The flustered woman wanted most to escape from the other customers staring in her direction. Trembling with shame, she'd gather her tea, sugar and margarine together, and hurry out vowing never to go back again. But next week the humiliation had to be repeated.

Most of it was unintentional, but sensitive women often cried. The unemployed committee, acting on complaints, asked the guardians to stop food vouchers entirely, and pay full relief in cash. The guardians could not agree to this because it was illegal. But they extended the voucher system to include all local shopkeepers, and gave recipients the privilege of obtaining groceries where they wished. Despite the guardians guarantee, food shops along the main streets would not handle the coupons. Grocers, butchers, bakers, and the rest, shook their heads at applicants, and went on serving the ready cash customers.

Poorer shopkeepers in the back-streets could not be so particular. Their poky little shops, scattered all over the slums, were generally owned by widows struggling to keep out of the workhouse. They obliged needy neighbours with weekly credit, charging higher prices than a big shop dared for fat bacon, scraps of cheese, and vegetables usually damaged. A penniless woman with relief coupons knew she was being overcharged, yet preferred it to the open humiliation of the big shops on the main road. Besides, there was a chance of wrangling a packet of cigarettes for her husband which was entered up as tea or margarine.

Though parish relief was now easier to obtain, thousands of people starved sooner than apply for it. The unemployed leaders told them they were legally entitled, and unless they applied quickly the guardians would say there was little destitution. The woman organiser, whenever she had time to come said that shame ought not to stop any unemployed person from asking for relief.

'There are certain favoured families in this country,' she explained 'who take thousands of pounds annually in doles. And they never blush. And they've rendered less service to the nation than many of you standing here.'

But this talk failed to inspire timid men and women. Committee-men had to go to the parish offices with them to give them moral support.

(I had taken several men and women. Then the Labour Exchange stopped my dole. The dole was only fifteen shillings; the poor-law scale of relief for me was twenty-six. Yet I hesitated in going for it. It was not a physical fear. Had new premises been opened it might have made a difference. But there was something repressive about the gloomy parish rooms with their miserable records of bygone paupers, and the conscious degradation of those now following them. A man felt uncomfortable; a woman usually fainted. They had plenty of cause. Pencilled all over the lavatory walls was a telling inscription: 'ABANDON ALL HOPE YE WHO ENTER HERE'.

In the district where I applied first, so few had been for relief that the old-time officials were carrying on without any additional staff.

My relieving officer was a very sympathetic man. It was a surprise to discover there was such a person. Old parishioners spoke to him without fear or embarrassment. He was an exception.)

Close by him sat a typical parish official, a callous busybody. He never smiled. He terrorised the old parishioners. Widows and deserted wives dreaded him coming near their homes. If the door was open, he pushed straight in, prying into cupboards, and lifting up pan-lids. If the pan was on the fire he went there first, then turned on the trembling housewife.

'What's this?'

'I'm making a drop of soup for the children, sir. It's so cold today, sir.'

'I never asked what you were making. I want to know what's in the pan.'

'They're a few mutton pieces I picked up, sir.'

'MUTTON PIECES! You're not given money to squander on mutton pieces. Get a couple of pennorth [sic] of bacon bones. They're plenty good enough.'

'Yes, sir. I didn't know I was doing any harm, sir.'

A slice of cheap cake on the table would send him raving. It was no use a woman saying she had stood in the queue for a couple of hours outside the stale cake shop that disposed of cake left-overs.

'You're not supposed to have cake,' he'd bawl. 'And well you know it.'

'I thought there'd be no harm in it for the children, sir.'

'You shouldn't have children.'

If she answered him back, off he would stamp, threatening her with a committee for her insolence. This meant a trial at the parish rooms. The guardians sat as judges. The relieving officer did the prosecuting. Against his interpretation the woman had no chance. She dare not contradict. An order to 'Shut up' would silence her immediately. She would be told to stand outside the room. Behind the closed doors the reasons were stated why her relief ought to be cut. When the guardians reached their decision she was called in again, and reprimanded. Then she would emerge – crying. The ratepayers had been saved two shillings. The relieving officer looked about him for another trembling victim.

Many an unemployed man longed to batter some of these ophidian-brained joy-busters. They were only deterred by the fear that while they were in jail their own wives and children might be bundled into the workhouse.

Some of the men could not always restrain themselves. One morning a group of six were walking down the street at the back of the relieving office. They had just been paid. About ten yards ahead of them was a middle aged woman in rags. Suddenly she staggered against the wall, clutching at it to keep on her feet. Being used to women fainting at the parish, the men dashed to catch her before her head hit the kerb. One man ran to a house opposite for a chair and a glass of water. Others helped the woman to remain upright.

Her lips were blue. Her whole body was shaking. She grabbed at the glass of water but refused to sit on the chair. 'No,' she kept repeating, 'He'll see me.'

'Who'll see you?' some of them asked. They thought that perhaps she had been separated from her husband and was afraid of him waylaying her. They told her not be afraid; there was plenty there to escort her home.

'Oh no,' she pleaded. 'Don't come home with me.' Suddenly she let out a frightened 'Oh' and ducked behind the men's backs. 'Please,' she cried, 'Don't let him come near me. Oh don't let him touch me.'

The men looked around to see why she was terrified. 'Mutton pieces' was coming up the street. One of them hurried down to meet him.

'Listen,' he said, 'You're not going up there. You go around the other way.'

'Out of my road,' Mutton pieces ordered. 'The very idea! Why I – I.' He tried to push past.

The man grabbed him by the lapels. 'If you don't go the other way,' he swore, 'As sure as Christ I'll stretch you out in the gutter.'

'By God, you'll pay for this,' Mutton snarled. 'I'll deal with you and that lady later.' He turned on his heel muttering.

All the men farted after him. A dozen gave in their names and addresses in the event of a court case. The woman would not give hers: 'You'll only get me into more trouble,' she said. They let her go. There was nothing more heard about the court case.

As the applicants for relief increase, the guardians began to impose test-work. This was not work in the ordinary sense that the men might eventually adapt themselves to, nor did it release them from the parish. It was the official reminder that they were on it, and as paupers had no say. Perhaps the clearest idea of why men resented it was given years ago in Dostoievsky's [*sic*] 'House of the Dead.'

'I did not understand,' he says, 'till long afterwards why this labour was really hard and excessive. It was less by reason of its difficulty, than because it was forced, imposed, obligatory; and it was only due through fear of the stick. The peasant works certainly harder than the convict, for during the summer, he works night and day. But it is in his own interest that he fatigues himself. His aim is reasonable, so that he suffers less than the convict who performs hard labour from which he derives no profit. It once came into my head that if it was devised to reduce a man to nothing – to punish him atrociously, to crush him in such a manner that the most hardened murderer would tremble before such a punishment, and take fright beforehand – it would be necessary to give to his work a character of simple uselessness, even to absurdity. Hard labour, as it is now carried on, presents no interest to the convict; but it has its utility. The convict makes bricks, digs the earth, builds, and all his occupations have a meaning and an end. Sometimes, even the prisoner takes an interest in what he is doing. He then wishes to work more skilfully, more advantageously. But let him be constrained to pour water from one vessel into another, or to transport a quantity of earth from one place to another, in order to perform the contrary operation immediately afterwards, then I am persuaded that at the end of a few days the prisoner would strangle himself or commit a thousand crimes, punishable with death, rather than live in such an abject condition, and endure such torments.'

That's how men on the parish were affected by test-work. Batches of them were sent to break stones or dig trenches to prove they were willing to work. Behind it they felt the insinuation that they were loafers. No wages were paid, only individual scales of relief in cash and coupons. Further humiliation came in an attempt to exploit them as cheap labour. A man in receipt of thirty shillings would perhaps be sent to use a pick and shovel alongside a corporation employee whose wages were three pounds. The corporation employee thinking his own job in danger immediately became antagonistic. The test-worker knowing why the other men despised him remained miserable and lethargic. Having no voluntary pride in the job, he could not put his heart into it. It was forced labour. Those who submitted, felt they had betrayed their manhood. Those who refused had their relief stopped.

The Unemployment Committee organised a strike. A leaflet was issued calling on the men to re-assert themselves. There was a rush to sign a printed declaration, that bad as their conditions were, they would not allow themselves to be used to worsen the conditions of others. 'I am willing to work,' the declaration confirmed, 'but those who offer it must pay me for doing so.'

Demonstrations marched to the jobs where test-workers had been sent. The men were glad to drop their tools. Other men refused to take their places. This caused the guardians to issue handbills at the relief depots threatening prosecution in accordance with the powers conferred them by the Poor Law Act of 1834.

The men's committee parodied the notice in a further leaflet which ran: 'Wanted. Able-bodied men for roadmaking. No wages. Apply, Sprayport Board of Kindness. Anyone refusing to take advantage of this wonderful offer will be prosecuted according to the laws laid down by Adam and Eve.'

Some of the committee-men applied for admission to the workhouse. The unemployed were advised to follow. The guardians saw the danger in them fraternising with ordinary inmates. Other factors may have influenced them to change their methods, but test-work suddenly stopped and was never again repeated.

Shortly after the strike, a circular arrived from the headquarters of the National Unemployed Movement suggesting a march on London 'for the purpose of interviewing ministers of the government'. So many distorted opinions appeared later in the newspapers that I quote from the preliminary circular of September 1922.

'Before undertaking this great trek,' it said, 'there is an enormous amount of detail [sic] work to be done as regards organising. What must be considered is the fact that hardships will have to be endured by all concerned to make this great national demonstration the huge success which it must be to be effective. We do not intend that the Unemployed Movement shall be stampeded into any premature actions, but are determined that the whole organisation of this march shall be carried out in a systematic and efficient manner. This will perhaps necessitate a month or two of preparation to assure its success, but a success it <u>must be</u>, that we are also determined upon. Each committee must consider <u>very seriously</u> the implications of this march and not rush blindfold into something they are not prepared to carry out. Every atom of energy will have to be put into it, and every participant must have at his or her heart the CAUSE for which we fight. The co-operation of all will be invited in rendering assistance, but on the deputation or deputations, only those who are unemployed and can therefore justly claim to represent the unemployed will be permitted.'

The marchers recruited through that circular set out for London 'to urge that the national exchequer to shoulder the burden of maintaining the unemployed, and relieve the local authorities.' Some of these bodies after the first twelve months of paying the new scales were only too willing for the government to step in. The Sprayport guardians supplied the local contingent with strong shoes and stockings just before they started off. A crowd of followers escorted them to the outskirts of the town. Then they proceeded alone, stopping overnight at a distant workhouse, and linking up with another contingent the next day by arrangement.

The marchers usually chose for leaders those who as non-commissioned officers had handled men in the army or navy. Their actions were controlled by a small executive council who set up each night to discuss the next day's activities. Because of spies, important decisions were occasionally withheld from the rest of the rank and file.

Most of them understood why, having walked in local street demonstrations where a dirty dungareed [sic] stranger was probably a member of the C.I.D. or a paid tout. All recognized the need for discipline in their determination to reach London. Being mostly in rags they looked like a rabble cadging for bread. They did not feel one as they marched four abreast.

Some had dyed their army great-coats black. Others wore Australian dinkum [sic] hats. All shouldered haversacks. The khaki puttees revived their past military training. Many a shabby overcoat hid a bare backside. Bad boots were the worst trouble. Men down at heel are down at heart. The old campaigners knew this and kept the contingent cobblers busy at their lasts.

This was their special job, but every man had something to do. Only the sick, or those with very sore feet were excused. The leaders took their turn at pulling the trek-carts and at washing dishes. Favouritism was debarred. Cycle scouts had their own particular job. There was a band too.

The fifes and drums quickened many a lagging footstep along the narrow country lanes. Two tunes mingled strangely together: 'Colonel Bogey,' and the 'Red Army March'. The men found inspiration in this song of the Russian Revolution.

On leaving a town, especially an inhospitable one, 'Rulers who sit in High Places' was played and sung through middle class residential districts. As windows and doors shot open, the scornful refrain of 'Colonel Bogey' quickly slammed them shut again. 'And the same to you' the marchers shouted as they went by.

The bandsmen, as much part of the morale as the food the marchers ate, were excused from the ordinary routine work of the contingent. Relays of men took turns-about in dragging the loaded trek-carts with their bulky canvas coverings. Hidden beneath, said the newspaper knowalls [sic], were spare parts of machine-guns. The marchers enjoyed that story enough to mischievously keep it alive.

At each stopping place, the selected men stood guard over the carts to prevent the covers being lifted up if strangers were about. Suspected loiterers, usually newshawks, were referred to the marchers' council, and beckoned aside to have the machine-guns story whispered in their ears. Always they swore to respect it as a confidence, then would dash off to scribble it down for immediate publication.

The police knew it was a hoax, for the trek-carts merely contained the usual odds and ends of camping equipment; spare cooking utensils, reserve sandwiches, cobblers tools, shaving gear, and a few battered storm-lamps for night use on the dark roads.

During day-time rest in country lanes the marchers would have an impromptu snack; the leaders, an inspection. Out would come the cobblers tools, while the barbers cut hair. First-aid men were down on their knees bandaging sore heels and swollen ankles. Men unfit to walk further were sent on in a friendly vehicle to the nearest hospital. They caught up the contingent a few days later.

The leaders, faced with this enthusiasm, dare not accept the scanty diet of the workhouse en route. It was not easy to refuse after a tiring all-day march. Yet the chief marshal, a five foot ex-soldier seldom got excited. His temper was well tested one night in a big northern industrial town.

He had sent two of the bicycle scouts ahead of the marchers to say they would arrive at about ten-o-clock. It was just after then when two hundred men representing six or seven towns limped through the workhouse gates into a dimly-lit yard. They saw sixty hefty policemen lined up, their helmets bobbing in the gaslight. The slightest mistake was likely to cause a slaughter. The marchers, hungry and sorefooted [*sic*], felt they had been walked into a trap. The police-inspector's sneering face seemed to confirm it.

The marshal managed to conceal his anger and addressed his men in a quiet tone: 'Comrades,' he advised, 'stand easy. Above all, keep your tempers. Be as silent as you can. Our job is to get to London. Don't forget that.'

With two of the marchers' council he was shown into along drab dining-room. The police-inspector kept hovering near. The workhouse master smilingly pointed to the tin plates of steaming skilly [*sic*] and the hunks of dry coarse dry bread.

'Everything's quite ready for you,' he said.

The marchers leaders looked at each other. The chief marshal, veteran of two wars, glanced at the rows of the tin plates again. 'My men won't have that stuff,' he declared.

The workhouse master seemed greatly surprised. 'Why? What's wrong with it,' he asked.

'Everything.'

'Well, what the – what the – am I going to do with it, then?' His voice rose almost to a shriek.

'You ought to know,' the marshal told him. 'Stick it where you stick your Christmas pudding.'

The police-inspector's face shot forward. 'Is this your idea of a joke,' he demanded.

Nobody answered him. The marshal turned away followed by his two companions. Outside in the yard the rest of the contingent stood waiting. The police had not moved. The marshal ignored them as he walked by. His own men were instantly attentive.

'Comrades,' he began, 'for obvious reasons we have decided not to stay here to-night. We will manage to stagger on for a few more miles. I have a place in mind.'

He glanced sideways at the sneering police-inspector, then continued. 'Remember,' he said, 'you came through that gateway as a disciplined body. I want you to leave in exactly the same manner and NOT as a disorderly mob. Do you thoroughly understand that? All right, then. Fall in! Everybody ready? Good! By the left, quick march!'

Back into the street limped the contingent. The band struck up 'Colonel Bogey'. The big drummer could not resist banging in a few whacks for his own gratification. The hungry men fell in to step.

Far away from the workhouse some of them broke ranks for chips and fish. On being reprimanded, the stragglers moved off in orderly formation again, balling their greasy papers in the roadway.

Long after midnight they reached a big field on the outskirts of the town. The cycle scouts led the way to a dilapidated barn. Here the men chucked themselves down on some old straw, huddling close together for warmth and a few hours sleep. The storm-lamps lined a passage to the exit. Luckily there were no rains.

The marchers' council, tired as they were, dare not lay down. There was too much for them to worry over. In undertones they discussed the next move. The experience at the last workhouse demanded a change in tactics. Unless pauper treatment was avoided the men's morale would weaken.

The marshal bore the added strain of checking a few hotheads who were bent on going back to town to smash the big shop windows in protest. They felt they had been tricked and insulted. But the marshal would stand no talk of going back. When somebody said outright he was afraid, he lost his temper for once.

'I'll be no party to any fancy heroics,' he roared. 'These men started out to march to London, and I'm bloody well going to get them there.'

Some of the marchers raised their heads from the floor. The marshal quietened down again.

'It's all right, comrades,' he said. 'Go to sleep. There's nothing the matter.'

The quarrel passed over. Different methods were freely discussed. Lamps were brought nearer, and maps spread out to decide on the next stopping-place. A railway time table proved an asset. Connections between neighbouring towns on the line of march were ticked off, also the times of first and last trains by which police might be drafted from one place to another. This was the danger. The marshal explained how a blundering skirmish now was bound to drive some marchers dribbling back to their homes. He suggested ways to avoid this. It was turned three-o-clock when the council lay down.

At six-o-clock, all the men jumped up shivering but glad of their water flasks. After a hasty snack of bread and cheese, which had been held in reserve, they were ready to move on. Two cyclists went pedalling ahead of them with sufficient money to buy more bread.

There were four other bicycle scouts in this particular contingent. Two, with a printed card 'NATIONAL UNEMPLOYED MARCH' strung to their handlebars, were sent on to a town the marchers were deliberately avoiding, to notify the workhouse master that the contingent would arrive at a late hour that night. By contact or examination of a directory they found out the number of police. This was reported back when the cyclist rejoined the contingent at an agreed spot on a fork road at noon. Meantime, the remaining two cyclists with no identification cards rode onto a town the leaders considered suitable, to make contacts there, find whether the workhouse was situated in a back street or main road, and if any police were being drafted in or out of the town. It was evening when they reported back.

Long before dusk the band had stopped playing. Just the single tap of a drum kept the contingent in step. The night grew very dark. In the narrow country lanes the men stumbled blindly along, bumping into hedges and each other, and cursing in spasms as the trek-carts wobbled over the humpy roadway. Two storm-lamps were carried at the front and tail-end of the contingent to warn off tooting motor-cars that whizzed by and vanished in the dark again.

At half-past ten the marchers limped into the town least expecting them. The sleepy inhabitants wondered what had had happened, so did the astonished chief constable. He might have been a kind man. He was certainly a wise one. He was told the men were ravenous and wild and could not be restrained for long. It was hinted they might help themselves from the shop windows. There wasn't enough police in that small town to prevent them. The marshal did not mean this as a threat. His position made him uneasy.

The chief constable stood pondering. 'What can I get them at this hour of the night,' he asked.

'They want eggs and bacon.'

'Eggs and bacon! My God! EGGS AND BACON? Why that's – Eggs and bacon!' The chief constable could hardly recover himself. 'Eggs and bacon! By Christ, I've heard of some things. Eggs and bacon? Oh-h,' he sighed. 'Eggs and bacon. Wait! I better see what the chairman of the guardians has to say.'

This bearded old man though also afraid of the marchers looting, saw no way of supplying such an order of eggs and bacon at that unusual hour.

'All the shops are closed,' he said, 'until the morning. We could find some eggs for you, but not a whole army.' He was worried. 'We can't put you up in the workhouse, either,' he continued. 'It's too small. Let's see. There's a spare ward in the hospital. Oh dammit, come along. We'll fix up something. Bring all the boys over.'

The marcher's council knew how inadvisable it would to accept eggs for some and leave others short. They agreed to cold meat, cheese and pickles for all, with plenty of bread, butter, and tea. The men were instructed to make as little noise as possible. They tiptoed through the hospital grounds, taking care to lessen the squeaking of the trek-carts.

At the suggestion of the marshal the hospital day-staff were left in their beds. A party of marchers were put in charge of the night-matron to help her prepare the meal. She was genuinely surprised to find they were flesh and blood beings who actually spoke English, and had never been in Russia or worn ferocious whiskers in their lives.

When the meal was over all the crockery was washed and noiselessly replaced on the kitchen shelves. Tables were lifted back against the walls, and the men bedded down for the night. Though the beds were on the floor. The floor was scrupulously clean and the ward comfortably heated. Soon everybody was asleep.

Before seven next morning, blankets were folded, beds rolled up, and all returned to the hospital storeroom. The chief constable seemed impressed by the discipline. Perhaps it did not coincide with what he had heard or read. Besides, there was something kindly in his behaviour. He stood by as the marchers filed in for their breakfast.

'There's your eggs and bacon, boys,' he said. 'I hope you enjoy them.'

They did. The next party of men on the rota were detailed to wash the dishes. The remainder smartened themselves up, then cheery and refreshed mustered in the hospital grounds. Those next in turn for the trek-carts grabbed the ropes in readiness.

The marshal came out, strapping on his haversack. Then men's chatter ceased as he held his hands up.

'Hush, comrades,' he cried. 'Please. Don't forget where you are. There must be no band nor no noise of any description until we are well clear of this building. Don't spoil things. Everybody here has been really decent to us as you know. I have already thanked them on your behalf.' A chorus of 'hear-hears' brought his hands up again. 'Shush! The whole bunch of you.' He looked them over. 'Are you all set? Good! Quietly now. No noise. Mind those carts. Quick march!'

The chief constable, stationed at the gate, wished them luck. They saluted briskly and wheeled past smiling into the street. At a safe distance from the hospital the bandsmen searched their music, then led the contingent out of town to a rollicking Irish jig. The distance to the next stopping-place was less than eighteen miles. About halfway the contingent was joined by a small body of twenty men. Each carried a strong walking stick. The night previous they had attended a crowded indoor meeting where the chief speaker, a parliamentary candidate, was also a prominent barrister. The leader of the small group saw an opportunity of getting some money for his men's immediate needs. He sat at the back of the hall until question time, then jumped up and asked for a collection. The platform taken by surprise allowed their stewards to pass the plates around. The barrister counted up thirty shillings. In handing it over he hoped that wherever the marchers went they could always behave as gentlemen.

In promising to do so they had no thought of walking-sticks. That only occurred to them the next morning when buying cigarettes at a small general shop. The sticks were hanging in the doorway. The men with badly blistered feet recognised their immediate value and twenty were bought at a reduced price. At once a difference was felt. As the men limped quickly along, the desire to act as gentlemen grew stronger in their minds. They visualised the advantage of walking sticks if they were attacked on the road, remembering that gentlemen were privileged to defend themselves against ruffians of every kind.

Members of the main contingent soon grasped the idea. During rest-halts in country lanes those familiar with trees cut out their own sticks, trying them first to make sure they were serviceable enough to lean on. Then they swaggered in behind the band.

The next town was reached in the early evening. A hot tea was waiting at the local workhouse. The hospitality here was fairly satisfying. There was no need for veiled threats or bluff. Perhaps a friendly phone call had come from the last place.

After tea most of the marchers went into the grounds for a breather. They made a startling discovery. Local families whose home-life had been broken up on entering the workhouse, were compelled as inmates to live separate existences. A high wire netting divided the workhouse grounds into sections. Through this, wives conversed with husbands, and children with their fathers. Some of the marchers stared in amazement as little tots pressed their lips to the wire in awkward kisses for their fathers stooped low on the other side of the netting. An explanation was asked for. The fathers complained that they only saw their children for an hour or so in the evening.

A marcher's deputation immediately tackled the workhouse master. He could see nothing wrong in the wire-netting arrangement. It had been the rule long before his time. So coolly was this said that the angry deputation threatened to pull down the wire netting, and perhaps wreck the institution unless the father-inmates and their wives and children were allowed to fraternise in the common-room that night. The workhouse master gave way.

The common-room was quickly crowded. Women and children bunched around the fireplace. Some of the marchers flew across to the harmonium. One began to play hymn tunes. Others were soon singing the parodied words that had often cheered the American I.W.W.* Ex-members of that organisation led with 'Pie in the Sky', 'Dump the bosses off your back', and 'There is power, there is power in a band of working men'. The choruses were repeated with gusto. The children tried to catch the swing of 'You will eat in the sweet bye and bye'. Their voices were at it as they went upstairs to bed. The women followed shortly afterwards and the singing stopped.

The men-inmates grouped around some of the marchers who were holding forth on this book and that book and what Marx really meant, workshops and workhouses, and the reason for the unemployed march

* The Industrial Workers of the World. A militant trades union organisation.

to London. The inmates were bewildered by the continuous rush of strange phrases that poured into their ears from all sides. Whatever they thought, the privilege of sitting up late and the solace of a cigarette was due to the marchers' protest.

How long the concession was to last nobody could tell. It had temporarily weakened the authority of the workhouse master who was much relieved to see the contingent depart the next morning.

The next workhouse was a gloomy and forbidding hole, both outside and in. The yard was like a rubbish tip. The master came out and wanted the marchers to do test-work. He showed the marshal a pile of stones that had to be broken according to the regulations. The marshal told him that the only stones the marchers were likely to break would be for their own use: 'And gentlemen do not use stones,' he added. The master threatened to call the police.

The chief marshal, unperturbed, reckoned up the large number of police that would be necessary to frighten a disciplined body of two hundred and twenty men who had spent years in the trenches and returned with plenty of grievances. He detailed what it would cost the ratepayers, the damage the marchers would do, the publicity it would get in the papers, and the bad effect it would surely have on people throughout the country.

'And what good will that do you,' he asked. 'Just for the sake of a few cobble-stones.'

The workhouse-master exploded. 'You've got enough men there to eat the bloody stones,' he roared.

'They don't want to eat them.'

'Don't forget I've asked you to break them.'

'We've no intention of breaking them. We've been in nearly a dozen workhouses and haven't broken a stone yet.'

'Why didn't you say that at first instead of starting all this argument.'

'ME! I wasn't arguing.'

'All right. It's all over now.'

The master provided a satisfying meal of roast meat and vegetables. Maybe it was to compensate for the cold sleeping accommodation. It was horrible. A row of crypt-like stone-floored openings off dark and musty passages. These rickety old premises could offer no better. The smelly horse-blankets must have been stored in a deep cellar for months.

In the morning they were piled in the yard to air. They needed airing; so did the marchers after a night under them. It almost spoilt their appetites for a breakfast of ham and eggs. This diet now had become quite ordinary.

As they were assembling in the yard to move off, a husky voice bawled from an outhouse: 'Get out, you gang of Bolsheviks. You ought to be bloody well shot.'

A few of the marchers dashed across to the half opened doorway. Inside was a raggedy unshaven fellow working his feet on a treadmill and not daring to stop. Between scowls and mutterings he wanted to know why the marchers had escaped test-work while he had to stay behind. They ignored his insults and invited him to come with them, but he persisted in shouting at the top of his voice that he was no bloody Bolshevik. The marchers could waste no further time convincing him that they were Britishers. They were too anxious to move on to a place with decent baths. The blankets had made them lousy.

In the main street a propaganda meeting was held. Speakers taunted the inhabitants about their vile and filthy workhouse. This did not stop the collectors from rattling their money boxes in the faces of the crowds. Within an hour the meeting was closed and the contingent was on its way again.

Just outside the town they met a meandering group of thirty. These men had decided to march at the very last minute. They seemed to have lost their way. One of them, a tall gawky chap, looked like a superintendent in charge of a Sunday School treat. He was at least six foot in height, wore a new bowler hat, and carried an umbrella. This he swung around in grand style as he jogged along, chest stuck out, humming gaily to himself. Probably he was unaware of the interest he was causing. It came out by mere accident that under his bowler lay plenty of romance. On overhearing the I.W.W.'s talking of America he sidled over to one of them.

'Have you really been in America, Mr. B?' he asked.

'Why, sure. I was there for twenty years. I tackled everything from steamboats to ranches.'

The big chap shook his head enviously. 'God, you're lucky,' he sighed. 'Really you are. I wish I could go there. I'd love to be a cowboy.'

Though the next town was a small one the general atmosphere was sociable and kindly. The two hundred and fifty marchers were allowed the free use of the baths. In addition, the manager of a variety theatre offered a hundred free admission tickets for the second evening performance. The men's council, chary of accepting, were persuaded to do so by the rest of the contingent who drew lots to prevent any grumbling. It was agreed that should a similar offer be repeated elsewhere, the first hundred men would automatically be passed over.

The cobbly [sic] conditions of the roads in this area blistered everybody's feet. Some of the men could hardly drag themselves along. The wheels of the trek-carts went lopsided. This caused plenty of swearing. The pace had to be slowed down and the daily mileage reduced from twenty to twelve. This and a heavy drenching rainfall compelled the contingent to diverge on a town renowned for its schools and culture.

As usual, two cyclists were sent ahead. They returned to report there was no big workhouse in the locality but that suitable premises would be in readiness to lodge the marchers on their arrival. The men's council had visions of a part of the school buildings being placed at their disposal.

At eight-o-clock that evening they were greatly surprised to be directed to a big tin-roofed barracks. On sitting down at the long mess tables, they were more surprised still to have dished before them the soldiers standby feed, bully beef. Most of them had thought they had finished with that stuff on being demobbed from the army. Yet here it was once more whether they liked it or not. That, and bread and tea.

They could only sit and stare at it in silence. Though hungry, they were soaked to the skin and all too lame to start a rumpus. They were in a barracks, not a workhouse. Reluctantly they ate what they could. It was as much the marshal was able to do to scrounge a few pickles.

The marchers council sat up that night to plan some way of giving this home of culture the horse-laugh. A mock military funeral was decided upon.

The 'corpse', a seven pound tin of bully beef, was saved for the purpose. Not a word was broached to the body of the marchers. The 'funeral' could only be a success if they were made to believe that one of their comrades had died overnight. As soon as they were asleep no time was lost in laying out the 'corpse'.

A dozen men, specially picked, were sworn to secrecy. All had had experience of military funerals. They went prowling around the barracks for the necessary props. A stretcher was found and taken to the bottom corner of the long shed. It was easy enough to smuggle a couple of white sheets and two pillows. The pillows were laid lengthwise on the stretcher, the tin of bully beef placed in the middle, and the sheets spread on top, ends tucked in. Before daybreak a large-sized union-jack had been draped over all.

Four of the tallest marchers mounted guard, leaning piously on their walking-sticks. One of the cyclists, a florist, rose early, and sneaked out to gather some flowers and foliage for making a wreath. There were a number of private gardens nearby to select from.

The awakening marchers sat up, heard the whisperings, gazed down the long shed, and were dumbfounded. On tip-toe they approached the supposed corpse. Alert guards motioned the over-curious away. For others, the union jack was sufficiently convincing.

During a bully-beef breakfast, there were gloomy guesses as to the identity of the 'dead man'. All were proved incorrect by glances across the table. It couldn't be so-and-so; he was lacing his boots. Nor was it 'What's-his-name', he was having a shave. Finally they agreed that the corpse was a little fellow who had been left behind in hospital three days ago before. Having died there, his body had been sent on. Everybody murmured 'Poor beggar' and looked downcast. It was worse when the cyclist appeared with his wreath. There was silence as the marshal laid it tenderly on the union-jack. He seemed to be taking the 'death' to heart.

Everything was now ready for the 'funeral': stretcher-bearers, an experienced firing-squad, a band to play the dead [sic] march, and a bugler to sound the 'Last Post'; everything apart from a clergyman.

Two of the marchers council were ex-Roman Catholics. Both could gabble Latin in pagefuls [sic]. One had been a serving altar-boy; the other, a chaplain's clerk in the navy. Both had travelled around the world in ships, and could wangle almost anything in a fix. The first had a blubbery priest's face; the second, the ascetic drawn features of a fasting saint. Though they fitted naturally into their respective parts, neither owned a prayer book. The 'priest' said he must borrow one from somewhere, if the 'service' was to appear real.

Arranging to meet the 'funeral' procession in the centre of the town, he slipped out of the barracks on his strange errand. It would have been easier to ask for money. Busy housewives jerked open their doors to the most absurd request ever made on a front step: 'Can you lend me a prayer-book, missus, please?' Thinking the man was a lunatic, the woman dashed in with fright.

The shops were now opening. Amongst them was a dirty-looking secondhand store. The contents of an attic had evidently been dumped into the window. The 'priest' spotted a bundle of broad linen collars and bought one for a penny. In a pile of rubbish on the floor, he found an old bible with a clasp. This cost threepence. More eager now to complete his clerical rig-out, he rummaged about for a bowler hat that that could be cut down to resemble a clergyman's. The few bowlers in the shop were on the small side. He suddenly became ambitious. Why not a tall silk hat? Church dignitaries wore them.

The old woman shopkeeper had none in the place. She mentioned an undertaker's where one might be bought cheap from one of the coachmen.

'Is it for a concert,' she asked. The 'priest' nodded his head and hurried out.

The undertakers yard was not far away. A cheery-faced stable-man was rubbing a horse down. His forearms were tattooed. This served as a helpful introduction. In a moment he was quite pally. The 'priest' explained in confidence what the hat was really for.

The stableman's round face spread in a grin. 'That's a good one, sailor,' he said. 'A right good one. Now just half a mo'.' He scratched his head while he pondered. 'Yes, I can do it,' he said. 'Come on over to the harness room.'

Very quickly the 'priest' was dressed: collar back to front; a piece of black sleeve-lining down his chest, and a silk hat on his head. The stableman next brought out a mournful-looking overcoat, buttoned it on the 'priest' then stood a few paces. While flicking off some pieces of chaff he burst out laughing.

'You look the real McCoy now,' he said. 'By Jeese [*sic*] you do.'

The road being clear, the 'priest' in his anxiety not to miss the procession went to run out of the yard. The stableman slowed him down to a correct funeral pace.

Crowds of wondering people were already squeezed on the narrow side-walks. Others gazed down from open windows. The police had stopped all traffic. As the muffled drums were heard, people craned their necks and stopped chattering. The procession slowly approached;

the band playing the dead march, while the stretcher bearers, heads bent, crawled just behind. The rest of the marchers followed with walking-sticks reversed. The six kettledrums were covered in black crepe.

The 'priest' watched for an opportunity to step into line. A section of the crowd respectfully eased a passage to let him through. Looking very downcast he joined in behind the 'corpse'.

The saintly ex-navy clerk lifted his eyes, gaped at the silk hat, and blurted out: 'A tall-shiner! Gawdblime [sic], that's the limit!'

Men on the pavement doffed their hats and stood bareheaded. Women grouped together were bitter in their denunciation of the government.

'Imagine poor lads coming home to that after fighting for their country,' said one. Some of her neighbours were crying. Even a few of the marchers were unable to hold back their tears. The 'priest' was compelled to keep his eye to the ground. By his side walked the ascetic-looking clerk, his hand joined in prayer like a church-window figure. As they drew near a stern-face policeman shook his finger warningly at some children sitting along the kerb.

The procession passed slowly by the famous college and halted a short distance away by a double-sized pillar-box that stood on a traffic-island in the centre of the main street. The flag-covered stretcher was lowered gently to the ground. The bearers moved aside.

The 'priest' solemnly handed his hat to the clerk, and then stepped across to deliver a short oration. His head was still bowed. With an effort he raised it.

'Friends,' he began with an ecclesiastical drawl, 'we are gathered here to pay a last tribute to our dearly-departed comrade, B.B. The greatness of our empire is in no mean measure due to him. He served on all fronts in the last war. A very old soldier, he saw service in the Boer War. He was always at hand, and could be rushed anywhere in an emergency. We are all mindful of the praise lavished on prominent generals, and don't begrudge the fame that belongs to two other names none of us are likely to forget, Tickler and Macconachie [sic]. With all due respect to them, our late comrade, B.B. was the real backbone of the British Army. The song says 'Old soldiers never die', but like everything else they must die eventually. And comrade B.B. has ended his days with us. May he rest in peace.'

Solemnly, the priest fingered the pages of the open bible. The ascetic cleric moved nearer to mouth the responses. The 'priest' mumbled a few sentences in Latin, then raised his right hand piously for the blessing.

'Dominus vosbiseum,' he chanted.

'Et sum spirito tuo,' responded the clerk.

'Requiseat in pace.'

'Amen.'

The bible was snapped to. At a signal from the marshal, the firing squad closed in on both sides of the stretcher. On the command 'Fire!' they cocked their sticks skyward. The six muffled kettledrums rumbled through the stilly silence. As the air vibrated there were broken sobs everywhere.

Three times the sticks were cocked, and three times the muffled drums rattled off a long drawn-out tattoo. Then the bugler stepped forward to sound the 'Last Post'. The crowd could no longer hide its emotion. Men and women wept openly.

The ascetic-looking clerk slyly nudged the 'priest'. 'Hey, Joe,' he whispered. 'Take a peep around. Some of our bloody fellers have gone wet-eye too.'

The 'priest' dare not look around. As the last lingering notes of the bugle died away, he stooped over the stretcher and lifted the wreath aside. The union-jack was thrown quickly over the pillar box, and after it the white sheets. The tin of bully beef was then set in the middle and the wreath hung like a crowning laurel.

The vast crowd stared and blinked. They were still uncertain of what had actually taken place. So were the marchers in the rear. Their doubts were soon settled by the marshal. Barking out 'Attention!' he ran his eyes over the bewildered men as they straightened up and reversed their sticks. Shouting to them to 'Be lively', he gave the order 'Quick march!'

The band struck up 'Colonel Bogey'. The contingent immediately swung into stride, and into song against bully beef culture. 'And the same to you!' was the roaring challenge that reached the college rooftops.

No other place was more stingy as this for food. In the more densely-populated areas, the marchers' midday rations were supplemented by local sympathisers. The workhouse fare was variable. In one big manufacturing town it was exceptionally satisfying, in spite of bare walls and tables. After supper, the chief of the C.I.D., a heavy-jowled [*sic*] giant, sauntered across with a body of detectives. He wanted to know who was in charge of the contingent.

The little marshal said 'We are,' and called the council over. The chief detective took stock of their faces. They took stock of his.

He seemed concerned about their comfort. 'You lads are only mugs to stay here with the others,' he said. 'I can get you fixed up at an hotel for the night. You'll be better off there, you know. But you'll have to come now.'

The marshal looked at him. 'All of us,' he asked.

'Yes, all that's here.'

'There's two hundred and fifty, remember.'

The detective's lip dropped. 'Hey don't come it,' he growled, 'I only meant you dozen or so.'

The marshal shook his head. 'Nothin' doing,' he said. 'We'll stay where we are. We'll be all right.'

'You must be very fond of these places.'

'No we're not; don't you believe it. But we prefer being with the rest of the lads.'

The detective stroked his chin awhile. 'I'll tell you what I'll do,' he said. 'I'll take a dozen of them.'

'Oh-no-you-won't,' drawled the marshal as he winked to some of the council.

The detective was watching through half-closed eyes. 'Just as you like,' he said. 'But you'll find there's no more empty beds upstairs. That's why I was making you the offer.'

'It's very thoughtful of you,' answered the marshal, 'but we'll stay here. It won't be the first time we've slept on a floor.'

The big detective shrugged his shoulders. 'You're bloody fools, boys,' he remarked, 'that's all I've got to say.' He ambled off down the corridor, his squad trailing behind him.

Though this was the only deliberate attempt at separation, the council had to be continually on their guard against anything that seemed like favoured treatment for themselves. One country workhouse they stopped at had the atmosphere of a convalescent home. It had been used as a soldiers' hospital.

The chairman of the local guardians was a pleasant old man. He was very deaf. He told the marchers there was time to wash themselves before they went in for the evening meal.

'We do everything properly in here, men,' he said. 'There's plenty of soap and hot water.'

In the long dining hall, the tables were all bare except for two small ones close by the door. These had white cloths on them, freshly cut flowers, and an elaborate display of cutlery. As the marchers filed in they kept staring back. Thinking that local bigwigs were about to join them they hoped there would be no speeches. A rostrum near the door seemed to suggest otherwise. In front of this was a harmonium.

A stout woman came in, twirled the stool-top a bit, and sat down. The old chairman followed. He mounted the rostrum. The marchers began to whisper across the tables: 'It's either hymns or the national anthem.' They looked around for the marshal or some of the council. There was no sign of any of them. This started a few grumbling.

'They ought to be cleaned-up by now,' said one. 'I suppose they're jabbering.'

'They know what they're up to,' said another. 'They've seen this stunt coming off, and they're dodging it.'

'Let's all get up and walk out,' urged a third.

'No. Not yet,' advised another. 'See what happens first.'

'I'm not standin' up for any singin',' said someone else.

'Nor me,' exclaimed several of them together.

Some of the workhouse staff came in carrying plates of soup. The old chairman rapped on the rostrum for silence. His face was beaming.

'I want all you men to be happy while you're here,' he said. 'I want you to feel that everybody is your friend. I suppose most of you are ex-soldiers. I've been talking to your officers outside, and I think they're wonderful men. You ought to be very proud of them.'

The marchers stared across the table. 'Officers?' they repeated. 'Officers: What officers. What the hell's he gassin' about?'

The marshal appeared in the doorway followed by the rest of his council. They were chatting together in pairs. Glancing casually at the decorated tables, they walked up between the packed forms looking for a place to sit. Only a couple of them managed to squeeze themselves in. The rest turned to stare at the decorated tables.

From the rostrum, the old chairman motioned them back. 'I want you all to sit at this end with me,' he said.

As none of them made any movement, he came down to the floor. Being deaf, an explanation had to be shouted into his ear. The marshal tried to do it as politely as he could as he pointed to the decorated table.

'It's very kind of you,' he shouted. 'But there are certain reasons why we must be treated alike. It's a bit difficult to tell you in a few words. Do you see what I'm getting at?'

The old man's eyes twinkled. 'Yes, yes.' he said, 'it's quite all right. I see now. Shall I have the flowers removed?'

'Nu-no,' answered the marshal. 'Leave them where they are. Some of us will swop places. It won't take a minute. So long as we're not all together at the one table.'

The changes were made. The marshal and half the council went up to the top of the room. The old chairman mounted the rostrum again, and rapped for silence.

'Now that's all settled,' he announced, 'I think we ought to make a start. It is customary for us here to have a prayer or a hymn. Oh don't be frightened. It will only be one; a very short one, too. Er, how many of you men remember the doxology?'

Some of the marchers had never heard the name before. Others had forgotten the exact words, but nearly all of them were muttering against the meal being turned into a Band of Hope meeting.

The old man beamed from the rostrum. 'Will you all stand up now, please,' he asked. 'The words will soon come back once the lady starts the music.'

The harmonium blared out a few notes. A scattering of marchers rose half-heartedly. The others remained seated. Practically all the men's council were amongst them.

The marshal, very troubled-looking was moving up and down between the forms. 'Come on, lads,' he appealed. 'Give him a bit of a show. He's a decent old stick. He's got a kink, that's all. Two of his sons were killed in France. That's why he's making all this fuss over us. Even if you don't know the words, get up and la-la the tune. He won't know any different. He's as deaf as a doorpost.'

All the men stood up. The ex I.W.W's, who were all grouped near the top of the room, whispered hurriedly, cleared their throats, then as solemn as a church choir, prayerfully joined their hands together, and as the harmonium led off, began to sing:

'Praise him for whom the workbells [*sic*] shine,
Praise him for bits of overtime,
Praise him whose wars we have to fight,
Praise rat, the leech, and the parasite,
    Oh-h-h, Hell-ll'

Heads bowed, they sat down amidst suppressed chuckling. The marshal alone scowled. The scowl was still on his face after the meal was over, when the workhouse staff were removing the last of the plates. The old chairman was up on the rostrum again, and saying how delightful the singing had been.

'I knew you could do it, men,' he said. 'It was a very fine effort. Now I'm leaving you. You can have the use of this room for a few hours, to write letters in, or read, or enjoy yourselves in your own way. Goodnight all of you, and may you all sleep well.'

Still beaming, he went out with the stout woman. Straightaway the marshal hurried down to the decorated table. As he approached, one of the marchers seated there asked what all the laughing had been about.

The marshal glared back up the room. 'That smart gang up there,' he grunted, 'and their flash hymn. They had no right to pull that over on the old chap. He's done no harm to them. Could you hear it very plain down here?'

'Not the words. But the singing was champion. It sounded like a mission hall.'

'Too bloody much like a mission hall.'

'The old man liked it, anyway. He was beating time with his hand.'

'He didn't know what to. The poor old devil.'

A few days later, the contingent marched into High Barnet on the outskirts of London. Lined along the kerb were hundreds of other marchers from Scotland and the North East coast. After five weeks on the road, they were standing at the salute, singing a music-hall ditty to which the arriving contingent kept time. These soon had the swing of the words:

'We won the war, we won the war,
You can ask Lloyd George or Bonar Law,
We fought the Austrians, the Germans, and the Turks

And that's just the reason now that we are out-of-works
We won the war, we won the war,
But next time the enemy's at the door,
Call him in and set him drunk, never mind the paper bunk,
For what's the use of fighting anymore.'

There were smiles galore, and a rush of handshakes. Limping men seemed full of the same questions: 'What kind of weather did you have? How was the grub? Did you run into much trouble on the road?' Replies were various, but few had regrets. To-morrow they would be in London.

Next day, twenty-three hundreds of them, including those from South Wales and the English Channel towns, marched through the cheering crowds in Hyde Park. Then they were allocated to the care of district committees.

This warm hospitality was a contrast to the organised abuse of the daily newspapers. Columns of print appeared, set up like extracts from a rogues calendar. Every form of vilification was used to infer that the marchers in the main were scoundrels. Scare headlines spoke of Moscow gold, intended rioting, and the certainty of bloodshed. The public were warned to keep clear of Whitehall. There were rumours of machine-guns, and of troops standing by. Offices and shops were advised to board their windows. Downing Street was already barricaded. Topping all this was a poster proclamation, forbidding the marchers to demonstrate within a mile of the Houses of Parliament.

A marchers' council, representing all the contingents, met overnight to discuss how to counteract the press. Some of the marchers had already become shaky. If the contingents went back to the provinces without interviewing someone in authority, the purpose of the march was lost. The Prime Minister, Mr. Bonar Law, had refused by letter to meet a deputation. The deputation decided to risk a batoning by going to see Mr. Bonar Law.

The following afternoon they marched through the crowded streets to Whitehall; behind them, a monster demonstration. Ahead of them, they knew, were hundreds of police. On the borders of the proscribed area, the demonstration suddenly broke off in the direction of Hyde Park. The deputation continued along Whitehall. Massed police were in waiting. Well-dressed men and women packed the pavements. They had come to see the Red Army savages, and only a dozen ragged marchers limped by, surrounded by hefty policemen.

The deputation halted, and gazed all around them. 'We've got so far,' whispered one to the other. They stared at the policemen and the government buildings opposite, and wondered if machine-guns were hidden behind the windows.

From one of the buildings a messenger hurried across to say that the Ministers of Labour and of Health were both waiting to grant an interview. The deputation paired off, and under police escort, were led over to a doorway and up a wide staircase. More police were grouped here, while inside the spacious receiving-rooms, several plain-clothes detectives lolled against the wall. The deputation eyed them with contempt, one of them muttering: 'This is as bad as Sydney Street.'

Through another door came the Ministers of Labour and of Health with them were <u>their</u> secretaries, and <u>their</u> secretaries, and <u>their</u> secretaries, until it seemed such jobs existed as official pen-wiper and blotting-man extraordinary. They settled down at the table in conference order, and began to thumb the foolscap that lay in sheets before them.

The ragged unemployed stood watching. One of the Ministers rose to speak. He was interrupted by the deputation's chairman who quietly announced, that as the Premier was absent, the deputation would not waste its time with subordinates. A couple of others briefly touched on the distress in their own localities, and asked that the government be persuaded to take over the unemployed. Then all withdrew, went downstairs, and caught the first bus going to Hyde Park. The rest of the unemployed had marched away there, but the problem had not marched away with them.

Six months later, the Sprayport organisation petered out. Unemployment relief being firmly established, there were no more demonstrations through the streets. The meetings dwindled away. Most of the leaders, including the man with the Stetson, left the town to seek employment elsewhere. The others hampered by family ties were compelled to stay behind to face additional privations. Far worse was the domestic life of the few too proud to apply for relief. One of these was the old police-striker. Most of his time was now taken up by a dreary house-to-house canvas for burial insurance. The ex-sergeant major, wearing somebody's cast-off pants, went around the back doors as a rag and bone man. The parson, poverty-stricken too, had to sell up his home, and emigrate to Canada.

I was keen on shipping to Australia, until returning men who had lost their jobs quickly changed my mind. My one hope was America again; the way to ship there, a pierhead [*sic*] jump. Each sailing day found me at the pierhead waiting alongside dozens of others. But there was little chance for anybody since the big liners had nearly all been transferred to Southampton.

I would try Southampton. Getting there was a problem. I had no money for railway fare, or nothing I could pawn; and unless on arrival I was immediately employed, the guardians could arrest me for leaving my family chargeable. Yet I had to get away somehow. After much hesitation I asked an old woman shopkeeper to lend me two pounds from her market money. Without any fuss she dug her hands down between her breasts, fished out her purse, and wished me luck. I dashed to the railway station in my rags.

The train drew alongside a White Star liner in Southampton. It was easy for me to skip up the gangway, and along to the firemen's room. There were men there who knew me. With their help I could stow away with safety. Just before sailing time, three of the crew walked ashore. I got one of their jobs.

In New York I deserted the ship, joined an American coaster, and though it was daily in and out of port, stayed aboard for four months until I could afford to buy some clothes. Then I hunted for work ashore. Conditions were not as favourable as in 1921. Wages had dropped. There was plenty of unemployment. The only openings were in seasonal occupations; building trades, and the like. I managed to average six months work in each twelve during the three years I stayed there. In between was the daily trudge around. This happened each time in the freezing winter months. Posting money home, besides keeping myself, very soon used up my savings. In the out-of-work periods there were frequent spells of hunger. But I dare not pawn my suit. On my tidy appearance depended a job.

'Americans for American jobs,' was the cry now. I had to spend a lot of time dodging the Emigration officers. They were more active than ever; raiding mission halls and employment agencies, and interrogating any aliens they found on the premises. Surprise visits were paid to works and factories, and all illegal entrants were rooted out of their jobs. Wholesale deportations followed.

I grew wearied of the continual dodging about. It meant changing my address, changing my name, and suddenly quitting a job if I had one. In the latter part of 1926, I worked my passage back to Sprayport. This time I had no savings; just two suits of clothes.

Right away I reported at the Labour Exchange and began signing on. Lacking sufficient stamps I could not draw benefit. Others in the queue were in a like fix. They were raggedy men, down-at-heel, who had not worked during the three years I was out of England. Most of them were about my own age, thirty. Their jaws were shrunken, they were heart-broken, and were wishing for another war. All of them were on the parish.

I had no desire to go there if it could be avoided. My tidy appearance would soon help me into a job. I looked up the 'want ads' and started the daily rounds of the streets. There were changes that impressed me immediately. One long thoroughfare that had once been busy with crowded shops, now had nearly half of them 'to let', and almost derelict. The windows were streaked with filth. Other shops had been re-opened as second-hand stores with second-hand furniture and second-hand clothes. The people along the street seemed to have gone second-hand too. In a much busier thoroughfare, the shops showed a different kind of change. Butchers, bakers, grocers, and others, who for years had curtly said 'No' to parish coupons were now competing for pauper custom. Every window displayed a large printed card: 'Relief coupons taken here. Best value given.' This made it possible for a man on the parish to occasionally sample a chop so long as the butcher marked it down as stewing beef.

My daily walks continued. The first setbacks did not dishearten me. While the tidy clothes were on my back there was still hope for to-morrow. The to-morrow soon mounted into a month. I had no money. The pawn shop routine recommenced. My clothes went in and the wife's clothes, my boots and her boots, to be followed by the rings she had stinted herself to redeem. Then the bedding was bundled together; next we started on the furniture. There was little of that worth selling. Being now really destitute, I applied for parish relief; there was no bread in the house. A visitor was sent around to verify my story. He gave me temporary food coupons to last a couple of days. I was booked for a parish committee.

In the gloomy parish building the clerical staff had been increased by more than twenty. Able bodied unemployed were now treated as a separate group from the ordinary parishioners. Dozens of them were jammed in a large room taking their turns in answering the routine questions of the clerks.

The smaller-sized committee rooms were at the top of a long passage. The guardians were supposed to sit from ten in the morning. None of them had yet arrived. Over fifty shabby men were standing in line, waiting to have their cases reviewed. There was a scattering of shawl women amongst them. A dozen or so were seated bent over on a couple of wooden forms. All were pale and careworn. Their lips moved; they did not speak. There was a sigh here and there, and an occasional graveyard cough that started off some of the wheezy men leaning against the walls. Most of them gazed weakly about them. The few whispering together, stopped each time a doorknob turned, and a relieving officer or clerk came out smoking a cigarette. Paupers were not allowed to smoke. They were not supposed to have cigarettes. Cigarettes were considered a luxury; smoking them, a vice.

One young clerk in the twenties seemed to have a roving commission. He bobbed about from room to room, a cigarette constantly in his mouth. Coming out of one door he dropped a lit end, stamped on it, and stood pondering a moment. Then he walked aggressively half-way down the passage between the applicants, and asked which of them had been smoking. Some nearest him mumbled indistinctly. Others further away raised their eyes and grunted.

The clerk stared along the faces at nobody in particular. 'You want to read the notices when you come in here,' he said. 'What do you think it's put up there for?'

A grey-haired man with faded war ribbons blurted out: 'It's you wants to read the notice.'

The young clerk reddened, and walked straight over. 'Don't talk to me like that,' he said. 'You've got too much to say.'

He hurried away, and appeared a few minutes later with an older official. Both stared up and down the passage. They talked animatedly, sniffed up together and nodded their heads. Then sniggering, they turned on their heels, and passed into one of the side-rooms again.

Men and women shook their heads despairingly at each other. Some swore under their breaths. One man broke out aloud.

'It's a bit of a beggar,' he said, 'when a young pup like that can ride over people. O sufferin' Christ, what we've got to go through.'

An old woman pulled her shawl aside. 'They can do just as they like,' she said, 'once they get you in here. God's curse to them.'

A door was suddenly opened, and all was silence immediately. A relieving officer came out carrying a heap of case-papers. He took them into a committee-room. It was a sign that the guardians were on the premises. Men and women stopped staring about them, and tried to sit up or stand up as straight as they were able. Their eyes were focussed on the committee-room door. Some of them folded their arms. Their toes beat a tattoo on the floor, while their heads dropped occasionally in a sigh.

A few of the men to relieve their nerves, nipped out to the backyard lavatory. Those with a cigarette stump lit up. One stood guard by the door. Their two minute conversation was mainly about individual guardians all of them had been before previously: so-and-so was a swine; Mrs. Whose-this was worse than of the men; old-what's-his-name did speak as if people were human; but Big-bust-the-po [sic], the bully, treated everybody like dirt.

'What gets me down,' said one man, 'is having to stand in front of them like a pelgarlic [sic] while they say just what they please.'

'I wouldn't be seen within a mile of this place,' said another, 'if I had a job to go to.'

'A job?' repeated a third. 'What sort of a thing's that?' He had already been on relief for five years.

They all dashed back indoors. At the top of the long passage an elderly clerk was calling out the names. The guardians were in the Committee-room. The relieving officer poked his head out, and beckoned the first woman in. As the door closed behind her, the rest of the applicants fixed their eyes on it. There was hardly a stir in the passage now. Even the elderly clerk stood like a sentinel.

Ten minutes elapsed. The door re-opened, and the woman came out alone. The clerk made her cross over to the opposite wall while the guardians discussed her case. She was about fifty, stringy-haired, and haggard-looking. Her eyes never left the ground. She seemed to be screwing her wedding-ring into her finger.

The relieving-officer beckoned her back into the room. A minute or two later she emerged, a sickly smile on her face. With a 'thank God that's over' expression, she raced down between the other applicants, then stopped, so lost in her embarrassment that one of the men had to go with her to show her the way out of the building.

Her smile had eased the tension a bit. As the other women followed in rotation, they went through the same procedure. Each stayed in the committee-room for about ten minutes, then had to stand outside until the guardians reached a decision. One woman almost whistled in relief; the perspiration teemed from her. Two came out crying. A fourth was scowling, and swore continually to herself. But all hurried down the passage as fast as their legs would carry them.

The men moved on to the forms. The first in was a young man about thirty, pale and half-starved in appearance. He dragged his cap off before entering. When he stood outside again he kept turning it around in his hands. They were all of a tremble. The cap flew through his fingers at times. Then it dropped on the floor. In stooping down to pick it up he nearly fell over. The elderly clerk stepped aside, glanced down, and curled his lip.

The door opened. The young man went to dart in. The relieving officer waved him back.

'Not so fast,' he declared. 'I'll tell you when we're ready.'

On being beckoned inside, he came out a moment later, dazed. The cap was still in his hand. He looked down the passage, then turned to a door behind him marked 'Private'.

The elderly clerk touched him on the arm. 'Hey,' he said. 'The other way out. Down there.'

The young man stared at the clerk but did not speak. He came clattering slowly down the passage. One heel was hanging off his boot. Both the toe-caps were broken. There was string instead of laces.

One of the men at the bottom whispered, 'How did you get on, chum?'

He smiled feebly, shook his head, and staggered away trying to fix his cap on.

Dejection settled on the passage again. The men took their turn in going into the room, stood outside again, and went back to hear the verdict, and passed quickly from the building. One or two smiled, but none of them stopped for a moment to converse with the other applicants.

One sprightly chap stood outside the room door winking for bravado. When he heard the decision, he walked briskly down the passage, his eyes blazing with anger.

'The bastards,' he was muttering, 'The bastards. The dirty shower of bastards.'

There was some delay in calling in the next man. This meant that the relieving officer was making a lengthy statement first to the guardians about the case to be considered.

When the man was called, a thickset grey-haired man stood up, and brusquely said 'Come on, you,' to a skinny young man in the twenties who was sitting beside him. As they crossed to the door, the clerk intercepted them to say that only one could go in at a time. He ordered the younger man back to the form.

The thickset man's head stuck out. 'Look here, mister,' he said. 'I am his father, or are you his father. Is he with me, or is he with you? Who is he with?' He turned to the son. 'Get in there,' he said, 'Never mind him.'

They were inside for about fifteen minutes, when the relieving officer came out and whispered to the clerk, who disappeared at once through the door marked 'Private'. The waiting applicants immediately broke out chattering. The general opinion was that the police had been sent for.

The committee-room door opened. The younger man appeared first. The father was shouting back into the room: 'I'd like to give you a ticket for the workhouse.' The relieving-officer pushed him into the passage. The thickset man was wild. He shook his finger. 'I've told you once already,' he warned, 'to keep your hands off. Now keep them off.'

The relieving-officer backed into the room, and shut the door. The son plucked nervously at his father's sleeve. They both came down the passage, the elder man talking very loud.

'Two shillings a week,' he was saying. 'Two shillings a week. For a lad of twenty-six. I've never heard the like. It wouldn't buy a baby its pobs. Two shillings a week. Two paltry bloody shillings. It's enough to drive a man crackers.'

A few of the men against the wall interrupted him to say that the clerk had gone for the police. They advised him to clear out the back way before he was pinched.

'Pinched?' he snorted. 'That's all they can do. Let them pinch me. You <u>can</u> open your mouth in a police court. But here – in this place, you mustn't speak. You're not supposed to say a word. Just stand there like a dummy, and let that bloody feller swear your life away. I'll swear him yet. Telling me to shut up. I'll shut him up. I'll shut him.'

The room door opened, and the relieving officer's head popped out. The thick-set man whipped around scornfully. 'Ger [*sic*] in, yer sheepdog,' he yelled. 'Ger in.' He walked casually around to the backyard exit, commenting all the time on the two shillings.

Another young man was called into the committee-room, and came out smiling. He blushed all the way down the passage. 'No change,' he kept murmuring to the men along the walls. 'No change.' They turned to repeat it one to the other. 'No change,' they said. 'No change.'

One who was not satisfied with this cryptic statement stepped out to ask: 'And they didn't stop anything, mate?'

The young man, still smiling, shook his head. 'No. Nothing at all. Just carry on.' Away he went. The men breathed a little more freely. Some indulged in repartee, and set the others smiling. A couple burst out laughing at their own private joke.

The door marked 'Private' suddenly opened, and the passage went silent again. The elderly clerk entered; two policemen were behind him. He tapped at the committee-room door. The relieving-officer stepped out to the policemen and began whispering. All of them looked very serious. The clerk hurried down the passage, went around to the backyard exit, and returned a couple of minutes later, shaking his head. The relieving-officer pulled a face, said something to the policemen, and they both laughed. One of them went out by the top door marked 'Private'. The other took his stand by the clerk. The next case was called in.

The man came quickly down the passage, head lowered, and his fingers across his lips. It was a sign that nobody must speak to him. The next out, glanced furtively at the policeman, and then hung his thumbs down for the others to see. About thirty were still waiting their turn. Those anxious about the time fumbled their vest pockets to see if anybody had a watch. None of them had one, nor would they dare ask the policeman or clerk; they could only guess it was near one-o-clock.

A stout guardian in a bowler hat came out of the committee-room, and nodded to the policeman. The clerk sprung to the door marked 'Private'. Two more guardians passed out the same way. They were followed by a man and woman in deep conversation. The relieving-officer was immediately behind carrying the case-papers.

He stopped to look down the passage. 'All back at a quarter past two,' he shouted. 'Don't forget. A quarter past two.' he said.

The elderly clerk took it up. 'A quarter past two, prompt,' he said.

The applicants whispered it to each other. 'A quarter past two,' and trooped out to the backyard exit where their tongues came to life again.

Some dodged off quickly through a side street. Others walked casually along, grumbling at having to come back. Four had found cigarette butts in their pockets. One man had a whole one. Two others took puffs apiece at it. The end was thrown in the gutter. Another man pounced on it and burnt his lips. A fellow with a lit butt crossed over to him.

'Here 'are,' he said. 'You might get a drag out of this.'

'Oo [sic] ta. Ta very much.'

All of them growled about being ordered back. 'Why don't they deal with us right away,' said one of them, 'instead of monkeyin' [sic] us about like this.'

'Aw hey,' said another. 'Be fair, yer know. The guardians must have their dinner.'

'And what about our dinner,' asked a third.

'Dinner! Blimey, I haven't tasted breakfast yet.'

'Breakfast on the parish. Never heard of it.'

They grouped on a corner for a couple of minutes, then scattered in different directions. At a quarter past two, a few faces were missing. These had cross-calls to make at different Labour Exchanges. The others were wondering whether the afternoon treatment would be worse or better than the morning. Morning committees were considered the worst.

'A lot depends on their liver,' said one man.

'They can be bastards in the afternoon too,' said another.

'Morning or afternoon, it doesn't make much difference,' said a third.

'Oh no, I won't have that,' said the first one. 'They're not all alike. There's a few good uns [*sic*] amongst them.'

A scraggy-looking chap bent forward on one of the forms. 'They wouldn't be half as bad,' he said 'if it weren't for the fellers deliberately coming here to kick up a shindy [*sic*]. The likes of that bloody disturber this morning with his son would get anyone's relief stopped. It wouldn't do if we all acted that way.'

A man opposite to him burst out angrily: 'It's a bloody pity we don't.'

The relieving-officer appeared with the case-papers. The elderly clerk took his stand outside the committee-room. Three new guardians entered by the 'Private' door and crossed over. There were a few minutes delay before the first case was called.

He was out in very quick time, and apparently satisfied. 'Good goin',' he whispered as he came down the passage. 'Good goin'.' The waiting men brightened up. Most of them were dealt with as quickly. These guardians were obviously determined to be off the premises before five-o-clock. This was an advantage to the applicants. There was not so much cross-examining. Only a few of their faces registered reductions. The last dozen men moved on to the forms.

There was only five left when I was called in. The three guardians sat behind a table. I stood facing them. There was no chair. The relieving-officer, standing too, summarised my case; I was a fresh application and had been three years in America; there was some doubt whether I was entitled to domiciliary relief.

The guardians took turns in plying me with questions; Why did I come back from America? Why did I go? Had I maintained my family all the time? Was the rent-book still in my name? Did I have it on me? And my seaman's discharge book? Had I prospects of work? Where did I look? Why not try such a firm? And so on.

The chairman handed the book back. One guardian sat twiddling his thumbs. The other pulled his watch out and murmured 'Twenty-to.' As there was a lull in the questions, the relieving-officer told me to stand outside.

The thumb twiddling guardian said, 'Wait.' I turned back. He began asking about New York. He had been there as a young man; there must be many changes; was the what's-this building still in use; he had read they were building a new one; America was a young man's country; he thought I was a fool for leaving it; if he had his time over again! So a routine probing developed into a reminiscent chat between the two of us.

The relieving-officer glanced at me, and bit his lip. The chairman fidgeted, but smiled tolerantly. The other guardian looked again at his watch and blurted out: 'Twelve minutes.' The chairman suddenly exclaimed 'By Jove, you're right.' He initialled my case-paper. 'You can go,' he said. 'Relief granted for four weeks.'

I had hardly reached the bottom of the passage, before the relieving-officer came out too. 'All right, you men,' he said to the others. 'Carry on as per usual for four weeks,' and went back in again.

The five applicants, all smiles, frolicked down the passage, playfully pushing each other. The elderly clerk shouted after them: 'Take it easy. Have you all gone mad?' But they ignored him and took a flying leap down the backyard steps. All rushed to the lavatory.

Applications for relief were mainly confined to Mondays and Tuesdays, the men being dealt with in districts. The large waiting-room was crowded from nine-o-clock onwards. Batches of thirty were taken through to the application counter, the top of which was partitioned into six sections. Behind each, a clerk sat writing down answers to his questions.

The clerks in the main were brusque and overbearing, the parish atmosphere being conducive to browbeating of men debarred from retaliation. Embarrassed applicants who for privacy's sake answered questions in a low voice, had their long-guarded domestic secrets bawled back at them for everybody's hearing. Every family detail was laid bare, even to the suspected pregnancies of the moment, and the pre-marital blunders of the hectic war period. Deaths were treated differently because there was less relief to pay out; the officials too would grab the burial money, although the applicant had struggled to pay the weekly premium out of his relief. Worse than the fear of the workhouse was the disgrace of a pauper's grave. If an applicant had had the temerity to buy a cheap suit for the funeral, the higher officials were brought to the counter to bully him and stop his relief pro tem. The roars came from all angles.

'Undertakers bills are no good to us. It's the money we want. Where is it?'

'Listen. On your own statement you had fifteen pound. There was a twelve pound for the hearse and coaches. That left three. Where is it? What have you done with it?'

'Yes. Where is it? You can go back and find it. You'll get nothing here.'

The applicant would feebly answer: 'I was in absolute rags. I had to buy this bit of a suit. The boots were only second-hand. I couldn't go the cemetery any old way.'

One of the officials would thump the counter. 'That's nothing to do with us,' he'd bark. 'You drew that money from the club and used it instead of bringing it here. WHY DID YOU DO IT?'

'Yes,' followed another. 'Why? You seem to think you can do exactly as you like. Get out, and don't show your face in here again for a few weeks at any rate. GET OUT.'

The applicant would stand dazed then turn slowly on his heel, and slink out past the other men. They had to stifle their feelings. To interfere meant the stopping of their own relief, and their appearance before a special committee where the relieving-officers and clerks had most of the say. The guardians, called in from their outside businesses could not help believing that the hangdown [*sic*] applicant standing in front of them was a liar and the worst kind of scamp.

At the counter, it was the clerk's job to ferret out all details of an applicant's means. The applicant had to declare every penny, and deductions were made according to the relief scale. Particulars were provisionally entered on a white card which bore the applicant's registration number, name and address, amount of rent, and names and ages for dependants. Below these were the income headings:

EARNINGS
UNEMPLOYMENT INS.
MILITARY AND NAVAL PENSIONS.
TRADES UNION
CLUBS AND FRIENDLY SOCIETIES
WIFE'S EARNINGS
ANY OTHER SOURCES.

After all the questions had been answered, the Labour Exchange card scrutinized, and the rent-book found clear, a pay-voucher and food coupon were handed over. Under the deduction system, a man with no income was interrogated less than anybody else. His ready 'noes' meant a minimum of work for the clerk and less irritation for himself. The question that would vex him most was: 'Is your wife working?' A definite 'No' would bring a suspicious glare. 'Are you quite certain? You'd better tell her to stay in the house so that the visitor can see her when he calls.' Which meant the applicant and his wife being tied in daily until the visitor felt satisfied there were no earnings on the sly.

It was this rigid deduction system that deterred a man from taking a casual day's work. Unlike the Labour Exchange which only stopped benefit for the day concerned and did not interfere with earnings, the parish virtually swiped the lot, leaving the man, who had already met stoppages for insurance stamps and paid for fares and extra food, financially worse off.

The most niggardly case I saw one morning was of a man a few places ahead of me. He had helped the police to recover a drowned labourer from one of the docks. Summoned to the coroner's inquest, he received the witness's fee of a shilling. Fearing that his name might appear in the press, he declared the shilling at the parish counter. It was deducted from his relief.

Ex-soldiers displaying their war-ribbons in the hope of preferential treatment were surprised at the questions fired at them. 'Any pensions? Gratuity? Savings? Army reserve pay? Quarterly retainer?' All the details were entered in the case paper, then the clerk looked up. 'All right, as soon as you finish it, bring it up here. Don't forget.' To escape this weekly pestering, they soon took off their ribbons. But periodically every applicant was asked this run of questions, and deductions made accordingly.

As the clerks were changed about, applicants answers were continually checked. Their homes were visited without warning. Doorstep investigators repeated the questions asked at the counter and marked them on a card. A man's wife might open the door. If her replies did not tally with her husband's, he was ticked off for an interview at the parish office, then got a reprimand for being out when the visitors called, and later a lecture from another official for staying in his home instead of looking for work.

An applicant seldom knew when he was doing right. There was always somebody finding fault. Even after parish-office hours, the feeling of being spied on never seemed to end. Investigators were supplemented by anonymous letters sent in by neighbours or spiteful relatives. Next, the applicant faced a committee to hear the relieving-officer detail the charges made by an absentee informant. He could deny the charge but was not allowed to cross-question. Then he had to stand outside the room until it was decided whether his relief be reduced or stopped, or whether he should be prosecuted.

It was risky for an applicant's wife to accept a couple of days charring, and tell a neighbour. The weary woman, after tackling a heavy day's wash, would sneak home at night like a criminal. If anybody rounded on her, her husband could be prosecuted for obtaining relief by false statements. The parish walls were covered with warning posters and penalties for this offence. About twenty dates were appended and the sentences printed alongside: Three months hard labour; two months hard labour; six weeks hard labour; and so on, but never less than a month. Other posters listed punishments for 'Deserting' and 'Failing to maintain'.

'Failing to maintain' usually applied to men who had not taken their relief home. Perhaps a racing-tipster's special had tempted one to risk a bet. If the horses won, the children sported a new pinafore or a pair of galoshes. If the horse lost, the man could not go home empty-handed. Unless the wife had relatives to fall back on, or something to pawn or sell, she could only obtain extra relief by having her husband arrested. These cases, and the occasional ones of drunkenness featured in the daily press, were blamed by other applicants for the harshness of the committees.

'Deserting' accounted for the most prosecutions. A desperate man on leaving the town to seek work elsewhere was deemed a deserter. Driven to tramp the roads he could not help leaving his wife penniless. Where there were children her handicap was worse. If she failed to find a job she had to apply for relief. The guardians would not grant it unless she first went to the police-court and swore a warrant for her husband's arrest. Refusal to do so meant the workhouse for herself and family. Whichever step she took, her home-life was broken up, for an embittered husband would not live readily again with a woman who had sent him to prison. Misunderstandings and despair often forced her to co-habit with somebody else, and provided doorstep scandal-mongers with another 'shameless bitch' to blab about.

Another wife fully aware of the additional hardships in store would nevertheless concur with her husband's leave-taking. Off he would tramp to some distant port where he believed there were more possibilities of a job, unconcerned that men passing in the opposite direction had similar ideas about his place.

Usually unsuccessful he was arrested on return, and sent to prison as a rogue and vagabond. Indifferent to the press-made distortions that greeted him on release, and still believing that his lucky days must come, he would have another try somewhere else.

A further police-court conviction inevitably followed with a heavier sentence as an incorrigible rogue. Though no more of a rogue than the magistrates who sentenced him, the parish solicitor could always prove in law that he was, and the man hearing his story so readily discredited realised the futility of looking for work at all. So back he went to the parish office that for months had not maintained him, and settled down in bitterness to the regular weekly routine.

A last alternative to a man taking to the road on his own was to drag his wife and children along with him, either to sleep behind hedges and risk arrest as vagrants, or be locked up overnight in a fetid casual ward. An application for outdoor relief resulted in them being sent back to their own parish again, homeless, disillusioned, and by prevailing standards were more shameless than ever.

In the general opinion, all the men on the parish were shameless. It was the lowest depth a family could sink to, and the trump insult that every screeching virago spat at a down-at-heel neighbour. Children were referred to as 'parish-reared brats'. On moving into a new neighbourhood they were warned not to mention the parish to anyone. But when the investigator came around with his questions and his answer-cards, curtains opposite were drawn aside, doorstep women leant on their broomsticks, and before long, the whole street knew that the new people were on the parish.

There was no escaping this parish consciousness. Men felt it and looked it. Their patched clothes, broken boots, and bare heels were all signs of the decline. Haggard faces and stooped shoulders followed; their hair curled untidily on their necks, and those unable to afford four pence for a cheap haircut grew indifferent to what happened next.

Regardless of biblical three score and ten the parish was the back-alley short cut to the grave. It was cynically referred to as the 'fish factory', where applicants were methodically scooped out, boned, and drained before the final boxing up. Here in the queues slouched the scarecrow battalion, the unbandaged casualties of the piece, the withered husks, the hollowed man, the careworn caricatures of a prosperous race, the devitalised and subjugated, scuttled wrecks, that nobody now wanted, not even the parish.

A sallow stubbly chin was the last stage before the cemetery. When a man had sunk that far down he crawled along the streets – alone. His death-face depressed the others. He kept to himself; he mumbled to himself; he was left to himself. His eyes had the look of being hunted to the grave. He wanted peace.

The other men lowered their voice in passing. On pay-days, in their rush to hurry home and buy a meal, they would sometimes bump against each other, apologise, and dash ahead. But they never bumped into a dying man. They spotted his lone figure in front, slowed their pace, skirted around him, and left him to drag behind.

He was an outcast. They were all outcasts. Without money they were cut off from every contact except the parish. They avoided former workmates and dodged through the back-streets. They were condemned to the parish, denounced for being on it, yet detested going near it. 'A pound of my own is better than a pound of theirs any time,' was a common saying.

The money they drew did little good. It was begrudged and watched. Within a couple of hours of receiving it there was hardly a penny left. Officials and their co-opted cronies had their own pet explanations for this; beer and gambling. They seemed unable to grasp that the parish was the last place an unemployed man went to; that beforehand, he had pawned and sold, borrowed where he could, and been semi-starved for months. Then with his body weakened, and hopes of a job gone, he timidly approached the parish where any official bounce could peck at him.

His parish money, though payable for the week ahead, was immediately swamped by household debts of the week before. Rent and coal, bread and margarine, tea and sugar, and burial insurance. All had to be paid for. No payment, no further credit was the rule, besides the risk of exposure on the front doorstep; for creditors would persistently call, and rave about money due to them until a debtor's private business became public property.

Any applicant's wife would have welcomed a few extra shillings ready money to spend in the cheapest cash grocer's, where she could select from the counter, stuff the purchases in her bag, and hurry home to her family with an appetising change. She seldom had that privilege. Week after week she was limited to the same dreary diet; bread and margarine, chips and fish, bone-spare hash, and occasionally cheese and bacon.

Her chance of buying new clothes disappeared entirely. The advertised bargains of the big shops were of no advantage to her. She never had any money. Children's wear at the lowest prices were out of her reach. Her own children's odds and ends were picked up at a rummage sale or off a pawnbroker's window-board. The only other way of dressing them was by means of a clothing-club check.

These checks were obtainable from canvassers on the security of a householder in steady employment. Most husbands disapproved of them because of the high prices charged. They were got without their knowledge. The woman householder signed for the check, and the money was paid through her to a collector. Repayments were spread over six months for boots and clothes of the shoddiest description. In less than six weeks, the children were barefooted and in tatters again, while their mother had to scrape together the weekly three or five shillings, and ponder where the next boots and clothes were coming from.

Fresh canvassers tempted her. In desperation she risked another check. Missing one to pay another, she defaulted under the strain, and after several doorstep threatenings [*sic*] finished up in the county court. Solicitor's costs were piled on to her other worries.

The court order was a constant drag. Its payment reduced the food allowance. The children had to be sent to school in rags, and on Sundays were locked indoors. It was a struggle to provide them with boots. In a pinch they wore cheap galoshes, and kicked the toes out in a week.

The mother herself dare not think of new garments. She depended entirely on cast-off skirts, cast-off knickers, cast-off everything. All had to be tacked together before she could put them on. The same pair of corsets would be worn by her for years; a night-dress was a rarity. Occasionally she flared up about not having a decent stitch and burst into fits of weeping. Then as she slipped down deeper into her sluttish servitude there was barely heart left to brush her own floor.

Her husband though condemned to rags had to have boots. He did most of the outdoor running about; to the Labour Exchange, the parish office, and wherever a job was rumoured; besides the incidental errands that an ill-shod woman could not do. As his boots wore down beyond repair and became more difficult to replace, his movements were restricted. His instep lost its spring, and his pace slowed to a crawl. And when his boots were too broken to carry him in search of a job, he was beat.

In the parish-rooms, hundreds like him waited their turns. As their numbers increased, they queued in the street four and five deep. They wore rags from the head down. Ragged caps, frayed coats, patched pants, baggy knees, and heel-less socks. Rags that had to be worn because no man had a second change. Greasy rags, stinking rags, and rags that were often lousy.

On a cold day, the men with old overcoats on would turn up their collars to shield their ears from the wind. It was common to see a bug crawl across a man's shoulder, and half-a-dozen brown fleas dug into the neck-seams. Men were so touchy, that the one behind dare not whisper to the fellow in front for fear it was taken as an offence. There was the risk too of attracting the attention of others. So the bug continued its crawling, and the fleas stayed where they were.

Sometimes a man would stroke the back of his neck, finger what he caught, and blushingly drop it to the ground. Others not so sensitive would pass their find off as a joke, while the men roundabout had to laugh.

One exhibited his capture openly, and said: 'I thought I'd killed that bugger in France.'

Another laid one on the palm of his hand. 'There's a bobby-dazzler,' he cried. 'Look at him. He's got clogs on.'

A third spoke as if he were fingering a wayward pet. 'I told you to stay in the house, didn't I,' he said. 'It's no use talking. You're after me wherever I go.' He rubbed the flea on the back of his hand. 'Now get!' he ordered, and flicked it out of sight; while he went on to make comparison between wartime trench lice and the whoppers that jumped around cheap cinemas.

Seeing fleas in the parish queue was quite understandable. At night, the men's coats had to serve as blankets or foot-warmers at the bottom of the bed. A new change of bedding was as rare as a suit of clothes.

Sheets disappeared from many households. Blankets were washed and scrubbed until they fell to pieces, and were only useful then as baby's napkins or floorcloths [*sic*]. To make up for their loss, old coats had to be spread on the beds. It was the only way to keep warm. Such conditions bred fleas, and if a man became bedridden, his body turned crummy too.

I've been lousy under these conditions. If nobody in the queue ever saw fleas on me, it was because my coat had been well-picked before I left the house. Bodily cleanliness was maintained by going to the baths for a three-halfpenny scrub-down, then changing one ragged singlet for another. Trousers, costing more, had to last longer. Whenever mine needed patching on the knees or backside, I had to stay in bed until they were ready. To hide these backside patches from other peoples' gaze outside, meant wearing my old overcoat, Winter and Summer, as if it were stitched to me.

In other peoples' homes, I was always too embarrassed to take it off. The excuse was that I had a cold, or expected to leave early. But very often my trousers had just burst in a fresh place, or else the quilted backside patch across them stretched from cheek to cheek.

Bare knees and backsides at the parish were signs that the owners did not have an overcoat, and lacked a woman's timely hand to help them cover up their nakedness.

Cold wet days were the most miserable in the queues. Men arrived already soaked through, their boots squelching mud as they stepped into line. Few had handkerchiefs to dry their faces. They coughed and coughed repeatedly, and gobbed [*sic*] big white phlegms [*sic*] in the gutter for the rain to wash away. 'Consumption buttons' they called them. The longer they shivered in the street, the more they grumbled and spat. The sickliest ones seldom spoke.

Going to the parish doctor's was a last resort. The waiting-room was in an out-building. The aged bleary-eyed crocks huddled together inside often frightened younger people away. The doctor being overworked had little time to properly examine a patient. He asked for the symptoms, scribbled a prescription, and said: 'Send the next person in.' Withered and white, they took their turn. If one suddenly collapsed, the ambulance was telephoned for. That was usually the end.

Pay-day was 'independence day'. Men were more sprightly, moved quicker, and risked jollying each other. They passed in single file before the two pay-clerks. There was no long waiting, no cross-examining, and no surly remarks. The pay-clerks pushed notes and silver across with an amazing rapidity and absence of error. Their only stops were when a confused man dashed away, leaving a coin behind him or else dropping one on the floor. He was brought back, made to count his money over, and had the missing coins shoved towards him. His flustered stare and grateful thanks sent a smile the length of the pay-line, which got into its stride once more.

The two pay-clerks could dispose of a thousand men in less than a couple of hours. Once paid, the men darted out of the building. The unmarried ones made tracks for the nearest cocoa-rooms. The married ones raced home. Pay morning meant breakfast morning, the one morning in the week when a relish was possible with the tea and bread. Smokers too could afford cigarettes out of their shilling pocket allowance.

Pocket money was the traditional domestic right. The small amount was recognition of the woman's struggle to pay her way. The burden of management fell on her. She answered all the door knocks; held off one creditor, humoured another, and reversed the process to fit her purse. She knew where every halfpenny was going before the parish money reached her hand.

The string of callers came knocking; the clubman, the checkman [sic], the coalman, and the rentman [sic]. It was the only day they were sure of getting any money. The rentman had to be paid. The parish-clerks never missed scrutinising the rent-books; the doorstep investigators always asked for club-books and rent-books. A woman was harassed in her efforts to keep them all straight, and before the afternoon was over she was almost penniless again.

A moidering [sic] husband would sometimes insist on being told how the money had gone so quick. It was soon totted up for him: 'You only get thirty shillings for five of us. You bag a shilling right away. Then there's eight for rent, two for coal, two for the clubman, and three shillings check. And there was close on eleven in the little shop. That's twenty-seven. Chips and beans for dinner cost tenpence [sic], and there was sixpence for boot-leather and sprigs. I've got a shilling for the wash-house; I can't break into that. That leaves me with fourpence [sic]. Do you think I drink that money? You're as bad as the parish man, rootin' and what not. Get out 'till I clean up.'

A man who lolled around the kitchen became an eye-sore and a hindrance besides a butt for his wife's fits of growling. There was only two places he could go to; bed, or the street-corner. Lack of money, and his rags, shut him off from anywhere else. At the street-corner others like him met for a chat, and were on hand if the investigators called.

A ragged penniless man, feeling he was looked on with suspicion, seldom ventured out of the neighbourhood at night. If he did and it rained, he hesitated before sheltering in a shop doorway. The first policeman who came along was sure to move him on. If two questioned him, he was at a disadvantage, for a man in a job was considered respectable; a man out of one was up to some mischief. Once the policeman said he was 'acting suspicious', denials were useless. An unsolicited word would land him in the bridewell on a loitering charge. To avoid this, the ragged man usually stayed at home and went to bed early. Sleep was an escape from his rags.

Some of these men succeeded at times in beating the parish regulations. They were those whose Labour Exchange benefit was suspended while their claims were being reviewed. They had been on the parish before, and found temporary employment to cover sufficient stamps to place them back on the Labour Exchange. Benefit there was now about parallel with the parish scales of relief, except that pensions, army retainers, and other forms of income were not deducted the same as at the parish.

A man who had previously been deprived of every extra cent at the parish felt bitter and revengeful when he had to apply again. He was handed a letter to take to the Labour Exchange, and brought back an answer in return. After the usual parish interrogation, he was granted relief on condition he paid his dole over as soon as he received it.

Maybe five or six weeks would elapse before a Labour Exchange clerk could tell him whether his claim was disallowed or his benefit had been re-extended. 'Disallowed' meant he became chargeable to the guardians. If benefit was re-extended he drew five or six weeks back pay, sometimes as much as ten pounds. Determined that the parish were not going to grab all that, he spent half of it on clothes and boots for himself, wife and family. Then with five pounds worth of receipts and five pounds in cash, he went back to the parish and spread the lot on the counter.

The officials bully and bounce did not upset him in the least.

They could not frighten him with a committee, force him into the workhouse, stop his relief, or chase him out to pawn the clothes. He was independent of all of them while he could draw from the Labour Exchange. As he never expected to go back on the parish again, the penalties of a next time never bothered him much. To prosecute him, automatically made the guardians responsible for his family. The man knew it was cheaper for them to let him go free, and swaggered off the premises with new underwear against his skin.

A parish-tied man for a less offence was raved at and ordered off the premises. Usually he was an army or navy reservist who had re-joined for sixpence a day, and drew his quarterly retainer of two pounds odd from the Post Office. Feeling at times he had a right to new clothes, he brought some instead of taking his money to the parish. The instant he mentioned receipts there, the tantrums started. The receipts were thrown back at him, his relief was stopped, and before it could be renewed he had to face a special committee.

The committee as punishment deducted a weekly sum until the two pounds odd was repaid, and threatened the man with worse if he again spent what they said did not belong to him.

Only one guardian seemed to realize that the man had tried to escape from his rags. This was 'old Fuzzy'. Fuzzy in committee counted so little against the others that he seldom opened his mouth. It was different on a day when the others could not attend. Then Fuzzy took charge.

He was an old man with a pinkish complexion and a mop of white fuzzy hair. Very few of the applicants knew his proper name. To them he was 'Old Fuzzy' or else 'Daddy Christmas'. If another guardian sat with him, Fuzzy tried to win him around. When Fuzzy was sitting alone, the whole passage soon knew.

The first man-applicant, barely a minute in the room, popped out smiling and holding up his thumbs. He tripped down the passage cheering the other men and women. 'It's a walkover, fellers,' he told them. 'A doddle; money for jam. Yer all right, missus; don't worry. There's only Daddy Christmas.'

A glum-looking man asked: 'Is he on his own?'

'Christ, mate! Don't act so soft. Be happy; it's yer birthday.'

Everybody at once broke into a chatter that the clerks could not hush. For an applicant to learn that Fuzzy was by himself was to feel entitled to breath [*sic*]. The men moved quickly along the forms, and were no sooner in the room than they were out again with thumbs up. Shawl-women swaggered down the passage, declaring for all to hear: 'God bless Fuzzyman wherever he comes from.'

A vindictive official seldom scored off an applicant, for Fuzzy always insisted on hearing the applicant's version too. One afternoon, a bawling official brought a man into the passage, then went into the room, leaving the man outside. He was about forty, very pale, and his lips all of a twitch.

The other men waiting made room for him on the form. He told them his trouble. He was a naval reservist. After nearly two years on the parish, he had spent that quarter's retainer to get his serge suit out of pawn. The suit was on him; the receipt was in his pocket. That morning at the counter, on reporting what he had done, he had met with the customary abuse. His relief was stopped. When he said that he was penniless, he was told to go home and pawn the suit. He explained that doing that would throw away his chance of a job. The officials would not listen, and ordered him off the premises. Two hours later, he returned with his wife and four children, and marched them up to the counter.

'You can look after these,' he said. 'Until I find a job. And when I do find one, I'll look after some of you.'

The wife tried to quieten him. His children started to cry. The officials seeing he was so determined, gave his wife food vouchers. There was no allowance for him. He must first appear before a committee. He sent his wife home to make some dinner for the children, while he stayed behind to find out what the committee intended to do. He felt faint. He had been on a dock-stand at six that morning, and was dropping for a drink of tea.

The men advised him not to worry; Fuzzy was inside. 'You're quids [*sic*] in, chum,' said one. 'Just tell Fuzzy about the suit. Nice and easylike [*sic*]; same as you've told us. Don't get excited or anything, or shout. If the relieving-officer aggravates yer, take no notice. Just go on talking to Old Fuzzy as if nobody else was there. He'll listen. But for Christ's sake, don't lose yer head. Just take it easy and never mind any one.'

The relieving-officer, a scowl on his face, peeped out of the door, and called the man in. Old Fuzzy, his arms on the table, looked up. The man stood nervously fingering his cap.

The relieving-officer rapped out. 'This is the man, sir. He spent all the money on this suit, and because he was spoken to about it this morning, he turned on the officers and threatened them.'

Old Fuzzy looked at the relieving-officer. 'Have you had trouble with this man before,' he asked. The officer went to turn over the pages of the case-paper. Fuzzy laid his hand on top. 'There's no need to go through that,' he said. 'I only asked whether you've had trouble with this man before. Have you?'

'No sir.'

'That's all I wanted to know.' He looked up at the applicant. 'Is that the suit on you?'

'Yes sir.'

'Stand over there 'till I have a look at it.' The man stepped back. 'Turn around 'till I see the back.' The man turned around. 'That's enough, thank you. Umm. Very neat indeed, how much was on it?'

'Two pounds, sir, beside the back interest, here's the receipt, sir.'

'That's all right. I can see from here it's worth every penny.'

The man fingered the inside of his cap. 'I've got to follow different stands up, sir,' he said. 'With a decent suit of clothes I have a better chance. In fact, I got this out of pawn on the strength off a promise sir.'

'Did you? That was very sensible. I hope it brings you luck. You – you look quite – tidy in it.' Fuzzy turned to the relieving-officer. 'Er, I think we can make this man's money up for four weeks. He'll probably be off our hands by then.'

The man smiled. 'I hope so, sir,' he said.

'I hope so, too,' said Fuzzy. 'You can go now. Take good care of yourself.'

'Yes sir. Thanks very much sir.'

An applicant treated courteously by one of the clerks walked off the premises as if God had touched his shoulder. Next week in the queue, he described the clerk to others, who in turn revealed whatever risky favours had been put in their way too. When the man trooped inside to the counter, all eyes searched around for this particular clerk. Those called across to his section stepped over with a smile. They answered the questioned readily, exchanged a joke in passing, and when their pay-card was handed to them, worked their way out in good spirits. The only time this clerk raised his voice was when a deaf man stood before him.

A deaf middle-aged man tried his patience one day. He had examined the 'Labour' card and rent-book, and handed them back again. 'Any change,' he asked, and got no reply. Staring up in surprise, he repeated the question and again got no reply. The applicant bent down and cupped his ear. The clerk understood at once. 'Any change,' he shouted.

'Yes,' the man shouted back. 'Norah's started to work.'

The clerk looked down at the case-paper. 'When,' he asked.

'Tuesday. Last Tuesday gone. She got six shillin's.'

'Where? I mean, where is she working?'

'Cleanin' at some women's house. I've clean forgot the name. It's gone out of me head.'

'Is it constant do you know?'

'Constant? I don't know. I can't tell yer that. Yer'll have ter ask the wife.'

The clerk looked down at the case-paper, glanced at the busy officers both sides of him, then lifted his face, and stared straight at the deaf man. His lips frame the words: 'All right. No change.'

The deaf man looked puzzled. 'Yes,' he shouted. 'Norah. She's started. She got six shillin's for last week.'

The clerk ground his teeth: 'No change, I've said. No change. Are you dense? It wouldn't buy her a pair of shoes. Do you understand? No change.'

The deaf man grew impatient. 'Yes there is,' he shouted. 'You're not gettin' me into any trouble.'

The clerk's face whitened. Another applicant stepped quickly over to him. 'Stop the six bob,' he whispered, 'if he hasn't nous enough to see that you're doing him a good turn. Don't make a fool of yourself over him. He'll spoil the next one.'

The clerk sighed as he stretched for the pay card. 'It's enough to break a man's heart,' he said. He wrote down particulars of the deaf man's statement, then handed him the pay-card with the six shilling deducted. 'You'll find that's how you want it, isn't it?'

The deaf man examined the card carefully, then turned towards the door, muttering. 'Thought yourself smart trying to catch me,' he was saying. 'I'm too lary [sic] for you, mate; too old in the nut. I've met your sort before.' He elbowed his way through the crowd and passed out. The clerk shook his head and called the next man's name.

As unemployment spread, the parish queues grew longer. Disallowed cases from the Labour Exchange were swelled by others from non-insurable jobs. Amongst them were black-coated professionals, orchestra players, small shopkeepers, music hall artists, gardeners, and similar types. They had spent their last penny before applying for relief. With shoes usually polished, their tidy habits marked them out in the queue. Their pants were creased, they wore natty hats, clean collars and ties, and carried raincoats over their arms. Holding themselves erect, they seldom spoke to anyone else, and hurried home by the shortest cuts.

A few months 'queuing it' broke them down. Their shoulders drooped, their faces turned pale. Their pants became baggy, bowler hats stained, and their shirt-necks tore at a touch. In some cases, collars disappeared altogether; just a tie hung around the neck. Shoes broke all over, and bare heels showed that darnings failed to hide for long. Some of the men wrapped black cloth strips puttee-fashion around their feet, and slouched along with the older parish clients from whom they were now indistinguishable.

There was no total adaptation. Men who had had a big social drop were reticent about speaking of themselves. Only in intimate conversations would a man's past slip out. One, for instance, aged thirty-four, had a pianist's career interrupted by the war. After the armistices, he resumed his training, and later toured the concert-halls. Cinemas and talkies forced the halls out of business. This man could not renew his bookings. He sank into poverty, and was living in one room with his wife and baby girl. Wealthy relatives in another town might have given him help. Too proud to ask them, he was finally driven to the parish.

Just temporary assistance he wanted; for himself, wife, and child. As soon as he got a booking, he would pay the money back; one booking would last him for years. He was granted twenty-two shillings.

Twelve months passed; no booking came. His hair turned white. He used to walk alone, his arms folded behind his back, and jerking his head from side to side. One day very worried looking he approached some of the other parish clients to ask them about a doctor's note; his baby was ill.

A couple of the men went back with him to the parish office, showed him where to get the note, took him next into the crowded waiting-room, and sat on a form while the doctor was disposing of a long row of snuffing bronchial cases huddled together in their stinking rags.

Scabrous hags jabbered incessantly across the jaundiced faces of young girl-mothers where crying babies out-howled the old man's spasmodic coughing and raucous spits. All heads swung around mechanically to the irregular clacking of the doctor's door, starting another general movement one more nearer along the forms.

The pianist fidgeted continuously as if he wanted to run out: 'It's a terrible place, this' he murmured. 'A terrible place to sit.' He questioned the men beside him. 'Will the doctor come right away to the house?'

'It depends on other cases. Is your note marked 'urgent'?'

'Yes. I must get him to come right away. I'll explain. Oh, I hope he won't be long.' He began to thump his knees.

The packed form worked its way around. He moved neared to the doctor's door. But a row as long again was already filling up the empty places. He stared around at them. 'It's a good job I dashed up here,' he said. 'You'd wonder where people came from. My God, what a place.' His row edge up a bit nearer.

He came out of the doctor's room wildeyed [*sic*], and dropped on a form. The other two men joined him. 'I've got to wait until he deals with all these people first,' he complained. 'Anything might happen. Anything. Oh Lord, this is dreadful. Do you know where I can borrow half-a-crown? I'll pay it back as soon as I draw my relief money. Truly I will. You can depend on it.'

The other two looked helplessly at each other.

He pressed the nearest one's knee. 'I'm sorry,' he said. 'I forgot for the moment. Forgive me.' He stared back at the doctor's door. 'Oh, hurry up please,' he kept repeating, 'Please, please, please.'

The aged patients stared at him and began to whisper. Suddenly he jumped off the form, and paced the room like a caged beast. 'Oh this is terrible, terrible,' he kept saying. 'How much longer will he be?' He gazed wide-eyed at later arrivals joining those waiting, then darted out into the street and disappeared.

Three weeks passed before the two men saw him again. He was strolling towards the parish, the baby at his side. He blushed and apologised for running out of the doctor's room. The baby was better now. His wife had pawned some clothes to pay for a private doctor's visit. She had since gone out to wash for twelve shillings a week; the parish took ten. That was not the worst. He had no chance now of an engagement because of minding the baby all day.

The baby raised her face inquisitively. Her crumbled coat bore the pawnbroker's tell-tale mark. The father released her hand as she dodged behind his legs to play.

He was bitter against his wife. 'She swears she'll shame me into doing something,' he said: 'She'll shame me! She says I could easily drop out of town each week-end unknown to anyone, and get a job at some free-and-easy; earn a few extra shillings that way.' His eyes blazed, he shook his clenched fists. 'The woman doesn't know what she's talking about. She's mad. Expecting me to play a lot of maudlin rubbish to a collection of rowdy sots. And then go around with the hat afterwards. My God!! I won't do it. I won't do it. I WON'T. NO. She can do what the hell she likes.' He lowered his voice. 'Someday I'll tell the baby a lot of things that she'll understand. She'll know then who's right.' He smiled as he patted one of the men on the arm. 'Don't mind me too much, friend,' he said, 'only I must have someone to talk to. It relieves me a bit. Well, I'm glad to have met you. I'll trot along now. Come on, Babs. Come on, pet.'

The baby toddled out of the gutter, her hand full of dirty matchsticks. She grabbed her father's pants, and they walked on towards the parish.

These daily meetings developed into night jaunts around the park after the baby had been tucked into bed. The pianist's mania was music and composers. Beethoven was his favourite.

He would suddenly halt in the middle of the footwalk [sic], his eyes aglow.

'Do you know this tune,' he'd ask. 'Tra-la-la-la-la, tra-la-la-la-la-la, la-la-la-la-la.' His hands would beat the air while his fingers jumped an imaginary keyboard. 'A marvellous piece of work. Only a genius could write that. But this is the one I really like best: la da, la dee, la la la la, la la la la la.'

The other two men had never heard of Beethoven before but they enjoyed each enthusiastic rendering. 'That's music,' he'd say, 'Real music. And the damned fools of people throw that over for hip-noise. Hip-noise, that's all it is; something to wag their backsides to like bushmen jiggling in the Congo. Oh God, I could SCREAM.' His fists would shoot up to his head.

Though his ravings attracted the stares of passers-by, his two companions had to humour him for fear he became unbalanced. They saw too that unless he got some piano practise his fingers would lose their touch. His own back-room had no piano: they had none in theirs. They questioned acquaintances, sought out those with pianos, and arranged for the pianist to call at night to comment on their respective tones. In that way he managed a few hours practice.

At no time in these back-street houses was his private history divulged. He was formally introduced, shown into the tiny parlour, and went right across to the piano. Opening the lid, he would strike the keys. If the tone was passable, he sat down on the stool, and played into a world of his own. If one of his listeners spoke aloud, he swung around glaring, then bent full weight over the keys. Gradually his body straightened up again, his finger touch grew lighter, and as he sat smiling absently to himself the listeners nodded to each other with delight.

One night in a little parlour he found a piano that gave him joy. His fingers glided over the keys until he was one with the instrument. Six men sat listening intently; four of them were on the parish. The other two: sons of the house, had jobs. Their parents had gone to the cinema.

The woman from the next house poked her frowsy head into the parlour. 'Oh,' she exclaimed, 'I didn't know there was company. I thought you were having a 'do'. Can the quare [*sic*] feller play jazz? Does he know 'Swanned'?'

The pianist spun around on his stool, his eyes flaming. 'Jazz,' he yelled. 'Bah!!' He spat, and swung back to the keyboard as if to bury himself into it, pounding the notes at lightning speed. The other men got spellbound as his temper came through the music.

The frowsy women, shocked instead, turned to one of the sons. 'Are you blind, Tommy,' she shouted, 'lettin' him carry on like that. He wouldn't do it if yer mother was in. Where in God's name did yer pick him up?'

The pianist swung around on the stool. 'Get out,' he snarled. 'GET OUT.'

The women clutched the tops of her blouse together. 'Well I like that,' she said. 'Go away you bloody barm-pot, it's a hammer you should have. You want lockin' up.' She bounced out along the lobby, muttering to herself. The pianist shrugged his shoulders, then bent down to the music again.

A few weeks later, he disappeared from the parish. The two men heard he had left the town to play at the 'free and easy' [sic]. Months afterwards, on the dock road, they spotted him in shirtsleeves in between the traffic. He was dragging a handcart piled with wire hawsers, his back bent low in his straining to keep up with the horse-lorries.

The men hailed him. He stopped, smiled feebly, and pulled over to the kerb. The sweat streamed from him. One of the men stared at the heavy hawsers, and swayed on the handcart shafts. 'There's at least half a ton on there,' he said. 'What made you take on a job like that? Your hands will be murdered in no time.'

The pianist flared up immediately. 'My hands', he replied. 'My hands. Who the hell cares about my hands? No one. Not even myself.' He quietened down again. 'Oh yes. You do. You two. But that's all. No one else.'

The flow of traffic forced him to struggle for a foothold. The men started him off with a push. As they walked alongside him, one of them jokingly remarked: 'Old Beethoven would hardly recognise you now.'

The pianist raised his face enquiringly as if trying to remember something. Then a smile aroused his lips. 'Oh yes,' he said. 'Beethoven. Ha ha ha ha ha. Beethoven in a handcart. Damned good. Ha ha ha ha.' And he laughed and laughed until his face went blank again. He jerked his head around. 'Don't come any further with me now,' he pleaded. 'The boss might see you.' The two men bid him 'Ta-ra' and walked away, very disheartened.

They lost trace of him for a year. Then one of them in a shopping street when crossing the tramline, saw him. His clothes were dirty and threadbare. His eyes, bulging and blood-streaked seemed overbig [sic] in his bearded face. The other man in a hurry asked him how he was doing, without venturing into details.

The pianist's eyes shone. Elbows pressed against his sides, his half-clenched hands jerked up and down in front of him.

'My hands are on the wheel that is steering the Universe,' he declaimed. 'One twist, and I can destroy mankind, and all these people passing.'

The other man patted his shoulder. 'That wouldn't do you much good,' he said. 'You'd destroy yourself as well.'

The pianist's face set. 'You're wrong, friend,' he declared. 'I am the indestructible. I am in control.'

A tram-driver clanged his bell. The pianist had to be led on to the pavement and left there, his hands still gripping an imaginary wheel that was keeping the Universe from disaster.

Every man on the Parish had to register for work, and signed once a week at the Labour Exchange. Inside here, though poverty was apparent, the atmosphere was not so repressive. In a dozen queues filing up to the counter, men chatted freely on football, racing, and politics. Here and there one had a cigarette stuck behind his ear; for the moment a clerk started to smoke, the men smoked too.

Amongst glum faces and smiling faces there was an occasional outburst of laughter. One big man with a bent nose always amused most of those standing near. No matter how glum others wanted to be he went on cracking his jokes. His belief was, there was enough misery in the world without adding more to it.

At times he became annoyed at the glum faces opposite. 'They'd sicken any one,' he'd say. 'Look at the mowies [*sic*] on them. If their faces ever froze, a bloody earthquake wouldn't shift them. Their poor wives and kids must go through torture with the likes of them in the house.'

One morning he took his cap off and exposed an absolute baldy head. 'I was thinkin' of goin' in for a perm,' he said, 'or my missus swears she'll leave me.'

The men gazed up at his shiny pate. One of them in astonishment asked: 'How did you get that baldy, Tom?'

'Lookin' for work,' the big fellow answered. 'Bein' too conscientious.'

'You'll never get a job now,' said another 'You haven't an earthly.'

'Aw don't worry. I'm not licked yet. I'm savin' up for a second-hand wig.'

As the men about roared laughing, they drew the stares of others from the queues nearby. A glum-looking man turned on them. 'I don't know how the hell yiz can laugh,' he growled. 'Yiz can't have much on yer minds.'

The bent nose man was angry. 'It's a crime to laugh now,' he declared. 'If yer out of work yer mustn't laugh. That's the new order.

And it isn't these fellers behind the counter that say it, nor anyone at the Ministry of Labour. It's walkin' corpses like you. You want to go into the library oftener and read 'The Bystander' and 'The Tatler' [*sic*]. All the gang in them pictures are laughin' and there's none of them in work.'

'They have somethin' to laugh at.'

'Yes; at boneheads like you.'

In the men's parlance this dole was the 'Old King Cole' and the Labour exchange card, the 'Yellow Peril'. Out of work was 'out of collar!' In work was 'in collar' or 'grafting'.

The parish men's queue was 'The Homeguard Battalion' [*sic*] or 'Britain's last hope'. Each man in it felt seasoned against the benefit-queue whiner who poured out his woes as if he alone was roughing it.

'It's miserable bein' out of collar,' he'd begin. 'I'm fed up already.'

'How long you out now,' one of the 'homeguards' would ask.

'Nearly three months. And it isn't for want of lookin' for it, either. I've searched everywhere high and low.'

'Three months? Blimey, yer only a novice. Wait 'till you get used to it. The first five years is the worst.'

'Five years! I'll be out in five years. I'll stake me oath.'

'Don't be too sure of yerself. We all said that at one time.'

'Aye, but some of youse fellers are noted. Yiz wouldn't work in convulsions.'

'You would, eh. A smart feller. Wait till you've had a spell of this. You'll know yer alive then.'

'There'll be no spell for me, mate. I'll make sure of that. I'll get a job somehow.'

'It'll be the way that others get theirs then; crawling around someone's behind.'

The queues diverged at the counter and the conversation ended. The counter was wired off like a post-office. The clerks pushed each man's policy under to be signed, a job that took only a moment. Questions were seldom asked unless a man was late. Some of the clerks were officious, but never with the arrogance of those at the parish. The men were dealt with alphabetically at a fixed signing time, none being signed before or after without a reasonable excuse.

From the entrance gate to the counter moved these twelve continuous streams. Above each clerk's section hung a box number, below it a printed instruction; 'Don't wait for the clerk to ask are you working. Before you sign, say not working.'

Nobody ever heeded it. The only occasion it was acted upon, the work of the exchange became disorganised. The men feeling that their presence and signature were sufficient resented having to say 'not working'.

The clerks refused to sign them on, and friction and arguments started. There was a deadlock at the counter. The swelling queues becoming mixed up and jammed, soon packed the building to the doors. Outside, more men were clamouring to get in, so as not to be late for signing on.

The clerks, behind in their work, warned the men nearest the counter that unless they said 'not working', their benefit would be suspended. Some from the back of the queues stepped forward to sign on. The men at the front stopped them.

'What time are you?' they asked.

'Quarter past ten.'

'Quarter past nine, us. Get back and wait your turn.'

'It's eleven-o-clock now. We'll never get out of here today with all this crush.'

'What about us? Don't we want to get away? We know what we're doin'. Askin' us to say 'Not working'. We wouldn't be here if we were.'

'It'll have to be said first as last.'

'We know that. But let's say it our own way.'

The late men went back to their places, and passed the word down the queue. The signing on began and became a dawdling ritual.

The first of the men stared through the wire at his box-clerk. 'Not workin',' he began, 'and don't forget I've said 'not workin'. All these fellers behind are proof that I said. It's five past eleven now, and I've been here since a quarter past nine. And yer can't say yer didn't see me here, because I've got all these fellers for proof. And I've told yer I'm not workin', so don't forget in case any questions are asked. Whereabouts do I sign?'

'There where the pencil mark is.'

'Where? Here?'

'There. You know where to sign. Don't act the goat.'

'Oh, here. I see. Shall I put my full name, John Joseph Smith; or will J.J. Smith do, or just the one jay?'

'I don't care what you put.'

'You needn't get yer rag out, mate. I was only asking a civil question. I best sign it in full, eh? John, Joseph – Oh crimey [*sic*], that's beggared it. I won't get it all in there now. I'll have to finish it off down here. Does it matter? Will that do?'

'Oh go on. Get out.'

'There yer go. On the muscle for nothin', and me tryin' to do the right thing. Don't forget, I have told yer about not workin'. Yer can't deny I didn't, because all these fellers were here.'

'FOR GOD'S SAKE, MAN, WILL YOU GET OUT.'

'Aw now, you needn't get ratty. I was only remindin' yer about me not workin' in case of any dispute.'

The men behind tittered and varied the performance, until the clerks grew even more exasperated each time they glanced at the clock. Working through their lunch hour put them behind with afternoon signings, until those disgusted with the instruction from the commencement signed the men on as usual. Their queues were soon cleared, but the regulation sticklers had to work late through the evening and finished hours after the others had gone.

After that, the regulation was dropped, and the queues went back to the ordinary. From nine in the morning, men came trooping in, according to the index quarter-hour marked on their cards. Most of the clerks were not too strict if a man arrived a few minutes late. They accepted his excuse and signed him on, with a warning to be early in the future. But the boorish clerks pushed a man's card back and told him to come in again at four o'clock.

The men hurt most were those who had been transplanted to the new housing estates five or six miles off. If they had no carfare, they had to foot it there and back, unless they owned an old bike. Usually they hung about the Exchange all day without a meal or the price of a smoke. Then after they had signed, they faced a long trudge home with the hope of a feed at the end.

One surly clerk persistently made the signings awkward, and though the men in the queue kicked in turn, they were silenced when he grunted: 'There's the clock.' On the slightest pretext he turned them away, until one morning about twenty to twelve he overstepped his powers.

The Exchange was almost empty except for a few men at the

counter, and those reading the vacancy lists that hung on the wall. Amongst them stood the bent nose man skitting [*sic*] about 'prosperity' and asking the others when it really did come, who would pay the dole-clerks on the dole.

Hurrying in past him came five shabby men who crossed to the surly clerk's counter. He glanced up casually, waved them away, and went on sorting some papers. Each of them pushed a letter apiece underneath the wire, but he swept them back immediately, and growled: 'Come in at four.'

The men stood gaping, and when one started to argue, the clerk got up and sauntered away to the far end of the room. The men waited awhile and seeing it was hopeless, turned slowly towards the door where the bent-nose man questioned them. They told him their dole had been stopped, and they had walked from the new housing estate. The letters they had were from the parish sub-offices there, and until their box-clerk initialled them they could not draw relief. The walk down had taken them nearly two hours, and unless they started before three they would be too late because the parish closed at five.

The bent-nose man glanced over to where the surly clerk was standing and asked: 'Have you explained this to him.'

'Oh he wouldn't listen,' said one of the men. 'He cleared right off and left us.'

'You should have followed him around the counter. Go and tell him now. It's only ten to twelve.'

'He'll take no notice. You know what he is.'

'He'll take none if you don't make him. Come on, I'll go with yer.'

They all went over to the far end of the counter where the bent-nose man beckoned the clerk. 'Here,' he began, 'Can't you fix these fellers up. They've walked five miles already, and they've got to walk back again yet.'

The clerk sneered through the wire. 'What do you want me to do,' he asked. 'Carry them?'

'No, I don't want you to carry anybody. But there's such a thing as stretchin' a point. These other clerks would do it.'

'I'm not concerned what they'd do. I run this box, my way. Besides, it would suit you better to get outside. You've been stuck in here all morning.'

'I'm looking for a job if yer want to know.'

'You'll not get one standing there.'

'And don't I know it. I'd need a letter from the Holy Ghost. But never mind that now; how about fixin' these fellows up. Come on, yer doin' nothin'.'

The clerk grunted and sauntered off to another part of the counter, the bent-nose man tailing him around. When he drew level, he pressed his face against the wire.

'Where's the supervisor,' he demanded.

'You want him. Look for him.'

The bent-nose man started to swear. 'If I had you this side of the wire,' he roared, 'I'd show you a thing or two.' He motioned the five men across. 'Here,' he said, 'Don't go away yet. Let's see the supervisor first.'

He rushed back, and to the surprise of the clerks, bounced through a counter-opening, and knocked at the acting supervisor's door. A voice called: 'Come in.'

He entered taking his cap off. The supervisor swung around in his chair. 'Well,' he rasped, 'What do you want? Who sent you in here?'

The bent-nose man began to explain, when the supervisor rose and stepped over to the door. 'If these men have a grievance,' he said, 'Let them come and speak for themselves.'

'That'll do me. I'll send them in.'

'You needn't bother. If they want to come, they'll come of their own accord.'

'But they won't. You know they can't get past that counter. I had to force my way in here.'

'Don't be so busy next time. When we want your advice we'll ask for it.'

'So that's it, eh. And what about the men? Will you fix them up yourself?'

'Their box-clerk will attend to them. He knows what he's doing.'

'Yes, and so do I. He'll leave them without anythin' to eat if they're too late tonight for the parish.'

'Don't talk nonsense.'

'It's you that's talkin' nonsense.'

'All right. No more of it. Outside, please. I've other things to do.'

The bent-nose man put his cap on, and sidled through the door. In his rage, he gazed along the counter and saw the clerk bent over signing the men's letters.

'Well I'll give up,' he exclaimed.

The supervisor glared at him. 'Are they the men,' he asked.

'Yes. Them's them.'

'It seems to me you've been making a noise over nothing. Don't you come here again wasting my time.'

The bent-nose man gulped, and made for the opening in the counter. Then nodding across to the men, he walked slowly off the premises. A group outside were waiting for him to tell what had happened.

Raving about the clerk, he passed up and down between them. 'When he comes out for lunch,' he swore, 'I'll bust him in the gob. He won't make a monkey out of me.'

'But,' one of the men broke in, 'what good'll that do? He'll get you pinched and once that happens there'll be no 'oldin' 'im back.'

'But someone's got to get pinched. Yer can't stand his sneerin' all the time.'

'Leave him alone,' advised the man. 'He'll fall by and by.'

'He'll fall when I hit 'im.'

'Yes, but that'll do more harm than good. They'll knock you off, and then after that he'll take his spite out of others.'

'I'll fix him someway then. He won't come it with me.'

Next signing day on his way to the exchange, he had a couple of pennies and bought a chocolate Easter egg. 'When I go in,' he'd thought, 'Sour-gob is bound to start, but when he gets this instead of hearin' me swear, he'll jump up and never come down.'

Chuckling at the silver wrapper, he put the egg in his trousers pocket, his only fear being that in the crush of the queues it might be squashed to bits. His hand never left it once he neared the Labour Exchange, and queued up outside with the other men until his own time-batch was admitted.

This signing-day being pay-day too, inside the building was congested. The men worked gradually around to the counter, signed their money-chits in turn, then squeezed through to a separate pay-queue. Delays occurred with the old men who could not read or write, because the clerk had to fill in each pay-chit himself and ask another busy clerk to witness it.

As the queues became jumbled up, the bent-nose man held fast to the egg, and apart from an occasional chuckle hardly spoke a word to anyone.

The men round about considered he was wise in doing so, instead of taking risks that might land him in more trouble.

One whispered to him: 'I see they've stuck a bobby in here to-day.'

'Aye,' he answered, 'They'll need one in case I faint.'

On breasting the counter, he pushed his signing card under the wire, then felt if the egg was all right. The clerk stared at him, glanced around at the clock, pushed the signing-card back, and motioned the next man in.

'Oh no you don't,' declared the bent-nose man. 'You'll sign me on first.'

'Ten-o-clock's your time, not twenty-five past.'

'It was ten when I came through that door.'

'I've no time to argue,' snapped the clerk. 'Stand back from the counter.' He shouted to the next man: 'Come on you with your card.'

The bent-nose man shoved it aside. 'There's no one signs here until I've signed first.'

'We'll see about that,' said the clerk.

He tore across to the acting supervisor's door, knocked, and went inside, while another clerk slipped around to the back of the queues to where the policeman was standing. The men near the counter warned the bent-nose man, but he only smiled as his fingers closed on the egg.

The clerk re-appeared, and with him the supervisor, furious at seeing the crowded Exchange almost at a standstill. He strode over to the counter.

'You again,' he barked. 'I had enough of you the other day. Now stand back from here or I'll have you removed.'

The bent-nose looked at him. 'Me removed,' he asked. 'What for?'

'You know damn well what for. Get right back from this counter, quick.'

'When I've signed on I will.'

'You've been told once, you're too late.'

'Well if I'm late, everybody's late.'

'WILL YOU STAND BACK, YES OR NO?'

'No. I'm stayin' right here.'

The policeman pushed nearer, as the supervisor broke out aloud: 'You, you,' he stuttered. 'You're a born trouble-maker. I've heard all about you, with your vile tongue, your constant interfering, and the sort of reputation that no decent man would own.'

The bent-nose man kept very calm. 'I don't like to contradict yer,' he said, 'but you're very much mistaken, 'cos I'm a boy-scout, and here's me one good deed for terday [sic].'

He gave the silver-papered egg a push and it wobbled across the counter. The supervisor's eyes nearly burst as he grabbed at it and swept it back under the wire.

His fist hit the counter. 'You-u,' he yelled. 'Take that damned thing out, and quick.'

The bent-nose man picked up the egg, and stripped the silver paper off it. 'I beg yer pardon,' he said. 'It just shows me ignorance. There; that's better now, I clean forgot about peelin' it.'

He sent the chocolate egg wobbling across again. The supervisor's eyes swept around the grinning men, the policeman who had turned his back, and the clerks who had sneaked away. 'You-u-u,' he growled, and he picked up the egg and aimed it high over the wire.

He turned on the surly clerk. 'Get him signed. Get him paid. Get him OUT.' He charged the length of the counter, bawling at the other clerks. 'Come on,' he roared, 'What do you think this place is? Hurry up, get back to your work.' He dashed into his room, and the door slam shook the partition.

The bent-nose man looked at the surly clerk. 'That's me thanks,' he said. 'He'll never get another. That was really meant for you, but I'll bring a great big one next week.'

Next week, the surly clerk was missing.

But even the most agreeable could startle a man by uttering the one word: 'Committee'. This was the warning that the claim was under review, and on a specified day a committee would decide whether benefit should stop or not. The moment it did stop, the man transferred to the 'Homeguard' queue, and from that time onwards usually drew relief from the parish.

No relief was granted where there was a son or daughter in work whose wages were equal to parish scale. Where they fell below, the parish would make up the amount, but few men cared to go near there for the sake of a couple of shillings.

A single man with relatives in work became an involuntary parasite, but a middle-age father suffered the most by the loss of his standing at home. Once his income ended, his privileges ended too, and this led to fits of brooding which made him cranky over trifles. While his unemployment benefit remained, he still had a voice in the house; but when it stopped, his authority weakened, and he began to feel in the way. Each casual act of the family reminded him of his dependence, and even for a smoke he often waited all week like a child for its Saturday penny. This was unavoidable where wages barely covered rent and food, and squabbles broke out until either the father himself or the working member left home.

The mother was buffeted in between manoeuvring to hold them together, while her husband raved of his working past as she schemed for the children's future. They had to have clothes, they had to have boots, and most of her attention too; and this began at six in the morning and generally went on until midnight. Their clothes needed mending continuously, and when possible were replaced, for they had a job to go to, the father had none.

His daily searching for one took him miles away from home, where he met others whose benefit had also been stopped for 'not genuinely seeking work'. This was the disqualifying term used by the Labour Exchange, and its wording embittered the men as they grumbled in the queues.

When one man told a committee he had followed the same firm daily for eighteen months, he was told in return he should have gone elsewhere if he really wanted work.

Another man butted in to say: 'But they told me the very opposite. When I gave them the name of places I'd been, they said if I had stuck to the one I might have become better known.'

A third man growled: 'I can't understand them. They know that trade is bad. Why don't they give the few jobs there is through the Labour Exchange instead of making us walk our lives away.'

'Because,' said a fourth, 'It's part of their game to make yer feel that you don't count.'

'We're just dirt in their eyes, then.'

Dirt or no dirt they had become good copy for paid scribblers of every kind. Profound pundits described them as 'Demoralised' and qualified what this meant by describing them as degenerates, wastrels and misfits. But their opposite numbers in daily contact with mass-misery knew otherwise than this and advocated schemes of social reconstruction.

Apologists for the status quo on rushing into print resurrected the stock silencer: 'Where will the money come from?' Their mesmerized disciples religiously applauding this magical password with the pan-philosophical stare of a Pilate asking 'What is truth?'

Library shelves were cluttered to prove that the nation's wealth was static, while others from the same sources calmly detailed the elastic quality of poor-law relief or the dole. Suggestions on how the poor should live piled up in innumerable listings of calories, vitamins, proteins and fats.

My wife and I had not the 'rocking chair' background to fool about with these lofthouse [*sic*] theories on living. We were daily facing the harassing problem of where the next meal was to come from, she more so than me. She acted on the very old fashioned principle that where there was growing children, food and clothing had a prior claim over furniture. Food was a daily necessity, clothing was infrequently renewed. There was never money for furniture. So through all these struggling years it was impossible to re-gather together the makings of a presentable home as measured by working class standards. Our furniture was our children and they could eat.

The lack of a decent chair to offer anyone always caused much embarrassment and often neighbours were left on the doorstep for no other reason. Being on able bodied relief saved us from intruders like 'heathen pieces'. Only neighbours with a similar predicament to ourselves were asked in. The bareness of our hovel was due to our pariah existence.

I seldom allowed a parish visitor over the doorstep. My <u>hovel</u> was still my castle despite its poverty. Until one day, just before noon there was a sharp knock on a street door. On peeping through the window, I saw it was one of the Parish visitors, a man between forty-five and fifty. At the parish round he moved silently along the queue, collecting the men's registration cards, searching for case-papers on the racks, and placing them in front of the different interviewers.

He knocked again; I barely opened the door ajar.

'Can I come in for a minute,' he asked.

'Come in?' I challenged, 'What for?' I demanded again, thinking it was an attempt to force some new poor-law legislation.

'There's nothing in it,' he explained, 'I only want to get out of the way for a few minutes.'

I was still uncertain whether it was a ruse to do some indoor spying. I felt safe enough. There was nothing to hide. I stared at him again. He seemed tired and full of trouble.

'Alright,' I agreed. 'Come on in. Don't wear the lino out.'

With a sickly smile he glanced down at the bare kitchen boards. I offered him the safest of the few rickety chairs we possessed. My wife had just made a pot of tea. There was nothing tasty to give with it, only bread and margarine. He refused the tea.

'No,' he said. 'I just want a rest. I've been walking around for two hours on calls. I'm glad to sit down.'

Being workless I had no qualms about accepting one of his cigarettes. We casually drifted into an intimate conversation. I was talking to a sensitive human being. I stared at the collection of parish cards in his hand.

'That's not a fit job for a man like you,' I observed.

'What can I do?' he answered, 'I don't like it. But there are two children depending on me. The wife's dead. I have a girl in college. The boy's learning the violin. I can't let him break his studies.'

Before he got this job, he had held a salaried position in a big commercial undertaking, trade depression caused cutting down of staff. He was dispensed with. I surmised, though I did not say so, that he had obtained this parish job through the influence of one of the local political big-wigs. Some of the additional poor-law staff had been pushed in that way. We came back to his job again.

'Yes, I detest it,' he emphasized, 'I feel terribly uncomfortable when the men in the queue glare at me. And honestly, Mr. Groundling, I wouldn't harm a fly.' He paused for a moment. 'Why are people that way?' he asked 'So full of, yes, hatred?'

With the presumptuous weight of a fully-fledged oracle I declared 'The system is all wrong.'

He stared blankly. My remark was obviously Greek to him.

'No. Do you know what I think it is?' he suddenly blurted out, 'it's the atmosphere there, it defiles everybody.'

I was back at him quick. 'There's some of your fellows up there don't need much defiling.'

'That's just my point Mr. Groundling,' he replied, 'they are not like that on the outside. It's whatever happens to them inside.'

My children coming in from school brought him quickly to his feet. He filed in the reporting card and was out on his way back to the Parish Office. There was never another meeting of this nature again, but whenever I spotted him hurrying along the back-streets on his rounds, it was with a feeling of pity.

Parish visitors varied in keeping with the cross-check system on applicants.

Uncertain of when they were going to call I was not always in. This meant them returning to the house at time when I might be in, or making other arrangements for me to be seen.

Arriving home one afternoon at 3.30 from the Labour Exchange where I had been standing about since 9, my wife informed me that the parish man had been. I was wanted at the office right away. Having been out all day without breaking my fast, I was in no humour for dashing immediately out of the house again. While I was drinking a cup of tea, the parish man knocked at the door again.

Answering him, I explained I had only been in the house about ten minutes and would slip up to the offices as soon as I had had something to eat.

'Don't be long,' he warned.

'But what is it about?' I asked.

'I don't know,' he replied, 'the boss seemed keen on seeing you tonight. He told me not to come without you.'

'You needn't wait,' I said 'I'll follow you up.'

'You won't be long?'

'No, I'm just having a cup of tea. I'll be there before five easy.'

On my way up I tried to figure out why this sudden call. I had written for a job as holiday-relief stoker in one of the city hospitals, and although there was now a direct connection between these and the poor-law authorities, I did not expect the appointment to come through the parish office. Perhaps it was an emergency call to fill a man's place that had been taken sick or died. If that were so, my period of employment would be longer and might lead to permanency. Happy with this thought, I skipped up the porch steps, and was immediately shown into the chief relieving officer's room. He pushed a chair towards me.

'Sit down,' he said.

I felt more confident. It was a job. Already I was thinking where I might borrow a pair of dungarees, and some coppers for fares if I had to report for work that night.

The relieving-officer perched on the table-corner eyed me curiously. 'Have you been in London recently,' he asked.

'No,' I answered. 'Why?'

'Are you sure?'

'Of course I'm sure, I haven't been in London in eight years.'

He stood up. 'Word has come through from head office that you were in London a fortnight ago.'

'Not me,' I replied. 'Though I wouldn't mind having a run up there if I could raise the fare.'

He stared straight at me. There was sternness on his face. 'Head office must have their information on good authority. Are you sure you haven't been in London?'

'Definitely. I haven't been there for years.'

His face seemed to pale: 'It will look bad for me if they can prove you were there.'

'But I haven't been there,' I protested. 'Why would it look bad for you?'

'If Head Office can prove you've been in London, working on the sly, then that means you've been getting relief here on false pretences.'

'How can they prove that?' I exclaimed, 'and if they could why would you be worrying?'

'Because I'm in charge here, and it will look as if I have shut my eye to something. And I can't afford to risk my job, Groundling. I have been up against it and I know what it's like.'

'There's nothing to worry about,' I tried to reassure him, 'I haven't been in London.' I stood up to leave, no longer kidding myself with prospects of a job. 'Is that all you wanted me for?'

'No, you have a special committee for tomorrow afternoon. Two-o-clock.'

'I'll be there,' I said 'I have nothing to fear.'

He crossed with me to the door. 'Honestly,' he pleaded. 'Have you been in London?'

'No,' I answered, 'On my word of honour. Does that convince you?'

His face relaxed a bit. 'I do hope you're telling the truth,' he said, almost as a prayer.

'Of course, I'm telling the truth,' I answered cheerily, 'what are you worrying about? I'm not worried and I've got a special committee.'

His face softened into a smile. 'That's a weight off me. Smoke?'

I accepted one of his cigarettes and hurried home, returning the next day for the special committee. Only once before, in the early nineteen-twenties had I appeared before one due to my own admission. As an ex-prisoner-of-war, I had received a small reparation grant. Familiarity with the parish method of swiping an applicant's income from whatever source had convinced me that they were not likely to use the money to my immediate advantage. As my home at the time had been depleted to two small chairs, one kitchen table and an entirely stripped bed, I immediately went to a second hand store, bought some bedding and kitchen furniture and as a precaution obtained receipts. Next I paid off some outstanding debts to impoverished friends who in their more prosperous days had unobtrusively helped me. With careful outlay of the balance left I was able to stay away from the parish for a few months.

My inability to find employment compelled me to return again and ask for relief. Declaring my reason for staying away I was ordered to appear before a special committee.

When I entered the small committee room, I stood facing the chairman's table, a dozen guardians, both men and women, sat grouped behind him. Amongst them I recognized some local shopkeepers.

The relieving-officer deputed to play the role of prosecutor trounced in after me, slamming the door so hard that it flew open again. Turning back to it, he fumbled excitedly with the lock then swung around, eyes a glint, and glared at me. There was no mistaking what his face contained: 'Now, I've got you at last.'

He spluttered and waved his arms about as if he would like to throttle me. All the detail of my parish record were emphasized; the time I had been on relief, the total amount I had drawn, my harmful reaction on parish discipline, and then on receiving this reparation money, instead of bring it up and handing it across the counter as I should have done, I had spent it.

Uncertain as to what my position was in law, I had to let him blaze away without interruption. A person of weaker make-up than myself would have trembled and been glad to escape from the room. It was no use of me going out empty-handed. Apart from the few extra sticks of furniture, I was as destitute as ever. I must have relief or else a ticket for the workhouse. And as this self-same relieving-officer had previously prevented me from getting such a ticket on the grounds that I wanted it for propaganda purposes, he was hardly likely to suggest I be given one now.

The guardians questioned me in turn without displaying any of his venom. I detailed the bareness of my home, where I had bought the furniture, and produced the receipts. They reckoned up how much I ought still to have left. What had become of that?

I explained I had paid off some outstanding debts to friends of mine.

'Who are these people?' demanded one of the male guardians. 'Tell us their names.'

I suddenly dried up. To me, it did not seem right to have the names of decent people bandied about in the Parish atmosphere. It would have meant investigators going to their doors to confirm my story, and given them a street publicity that their means had so far helped them to avoid.

'Tell us their names,' urged another guardian.

'I'm sorry,' I replied, 'I am not prepared to disclose them.'

In answer to a chorus of 'why's' I gave my reason. There was a silence. Then one belligerent lady member burst out, 'You've no right to contract debts on the parish!'

This was my chance. Ignoring the lady member altogether, I addressed myself to the guardians generally. Being on the parish had placed me under private obligations that were unavoidable. My parish relief was less than half my working wage. There was some excuse for myself and others in the same plight, but what about the apparently prosperous people not on the parish who were in debt. Local shopkeepers for instance, on this committee. Had all the goods being displayed in the windows been paid for? Was not the whole process of business based on the credit system? In fact, was there anyone in that committee-room like the proverbial village blacksmith?

Pausing, I searched their faces: 'How about you, Mr. Blank?'

I got no answer. 'Well, how about you Mr X?'

Startled, Mr. X replied: 'I wasn't speaking.'

The Chairman interposed: 'The circumstances are not quite the same,' he said.

'No,' I replied. 'If anything mine are worse, I have no wish to be in debt. I'd much rather be working.'

The reliving-officer pouted at me in derision: 'This man doesn't want work,' he declared, 'he is known to us as an agitator. He spends most of his time speaking on street corners.'

I did not deny this. 'As for the officer's charge of not wanting work,' I continued. 'You ladies and gentlemen can put that to a test. Increasing unemployment will mean more people applying for parish relief, and the engagement of additional staff. Out of the experience I've had and the knowledge gained, I think I am as competent as some of the clerical workers in this office. If you are prepared to give me a trial, I won't refuse it.'

The chairman turned around to the committee: 'Does anyone want to ask further questions?' There was a succession of 'noes' broken only by the hostile lady's mutterings. The chairman turned to me. 'Alright Mr. Groundling,' he said 'Stand outside.'

The door closed behind me as I retired to the corridor and plumped myself down on a form, wondering whether my suggestion of a job would be taken seriously. If it was it would be very unusual, particularly as the reliving-officer had made it clear to the guardians that I was not their kind. And the applicants who knew me would be more than surprised to see me in the role of Bumble.

Nearly ten minutes elapsed before the reliving-officer opened the door and beckoned me inside again. I faced the table to await the committee's decision.

The chairman rested his hands on my case-paper. 'We think you acted most unwisely with that money,' he began. 'You should have come up here—'

'I had hopes of cutting myself entirely adrift.' I broke in again.

'Let me finish. We have decided to grant you relief, but we have no power to offer you employment.'

'Thank you, I understand that.'

'You can go now.'

'Right. Good day.'

I winked maliciously at the disappointed relieving-officer and hurried out. There was a big load off my mind. If he had changed his earlier opinion about a workhouse-ticket and pressed for one, it would have placed me in an awkward predicament. Though I had no qualms about finding out what the local workhouse was like inside for myself, I did not relish the idea of lugging my wife and children along with me.

Now for this second special committee, there was nothing to worry over, nothing to wriggle out of. I had certainly not been to London. A few other ragged men in the passage were whispering together on a form. I was the first called in. To my surprise, there were only three guardians present.

The chairman, a slightly bigger man than myself, I did not know; the second, I knew by sight but not by name; the third, had once been under an obligation to me. In the event of any squalls, I banked on him for moral support.

An old committee clerk in attendance closed the door, and backed into the near corner of the room. I stood facing the table. The chairman opened my case-paper, and then leaned across.

'What were you doing in London on such a date?' he asked.

'I was never in London on that date,' I replied.

'And when were you in London?'

'I haven't been in London in about 8 years.'

'I want none of your lip,' he shot back. Glancing down to a scribbled note on the case-paper he re-read it, then looking hard at me again, asked in a slow accusing tone: 'What-were-you-doing-in-London-on-such-a-date?'

I was cocky in my reply. 'I've already told you once. I wasn't in London on that date or anywhere near it.'

His head shot up. 'I'll punch your nose if you talk back to me in that way.'

'You'll what?'

Staggered by his wild slip I stood staring at him. In all the queue complaints I had never heard one as blatant as this. But I was not frightened. Life had taken me into some of the toughest ports in the world, where around the docksides at night Moleskin Joe's philosophy 'The man who puts forth his fists is always respected' was a constant necessity, and the Marquis of Queensberry rules did not count. I glanced at the guardian I knew to see how the threat had affected him. His hand was stretched restrainingly [*sic*] on the chairman's wrist.

'You heard what this fellow said,' I charged him. He did not answer.

The chairman placed my case-paper on the side of the table. 'Now you get out quick,' he ordered. 'You'll get no relief here.'

Knowing I was in a strong position I did not budge. 'Sign that paper first,' I said 'then I'll get out.'

'Sign the paper?' he exclaimed. 'Huh!' He turned to the old clerk. 'Put him out,' he ordered. 'Put him out.'

The old clerk hesitated in his approach. I felt sorry for the dilemma he was in. In any previous contacts with him at the relief counter, I had always found him civil to myself and others and unaffected by the blustering officials on either side of him. Impossible to bear malice against him, I was now troubled with the thought of maybe having to knock him down.

'Please, dad,' I pleaded, 'don't lay your hands on me, or else I will be tempted to do something I have no wish to do. Let HIM put me out. He's big enough.'

I had already sized up the chairman and weighed my chances. My only fear was that with his superior weight and strength he might grapple me and pin my arms. On the other hand, if I could dance clear I had every confidence of knocking him out. There was still a punch left in me.

The chairman rapped out to the old clerk, 'Go for the police.'

I backed quickly to the door. 'No dad, not you. Let him go for the police. He wants the police.'

The chairman grasped the table edge. 'I'll soon shift if I get up,' he roared.

'I wish you would get up,' I retorted. 'Don't forget, you've threatened to punch my nose. You have all the advantages. Let's see what you really can do.'

But for the new fear that the old clerk would dodge out of it if I moved from the door, I was bursting to rush across the room and yank the chairman over the table. My blood was aroused. I wanted to make him fight. The other two guardians were silent but interested spectators.

Turning to the one I knew I asked.

'So-and-so, what's this fellow's name?'

'Mr. Draco,' he replied.

So this was the notorious Draco. His name was a byword on the queues. I was keener now than ever to have a poke at him. The longer he delayed getting up, the easier proposition he appeared to be. But I dare not waste much more time in case some other Parish official suddenly pushed the door from the outside. I stared at the chairman.

'Your mind's made up about my relief?'

'You'll get no relief here.'

'I'm destitute, remember.'

'You'll get no relief here. I've told you.'

'Alright. Then give me a ticket for the workhouse.'

The guardian I knew gaped at me as if I'd lost my senses. The other one smiled across at him. The old clerk hurried around to the back of the table and whispered into the chairman's ear, who immediately pulled my case-papers towards him and turned over the pages. The other two turned their chairs towards him and went into a whispered pow-wow and nodded their heads. Then the chairman initialled the case-paper, handed it to the old clerk, and stared across the door at me.

'We're granting you relief for four weeks only,' he said. 'Don't ever let me see you up here again.'

With a parting defiant glance at him, I opened the door and stepped into the corridor. The few men outside jumped to their feet, anxious to know what all the shouting had been about. Before I could tell them, the old clerk emerged with my case-paper.

'This way, Mr. Groundling.'

I accompanied him along the corridor. 'I'm glad it ended that way for you.' I remarked.

'It had looked a bit ugly at first,' he murmured.

'The silly stewpot [sic],' I ejaculated.

He made no further comment as we hurried through the front office for my relief card. I was glad to get out into the fresh air again. But the punch in the nose threat was still in my craw and the more I thought of Draco, the more determined I was to have a poke at him. Posting myself at the street corner a few blocks away I kept my eyes skinned for his coming. In half-an-hour at most I reckoned he would come past that way.

After a while a pauper-friend came towards me. When I told him of my intention and detailed the incident in the committee-room he stared at me in surprise.

'I gave you credit for more sense than that,' he remarked. 'Bothering your head over a big sappy-headed schoolboy. It's not him you want it's whoever sent in the information, you should go after them.'

'I wonder who it could be,' I said, as if he might know the answer.

'Whoever it is,' he replied, 'it's a dirty piece of business.'

I started to walk home, trying to figure out who it was who tried to injure me in this fashion. My friend was right: it was a dirty piece of business. Bad enough to be on the parish and bad enough to have its meagre relief as my sole income, but that somebody in the background tried to separate me from that was vile. It was not so much an attack on me as it was on my wife and children. It put me in a murderous mood. My lips were full of ugly oaths. I would find out the person responsible. My visits to a couple of suspects only brought forth denials, and I could prove nothing. To save myself a lot of unnecessary hunting around the town I decided to go to the parish head office. Somebody was bound to know.

A simple note from a member of Parliament gave me an immediate interview with one of the poor-law high-ups. The office was like a comfortable private study. There was no austerity here, I could not charge myself as I half-huddled on the edge of the easy chair, and agitatedly explained the purpose of my visit. Told the information had come by letter, I demanded the name of the sender.

The higher-up looked at me calmly from his chair: 'We get heaps of letters,' he said, 'but we never divulge names.'

I was flabbergasted. 'Does that mean then,' I asked, 'that a pauper has a lower social status than the worst criminals in an Assizes Court. He at least can see the witnesses against him and challenge them to prove their evidence. Yet a pauper is not entitled to that privilege. Do you think that's fair?'

'As a civil servant,' he answered, a picture of placidity as he sat there twiddling his thumbs, 'I am not allowed to make a comment.' Disappointed and embittered I rose to leave: 'If I knew who it was,' I declared, 'I would cut their heart out.'

'You'd better forget it,' he advised. 'Try and cool down. Consider the incident closed.'

'Closed?' I repeated, 'it's not closed for me. What about Draco? I've got another committee in four weeks. If I go before him again, there'll be more trouble.'

'Don't let him worry you. You won't appear before him again.'

He crossed with me to the door and in shaking hands pressed half-a-crown into my palm. I stared at the half a crown and back at him, doubtful whether to return it or not.

'Do I declare this as income?' I suddenly asked.

He shrugged his shoulders, and smiled as he opened the door. I was stull puzzled by the half-crown, wondering whether it was a trap, and yet disliking the idea of returning it because of the simple manner in which it had been given. Whether it was meant for a drink or a gamble I do not know, but on my way home I spent it on a rag doll for one of the children and irritated the shopkeeper by insisting on a receipt.

I never met Draco at any future committees. Even the mutual ones. The gaps between these lengthened as more men were drawn on the parish. On relief days, those living in the same neighbourhood usually walked together in small groups to the poor-law offices. To have somebody to talk to was an antidote to melancholia and full on depression. Socially shunned as we were and extremely bitter about it, we could still laugh freely in each other's company. We were at least alive in that respect.

I was approaching the poor-law offices one morning with one of these groups, when the relieving-officer in charge who only a few weeks ago had warned me for the special committee, stopped me outside the back gate.

'Don't go in there,' he said. 'Come around to the front office, and I will get you your cash card right away.' I glanced around a group of men who had halted and saw I was being treated as a privileged person. There was something peculiar about it, at least I thought so. Some of the men were not of the same opinion. 'Go on,' they urged, 'you'll get away earlier.'

The relieving-officer began walking away. 'Come on if you're coming,' he said.

'But why,' I asked. 'What's up? I'm going in with these chaps. I'm alright.'

He stepped back and grabbed my arm. 'You'll walk bang into trouble,' he warned. 'There's a government inspector inside.'

'Oh, let's have a look at him,' I answered. 'He can't be any worse than anybody else here.'

'You're a damned fool,' he exclaimed.

'Maybe I am,' I replied.

However good his intentions to steer me out of trouble he might have known I could not funk meeting a government inspector in front of my parish pals. With a reassuring 'I'll be alright' I turned away from him and followed the other applicants through the back gate. Inside the premise, hundreds of men were queued for a committee. These fell in a single file behind a long line which shuffled slowly along the walls of the two largest board-rooms in the building as it headed towards an ante-room being now used for committee business. As each applicant came out of there, a waiting parish official ushered him off the premises through a side door. There was no chance of asking any of them who was inside, what was happening, what were they like?

Here was the usual parish inflicted silence on the queues. The section where I was moved up gradually. My turn came to move on. A clerk opened the door and called my name, 'A. Groundling'. Entering the small room I stood waiting for the routine cross-examination. Seated behind the table facing were half a dozen male guardians. I had never seen any of them before, behind them perched against the side-wall on a tilted chair was another stranger, eyes half closed; he was apparently indifferent to what was going on. I surmised this was the government inspector.

The committee chairman opened my case paper and glanced up: 'Will you sit down Mr Groundling,' he pressed. I looked around me. There was a chair. I could hardly believe it. It was the first time in my living parish experience I had known a relief applicant to be offered a chair. I sat down and was instantly at ease, 'Mr Groundling' had been said so sweetly that I was convinced I was to be offered a job, and it made me feel as carefree as a club member.

The chairman turned over the pages of my case-paper and 'you've been coming up here a long time, haven't you, Mr. Groundling?'

'Yes' I answered. 'I would about find this place blindfolded.'

The chairman gaped. The other guardians' necks jerked out of their collars as they leant across the table to scrutinise me. The man in the background gazed his widely blued eyes in my direction. There was a few seconds silence. Then the atmosphere relaxed a little. I was still being scrutinized.

The chairman leant towards me in a patronizing manner. 'Have you any prospects of a job at all, Mr. Groundling?' he asked.

'No, but I am still ambitious.'

'You will try and do your best now,' he pleaded, 'won't you?'

I jumped to my feet fuming. 'Listen,' I retorted, 'I would do anything to get away from this hole. ANYTHING.'

The father-confessor tuck was still maintained; 'Ah well, keep trying Mr. Groundling,' he said, 'keep on trying. Your luck will turn someday. Good-morning.'

The clerk showed me out, and I was ushered through the side-door into the back-street, wondering what lay behind this suspicious coddling. Was the government at last going to end the poor-law repressiveness? Hope came to the queues with the parliamentary election of '29 when the Labour Party proclaimed its 'crusade against unemployment'. The propaganda was irresistible, for the writers knew the conditions and underlined them in handbills which were distributed by the bulletin.

'Unemployment is the terror,' said one. 'It is the most intolerable evil of our social system. It breaks the morale of skilled and conscientious workers. For many it is 'stopping the career of laughter with a sigh.' Break the cold paralyzing grip of unemployment, VOTE LABOUR.'

'The Labour Party' declared another qualified pledge to deal immediately and practically with this question. Its record on unemployment is a guarantee that this pledge will be kept.

'A further result of Tory policy,' went on a third, 'has been to drive the unemployed to the Poor Law. But here again the Tories have tried to hound down the unemployed. If you want fair play for the unemployed, VOTE LABOUR.'

'VOTE LABOUR,' urged a fourth, 'and see that the Unemployed are treated like Human Beings.'

As they wanted this more than anything else, they turned Labour, and talked nothing but Labour, until even the cynics in the queues had to agree to 'give Labour a chance'. They crowded the candidates' rooms, to write poll-cards and help with the canvassing, and volunteered for all the menial tasks that the limelight orators conveniently dodged. Night after night, squads of them spread through the quieter streets, to chalk meetings, bill-post slogans, and rouse the people for Labour. And on election night when they gathered in their thousands to see the results flashed on an outdoor screen, they cheered Labour wins, threw their hats in the air, and went home singing because their hardships were about to end.

The Labour government came into office in the May. For nearly twelve months after, the Exchange queues grieved worse than before. Thousands lost their benefit for 'Not genuinely seeking work'; there was another shock for those on the parish.

In Sprayport, after eight years of able-bodied relief, men for the first time were asked to sign that all relief was a loan. Those who refused were turned away without a cent, and later had to submit or starve, or else go into the workhouse.

Married men were further faced with the third alternative of prison, for no wife could personally obtain relief without a warrant for her husband's arrest. Despite this, at one office, a hundred and fifty men walked out in protest, but later in the day dribbled back to sign when they realised the trap they were in. The galling part to them was its happening under a Labour Minister, and not one could reply when a relieving-officer sneered: 'I suppose this is what's called 'brotherly love'.'

It bound a man to the parish for life. At every turn he was cornered. He had to ask for relief or let his family starve. If he left town to seek work elsewhere he faced arrest as a deserter, yet the longer he rotted on the parish at home, the less chance there was of a job. If by some means he found one, the parish had power to attach his wages, and an employer neglecting to hand them over became liable in turn for the debt.

It made the queues gloomier than ever. There was a bitter reaction against Labour, and men who had worked hard for the government's return hated others reminding them of it. 'Your gang's responsible for this,' was a stock cry now at the parish, and men were too ashamed to deny it after years of boosting up Labour. Luckily, Sprayport escaped the test-work that was being enforced elsewhere.

There was discontent at the Labour Exchange too, for whatever jobs cropped up were invariably given to men in receipt of the highest benefit. Those who never got a chance at all alleged the Employment clerks had their favourites and went to their houses at night whenever anything suitable came in. Another general grievance was that men were put off from seeing the manager, although a notice on the wall stated he could be interviewed at certain hours of the day.

Through a letter to the Ministry of Labour I forced an interview. The manager seemed surprised to hear I had been out of work for nearly four years. He said there must be a mistake. I told him there was no mistake, that if he cared to come outside to the street I would show him two hundred men who have been out of work much longer. He picked up the phone. 'I think I can fix you up,' he said, and rang through to another Exchange. They had nothing to offer.

Within a week I received a letter to call in again, and was sent to the Employment room. As I opened the door, a grey old man on his knees at the table was whining up to the clerk and begging for a job. The clerk told him he would have to clear outside, that he could do nothing for him.

The old man, unaware of me, dragged nearer the clerk on his knees. 'I'll go anywhere,' he pleaded. 'I'll take anything. I don't care what it is. Only, give me a chance. Will yer? Don't have me sufferin' like this.'

I was tempted to offer him my job-card, then remembered that I dare not. The Labour Exchange would inform the Guardians I had a job and turned it down. The Guardians could prosecute me then for failing to maintain my family, and in a police-court my motive would be twisted about to mean something different. 'This man was too lazy to take this job,' would be the charge, 'but he had no objection to an old man being sent to do it.'

The job-card was in my hand. The old man was still lost in his grovelling. The clerk, glancing across from him to me, jumped off his chair and hauled him up by the armpits.

'Come on,' he ordered, 'you'll have to get out. You've been here long enough.'

The old man stood trembling. 'Well why don't you give me a job,' he pleaded, 'and then I can get out for good.'

'I can't give what there isn't,' the clerk barked back. 'I don't grow jobs to order.'

'I'm not saying' yer do. But others can get them alright. You've been passing' me over for months.'

'I don't know what you're talking about, man. Come on, now. You must go. That's enough of it for to-day. No more. Outside.'

The old man stared suspiciously at me. 'Well what about all the jobs this morning,' he growled. 'There's been piles of them. I know.'

The clerk grabbed his arm. 'There's been no jobs this morning.' He emphasised. 'Can't you be told. Now get outside. I'm not arguing with you all day.'

The old man backed slowly to the door. 'There have been jobs this mornin',' he persisted. 'I'm not blind. I've seen them all comin' out with their cards. Dozens of them. Yer know the ones to give them to all right.' He glared at me and went out muttering.

The clerk closed the door and shook his head. 'Lord, what a pest,' he exclaimed. 'He practically lives in here, that fellow. I don't know how he gets past the counter day after day. I'm tired of telling them about it.' He crossed to his chair, took my card, and drew some papers towards him. 'This is for a road job,' he said. 'Have you done any pick and shovel work before?'

'Not pick work,' I answered. 'I've done plenty of shovelling.'

'This isn't the same,' he said. 'You'll find it pretty hard.'

'I don't mind,' I told him. 'I'll have a smack at it.'

The job was government-assisted, he explained; the wages higher than those paid to seamen. He wrote some details on a paper, then handed me a green card. 'There you are,' he said. 'Report there at seven-thirty tomorrow morning. It will be advisable to start out early. The trams are generally packed going out that way.'

I left the house as per usual, in rags and broken shoes. There was no means of buying new ones. The Corporation stone-yard was four miles away. Inside the gate were gravel heaps and stacks of setts. The regular workmen lined-up at the time-office and went off to their different jobs. About fifty ragged men were left standing by in groups. Most of them were strangers and had come from different Exchanges. Nearly all were pale and scraggy. As they stared about and took an occasional squint at the time-office clock, their chief concern was: 'I wonder where we're goin'.'

After twenty minutes, a broad-built elderly ganger strode up. He wore corduroys and hob-nailed boots. His face was a windy red; tobacco juice trickled down his chin. Spitting a stream out, he wiped his mouth with the back of his hand. Then he weighed up the men.

'Are yiz all from the Labour?' He asked.

'Yes,' was the answer.

'Stand back a bit,' he ordered. 'Let's have a look at yer.' The men spread out. 'More in a straight line,' he ordered. 'That's better,' he counted the fifty. 'All right,' he said. 'This way the lot of yer.' He strode ahead out of the yard and on to the main road, the men trailing behind like a pack of wondering emigrants.

About a mile away was a new housing estate and fields stretching beyond it. The ganger led the way across one of them. Through it flowed a muddy brook glutted with old bedsteads, and other household rubbish. The bloated body of a dead dog lay on its side by a sack.

A motor-wagon drew up nearly heaped with spades and clay-picks. The ganger shouted the driver to tip them on to the grass and hurry back to the yard for more. The men without being invited rushed to grab those that were there, and a few started squabbling amongst themselves as to who had first claim on a handle.

The ganger swung around glaring. 'Hey,' he roared, 'what the 'ells the matter with yis there? Who told yers to touch them things? Put them down where yer got them. You'll be usin' them time enough. Yer won't be so bloody eager then.'

The men meekly replaced the tools on the ground and stood by waiting for instructions, while the ganger kept staring towards the road and occasionally peeped at his watch. As he stood muttering, a young navvy cycled up and dismounted. On his back was strapped a theodolite and a couple of groundsticks [sic]. The ganger snatched them off him and strode across to a concrete archway overtopping the road end of the brook. From here he took sights and shouted orders to the navvy, who rushed about measuring the ground and pegging a patch out diagonal to the brook.

When an oblong had been marked off, about eight feet wide and thirty yards in length, the ganger shouted from the roadway: 'That'll do for now.' Turning towards the men, he let out a roar. 'Come on over here,' he bawled. 'Bring all that gear with yer.'

The men scrambled for the spades and picks, and hurried across to the marked-off patch. Most of them made clumsy attempts to break the surface of the ground. Being crowded into a small space, some were afraid to swing the picks for fear of hitting the men nearest them. Those accustomed to shovelling with a horizontal thrust found that of little use in digging a clay tool downwards.

The elderly ganger stood by, disgusted with them. 'You're like a lot of bloody 'ens scratchin' in there,' he said. 'Gerrowrer [*sic*] me way some of yer.' He stepped over on to the patch and took a pick from one of the men. 'Stand aside,' he ordered. 'Further over. Now watch this.'

With a few swings he loosened the ground about his feet, then took a clay tool and drove it down with his heavy hobnailed boot. Soon he was throwing soil and grafts of clay out past the peg-marks.

He handed the spade back. 'That's the way,' he said. 'Like that. Take it cool. Dig in the one spot until yer've got a footin' first. It'll soon come to yer. Why in a few weeks from now you'll come out in Australia.' He walked off with a sly wink, and went to another part of the patch.

The men copied what he had shown them or learnt the knack from each other, piling soil and clay both sides of the patch as they hacked it out in potholes. Those with broken boots had to depend on the sufferance of others, and all were dead-tired that night after the first day's work in years.

During the next few days, those with blistered hands hardened them with their urine, but they all shaped now with a better heart as their bodies loosened up. Faces lost their gloomy queue-cast, they chatted freely together; for by all the rumours they had heard, the job was good for at least two years.

There were joiners digging amongst them; clerks, seamen, iron-workers, and others; and the ganger adapted them all by degrees to the requirements of the job. New stretches of ground were opened, excavations went down to nine feet, and long wooden frames were lowered parallel to the sides to hold cement mixings for the walls of a culvert. A floor was laid the same way and a roof built over the top, and when this was re-sodded, the gang collected the tools, and moved further along the field.

The fine days in the open-air restored them to health and strength, and they became so keen on their work that few were ever late. Rainy days were the drawback, men were sent home minus their pay, and on re-starting again had to stand ankle-deep in wet clay that glued their feet to the earth. Most of it stuck to their spades and could not be thrown very far, for the men dare not risk their usual high swing without rupturing themselves or cleaving each other.

Standing in sloppy clay all day deadened a man's body and limbs, besides dragging his brains down his boots, and making him slow-witted and awkward. He floundered about or tripped over, and cursed, as each spadefull [*sic*] fell short of the bank and at the end of the day had little to show for his toil except the extra muck on his clothes. Some nights he was hauled out of the trench with a mould of clay caked to his boots, and dead-beat and chilled was glad to reach home and crawl off early to bed.

Every time it rained was the same. Good men's tempers were broken. It knocked the heart out of their efforts; it knocked the conceit out of me. Living in a town, I had the typical townsman's outlook that political progress was hindered by the half-baked yokels of the countryside. Then I got my feet stuck in wet clay for the first time. After standing in it for hours, I was so dog-tired and stupid at night, that on arriving home I was seldom able to read a newspaper.

This was not due to an ordinary physical exhaustion. I have stoked some of the hardest ships afloat; in the Red Sea, down the Indian coast line, and up the Amazon river; places recognised as the hottest parts of the world, and dreaded by many ship's firemen. And though I've staggered weakly around stokeholds and wished for the end of the trip to come, my mind never deadened like wet clay deadened it later. It was as if the earth had sucked my senses down through the soles of my boots and reduced me to a surly clod.

At home, I became cantankerous. Cramped up in apartments, there was no place to hang my mucky clothes. Each night they were bundled away in a curtained-off corner of the living room, and my boots kicked under the sofa to make more dirt. About every seven weeks or so, they had to be renewed; and my overalls, about every nine. Saving up for these spoiled all prospects of a suit, though I managed to buy a second-hand coat and vest. As I needed extra food and cigarettes, my wife financially was little better off, except that she could lay out her money without feeling she was watched; the parish man no longer came to the door.

There was another compensation; in return of the work touch. On the blackest of winter mornings, men starting work would grope in the piled-up tool box and seldom make a mistake in picking out their own particular spade, or clay-tool. It was not a case of the size of the tool related to the size of the man. It was the response of each particular tool to its own particular owner.

The old gaffer with his genius for organizing found light jobs for the few men physically incapable of being adapted to rough work. Then he selected nine of the ex-stokers for the concrete mixing gang. On some voyage in the sea-going days they had sailed with one or the other. A pre-existing work link was quickly rewelded [*sic*]. One handled the sprinkling can. The other eight poured into twos, shovel-turning the mix from one pair to the next, until in its thickened sloppy condition it was thrown down the culvert into the wooden frames.

Back once more came the feel of the shovel, the uniform swing of the shoulders and the tricky twist of the wrist in a tempo that never lost a beat. Left hand or right-handed swing made no difference. They were ambidextrous. What had started as painful gruelling toil was now child's play. We revelled in it. We speeded up the tempo and began showing off.

The floor-levellers in the culvert appealed to us to slow down, we could not. The job was no longer running away with us. We were running away with it.

Surface men bearing gravel, sand, and cement replacements to us could not bring it fast enough. We became a gang of gangers of our own, shouting orders to the others to hurry up. More barrows were added to keep us going. We strove to outpace them, enjoying our bit of fun we had to pay the price. The job finished ahead of schedule time, and in nine months we were back at the Labour Exchange.

Having more than seven months' stamps qualified me again for the dole, and I began signing on twice a week. The queues were longer than ever, and from the men's conversations it was useless going to the docks; there was always a mob down there. What was happening at the ships could easily be imagined from the occasional uproars in the employment room close to the Labour Exchange. The moment a ships' officer stepped in there, and said he wanted a crew, men rushed at him from all sides until he sank down like a player in a rugby scrummage.

Those standing on the outside would roar: 'Let the man up, why don't you,' and the bewildered officer on being helped to his feet had to select a score of men from a hundred clamouring around him.

The men longest out of a ship kept clear of these scrummages, having years back been passed over for being too long ashore. They were restricted from transferring to another exchange in the district although they believed there was a better chance of obtaining employment there.

I was in this category and continued to register as an unemployed fireman meanwhile writing for shore-jobs which brought very few replies, besides the loss of stamps on prepaid envelopes which I could ill afford. The stated previous experience in adverts narrowed down the chances for a sea-redundant like me, while personal interviews dropped to a hopeless note as soon as I mentioned I had been a fireman.

This was maybe because of strong local prejudice that regarded a ship's fireman as legendary "bucko" who always got mad drunk in port, and finished up by bashing inoffensive policeman about. This prejudice like many others is due to ignorance. A ship's fireman in regular employment has less opportunity for getting drunk than any shore worker. At sea, most British ships sell spirits and bottled beer to the officers, but not to the crew. Several weeks voyaging between port and port before the crew have a chance of setting ashore, as so many foreign ports lacked docking or quayside accommodation where a ship might tie-up. Even then, no matter what balance of wages is standing to the crew's credit, they can only draw a small proportion 'at the discretion of the master'. Consequently when a seaman returns to England with a couple of pounds to spend, it takes very little beer to set him drunk. And whatever chances he had of a splurge were disappointed in the Labour Exchange.

Shipping became worse. Engineers were grabbing fireman's jobs; deck-officers grabbing seaman's; and middle-aged captains were sailing in their forecastles for an A.B.S. pay. These displaced the lower ratings of 10 and 20 years service in the companies, and their oft proclaimed indispensability dropped to a sullen silence on the dole.

One tan-faced officer kept to himself. He was tall and wiry, and wore a serge double-breaster [sic]; and every day outside the Exchange patrolled a stretch of ground about the length of a ship's bridge. Up and down he swings between the ragged groups on either side, pausing only to stop whenever a passer-by crossed his path.

One group taking stock of him resented his aloofness, and hoped that unemployment would keep him a long time walking the flags. Aboardship [sic], divisions between officers and crew are rigidly observed, but in the queues they soon disappear; all men are equal on the dole.

This officer did not seem to think so, and kept solely to himself, doing his daily patrol, and smoking one cigarette from another. After a few weeks, his double-packets ceased; smaller-sized ones appeared at intervals, and in less than six months he was rolling cigarettes from tobacco scraps in his pouch.

Some of the ragged group watching him, gloated over his come-down, and prophesied that within a few more weeks he would be without a smoke at all.

'It'll touch him up a bit,' said one. 'Dyer notice the way he stares at yer?'

'Aye. And he walks up and down,' said another, 'as if he owns the bleedin' Maury [sic].'

One morning, instead of the double-breaster, he was wearing a grease-stained Norfolk coat, and a pair of washed grey pants that ran up past his ankles. He was smoking packet cigarettes again when he started his patrol, and occasionally smiled to himself, or shook his head in a chuckle.

One of the gossipers remarked: 'There's something ticklin' me laddo. He could do with a sprinkle of sugar in his boots to coax his trousers down.'

Another fellow said: 'I'll tell yer what; if he'd only learn to stand still, he'd make a damned good scarecrow with his arms stretched out in a field.'

The tall officer went on patrolling, never once speaking to anyone; and daily smoking his packet cigarettes until they were finished and he was back on the roll-ups. His face became gaunt and greenish, and his head was usually bent, as he now paced up and down a shorter space, one hand stuck in his pocket.

The group who had months before sneered at him, now rarely mentioned him except sympathetically as they noted his slow decay. Had he asked any of them for a match, they would have drawn him into a chat, sooner than see him parading like an outcast mumbling continually to himself.

One day he broke out jabbering, and made a short dash forward; then halted, swung his head like a horse, and neighed out a laugh that bared all his teeth. Snatching off his cap, he bashed it down on the ground in front of him; then picking it up, dashed the opposite way, and neighed out his horse-laugh again.

All the men turned to stare at him, as he halted, legs apart, grinning at those around, then charging off with his head-toss. They watched him, bemoaning their helplessness; here was man going mad, but because he remained on his feet, no one felt free to approach him. Had he dropped down in a fit or a faint, men would have rushed across to his side, patted his hands and face, and carried him to a seat. Now instead they were waiting to pile on him the moment he ran berserk, before he did harm to himself or maybe people passing.

He grinned at them in his dash-spasms, swinging his head like a horse; the slobber bubbling from his mouth each time he laughed aloud. A few of the men, creepy through watching him, found excuses for sneaking away; the others standing by for the fall that would give them a chance to talk. Not one had the price of a meal to offer, or a packet of cigarettes, only advice about the parish and how the officer might draw relief.

He grinned and glowered alternatively, then suddenly turned on his heel, and was off along the street, tossing his head as he went. The following day, he was back at the Exchange, doing his normal patrol and mumbling most of the time, except for the occasional whinny.

Days passed before his next outburst; meanwhile, his boots split apart, and a long black patch on the knee of his grey pants made his gawkiness more pronounced.

His laughing attacks were periodical; and as the men grew accustomed to them, he became another of the 'harmless loonies' who loiter around every Exchange. Then for weeks, they all lost sight of him, and thought he had gone to an asylum, or maybe hacked his throat, or else been found a job.

Until one afternoon during the council school holidays, from a street by the Labour Exchange, hundreds of little boys and girls ran out screaming, dragging smaller tots along. Older boys called them back, and they timidly returned, forcing the tots to go with them who were howling for their mam's. The droves of children attracted more children, who raced and yelled behind; halting when the crowd in front halted, and craning their necks for the sight.

In the middle of the road was the officer, hands behind his back, prancing about like a warhorse, and neighing into a laugh. When he galloped forward, the children ran jeering; when he turned around, they scattered and screamed, pulling up at a safe distance to watch him caper and stamp.

Some workingmen chased them all back; and one fellow, stepping off the kerb, grabbed at the officer's arm to lead him gently away. With a toss of the head he broke loose, and shot off down the street; his chin covered in froth and on his face a maniacal grin. Where he got to afterwards nobody seemed to know, but he was never seen again in the neighbourhood of the Exchange.

There were more setbacks for the men in the queues. The Labour Government had passed out, leaving behind disillusionment and an Anomalies Act which increased those lined up with the 'Homeguards'. These men, though compelled to sign weekly, no longer drew any pay, and could not go to the parish because someone at home was in work. Many of them, ragged and penniless, were worse off than their mates on relief, and were usually more miserable-looking than anyone else in the queues.

Rags became worse; everybody's. There was no chance now of a man with back dole spending part of it on underwear and socks, and taking the receipts to the parish. The new Public Assistance Committee had superseded the old Board of Guardians, and by arrangement with the Labour Exchange, overpayments were blocked at the counter.

It was only on this they agreed, for from now on the Labour Exchange swiped hundreds of men off benefit and drove them on to the parish. The National Government was reducing its unemployed figures by piling them on to the Local Authority, and buffeted in between was the broken-down wretch of the queues.

Haggard, white, and tattered; rationed for years on tea, marge, and bread; no job-break to vary the diet; and dissocialised because of his rags. Sole income, the dole; relying on that for at least pay-day's warm meal; and then, one day breakfastless [sic], reaching the counter to be told without warning; 'There is nothing'.

The clerk would repeat: 'Nothing for you', and the man would gasp: 'Nothing? Oh, Christ', then push his way out past the others who knew by his face he was stopped.

The clerk was not to blame; he merely sorted the policies, and did not know until seeing the slip whether payment had stopped or not. It was his job to say: 'No money'; and be a butt for any abuse, while the 'higher-ups' sat back in their offices secure from every attack.

I have heard thieves out of jail discuss how easy it would be to waylay the pay-clerks, and get clear with hundreds of pounds that they carried in their bags. 'But yer couldn't do it,' I've heard them contend, 'and leave any of our fellows without any money; make their kids wait a day longer for bread. Yer couldn't have the heart to do it.'

Yet the 'higher-ups' showed no such qualms in suspending a man's dole without warning, leaving him hunger-sick at the counter ill-fitted to stand a shock. The defence was, they were not really cruel men, would not deliberately do anyone harm, and whatever happened through them was in ignorance; they had no idea that men suffered so bad.

The queue scapegoats were not convinced. To them, it was a simple sum in subtraction; thirty shillings from a married man's thirty, left nothing; seventeen from a single man's seventeen the same. But there was still the parish to turn to if a man could dash up there in time.

A rainy day's slush was cold to the feet. A man was shivering from the start; drenched through on his way to the Exchange, to stand there sopping in the queue. At the parish there was another queue-soaking before reaching the counter inside, where after the routine questioning he was given a note for the Labour Exchange to confirm that his dole had stopped. Until he brought an answer back, he and his family remained without food, and delay at either end meant another day's double journey.

These journeyings [sic] to and fro seemed designed to humiliate him further, for he could see no reason why the Exchange did not give a letter at first. They had an arrangement to block overpayments, but when a man drew no money at all, he was shunted from one to the other as if his feelings did not count. Sick or foodless made no difference; the 'no dole' routine was always the same, except that afternoons left less time for the parish, and a man legged home, empty-handed. It was a neat way of smashing his spirit, doing it quietly according to rule, and afternoon was the time it hurt most, when it was raining and there was a long way to walk.

One afternoon, the Exchange was crowded; sopping men shivered in the queues, blowing their hands for warmth as they shuffled around to the counter. Coughing spread so quickly amongst them, that smokers put out their cigarettes, and only an occasional man here and there ducked his head for a sly puff.

One young chap's cough doubled him in two, ending each time in a groan, and as he staggered for a fall, several hands shot out to save him. His queue crawled so slowly around, that a couple of them stood him by the wall, to wait there until his turn came, then he could cross to the counter.

From his ragged cap to his boots he was soaking, his fingers trembled on his forehead as he moaned, and though he thumbed mucus strings from his nose, another one soon dangled from him. His head lolled from side to side; his eyes were closed most of the time, except when he stared at the counter to see if it was his turn to sign.

Since early morning he had been at the docks, hanging about in the rain, and after getting a ship-job that was promised him, the doctor had turned him down. He had been two hours dragging back to the Exchange; had taken that long through sheltering, and the moment he drew his few coppers, he would be glad to jump a tram home. His body lurched forward: 'Oh Lord,' he sighed; his face was twisted in pain, and as he fell back against the wall, the men grabbed him from slipping.

'Oh, I'm knackered,' he groaned, 'rightly knackered. Oh, I wish I was home in bed, 'till I get some of this sodden gear off. Do you think those fellers will ever get paid?'

He retched to a fit of coughing until his body seemed to sag, and the water streamed from his eyes as the men round-about held him upright.

'You ought to see a doctor,' one of them advised. 'You can't carry on in that way.'

'Oh I know,' he groaned. 'But they want half-a-dollar, and I've no half-dollars to give.'

'Well,' broke in another one. 'Why not touch the parish? They'll give you a bottle of some sort, and it won't cost you a sliver there.'

The young chap's head swung around, eyes wide open. 'Me?' he gasped. 'Go near that dive. Oh Jesus Christ, no mate. Here's bad enough. But up there! Oh no mate. Oh no.'

'It's not as bad as all that. It's the name; some of the doctors are really all right.'

'Oh, I know that mate. They're, they're all alright. But I'd … I'd sooner pay for me own.'

'So would any of us for that matter.'

'Oh I, I didn't mean any harm. I, you know, I–'

It was near his turn to sign. There was only three other before him, and when they motioned him over, he staggered away from the wall. Drawing himself along by the edge of the counter, he stopped in between two queues, the men allowing him to loll there while he fumbled for his card. He pushed it under the wire to the box-clerk, who fingered through a stack of policies, and pulling one from the back, glanced at it and pushed it across.

'There's nothing for you,' he chanted. 'Just sign there where that tick is.'

The young chap swayed as he stared through the wire, taking no heed of the policy, and making the clerk impatient having to wait for it to be signed.

The clerk pointed to a chained pencil. 'Hey, Lightenin',' he said. 'By your hand. It'll bite you in a minute. Come on you're delaying the queue.'

The young chap, breathing heavily, clutched at the bottom of the wire, and as his legs suddenly sank under him, crack went his chin on the counter. The men quickly eased him upright; one whispering to the clerk: 'He's sick': as the young chap groaned out 'oh,' and laid his head on his arms.

The clerk pushed the policy nearer. 'Try and make your signature,' he said. 'It isn't my fault there is nothing. For goodness sake don't blame me.'

'Not blamin' you,' was the answer. 'Saaallright [sic]. Not blamin' you.' Scrawling his name, and still dazed, he edged back along the counter; the men stepping out to let him pass as he made his way to the wall. There he leant, stroking his forehead, ignoring those who spoke to him, and after a weary gaze at the queue, started to grope towards the door.

The men glanced across to watch him. 'I think I'll slip him this penny,' said one. 'It'll pay his carfare home, or else he'll never get there at all.'

The young chap pushed the penny aside, then thumbing a mucus string from his nose, turned up his coat collar, and limped off into the street.

The state of him finished dock trampings [sic] for me. I would not be kicked down that far. If the Exchange had a job to offer, I was at hand, and they knew how to reach me. But for me to consciously tramp my guts away for something that was non-existent, I had not the slightest intention, and seldom moved beyond the Exchange.

It was futile looking for work; most men knew it from daily experience, and Cabinet ministers in their speeches were admitting they knew it too. Economists knew it, and newspaper editors; and the B.B.C. through its talks to listeners; most people in the country apparently, except the Courts of Referees.

Although the 'Not genuinely seeking work' clause had been abolished to lessen injustices, the court found a way to get around it, and disqualified more men than before. Reports were marked: 'Efforts restricted'; leave was seldom given to appeal, and men took it for granted beforehand that their dole was definitely stopped.

My own turn came; it was fully expected. Luckily, I signed in the mornings; and when the clerk told me there was no money, I had time to rush to the parish. Next, came a letter from the Labour Exchange for an interview with an official, who questioned me on my employment record, and where I had been for work. As I answered, he scribbled it down; 'That's all for today,' he said. 'You'll probably hear from us soon.' A fortnight later I was warned for a court.

The Court had a room in an office building. Cases from all the Exchanges came here, and sat outside in the passage until the clerk called them in. There was less than a dozen when I arrived; mostly young men in the twenties, and two girls chatting together in a separate bench on their own. Though the young men were all tidily dressed, they were bent over, silent and miserable; staring down at the floor, or glancing nervously around. They were not young soldiers suffering trench-fright, or desperadoes fearing the cat; they were ordinary artisan youths outside a Court of Referees.

To me, the Court was a farce. I would get half-a-crown raise at the parish; but if these young men lost their dole, it might mean their leaving home. Common lodging-houses were multiplying to welcome the likes of these, for whom an alternative address was necessary before they ... [Page 151 of the original manuscript is missing].

I stepped out, and the clerk told one of the girls to be ready. She was next. The young men raised their heads to question me, 'How many were on the court? Who were they? Did I know any of them? Was the workers' representative any good? Did I think my dole would be stopped?'

I could answer this last question rightly, I expected my dole to be stopped, and would be half-a-crown better off as soon as I was back on the parish. These young men were less favourably placed, did not want to go near the parish, and hoped to be called in the office room before the employers' representative came.

The clerk looked out and handed me the report paper. I glanced at it and grinned. It was exactly what thousands have been receiving for months, the stereotyped findings of the court:

EFFORT RESTRICTED.
Claimant is not normally employed in insurable employment,
And will not normally seek to attain his livelihood by means of
Insurable employment. Article 1. Unemployment Law.
(National Economy Order.) Unanimous decision of the court.
CLAIM DISALLOWED.
Signed, chairman

The chairman had not surprised me. He had acted according to the pattern, and should have known I had as much chance of a hod-carrier's [sic] job as a shop walker had of a diver's. It was the workers' man was the big disappointment, on him, these young people depended, yet he had not uttered a helpful word during the time I was in the room. I could only advise these young people instead to do at once what they must do later; find a cheap room to sleep in and then go right on to the parish.

My own change of address had landed me at another parish depot, a grey two-storied building where a fog [sic] had been bricked up for years. Inside, along the dark passages, a few naked gas-jets flickered the walls, picking up patches of crumbling plaster and perished paint which peeled off at the touch.

Hundreds of men queued in a large backyard for admission to the case-paper room where a clerk collected their cards and marshalled them into relays. Filing through to the oblong relief-room, they were reallocated into groups of eight to each of a dozen more clerks spaced out behind the long tables. These preceding-boards on trestles extended the length of the room except for a body gap in the centre and one at each end by the walls.

Calling relief 'public assistance' was supposed to remove the pauper stigma for by enactment the parish was dead and its methods a thing of the past. But many of these clerks seemed unaware of it, and insisted on servility as if the money came from their pockets and not from a government grant.

'Doff your cap' was a fit rule here which had lost some of its force because many of the recent applicants belonged to the no-hat brigade. How the rule originated nobody seemed to know, but it was despotically enforced as a condition of relief. Men wearing hats or caps sheepishly took them off at the door, and crossed mutelike [*sic*] to their groups for even whispering here was taboo.

Into this dismal den, one morning, behind a bunch of scraggy applicants came a barrel-built 'Twinny' O'Beese, wearing a paint-splotched cap, a relic of his seafaring days, he made no attempt to remove it though the rest of the men around him were standing cap in hand.

Cast ashore by the shipping slump, he had had a third run of work at the docks by using another man's tally at a firm where a relative was foreman. Even in the blackest of weeks, he managed to fiddle a couple of days, for if only a dozen truckers were on, Twinny was bound to be one of them.

Merry-faced and still in his forties his nickname came from his huge barrel-stomach which started to ball from his shoulders and ballooned all the way down past his thighs. His broad brass-buckled belt that could have been used for a horse's belly-band, hardly held the bottom of his stomach in place and was almost hidden by its overhang.

Years before at sea in the crew wash-house of a liner, a sailor gaping at the gargantuan growth had blurted out admirably: 'that's a tidy old gut you've got there, chum.'

To which Twinny replied casually, 'I have had it a long time now.'

The sailor was encouraged. 'I've never seen one like that before,' he said 'what are yer carrying?'

Twinny stopped soaping himself, gravely prodded his immense stomach and whispered in a helpless voice: 'It's twins, God help me!'

The stomach was no mere extension of himself. It was himself; something he carried about with ease, nimble on his feet, he could jerk it from side-to-side like a big bass drum. Often on a ship's deck he would mischievously collide into a group of conversing men, and with a screw-like swing of his ponderous gut knock a couple of them sprawling. Chuckling, 'Sorry you chaps'. He would dash for the nearest alley-way followed by every type of sea oath and filthy aspersions against his berth. Sometimes one of the men would take a flying kick at his stomach, causing him to yell out in mock horror: 'chuck it mate you will kill the poor babby [*sic*].'

But those days of after-watch horse-play were gone. And here he was at the parish for the first time, cap still on, standing unconcerned behind one of the groups crawling towards the nearest trestle table.

His turn came. Twinny rolled gingerly forward. The clerk's hand automatically reached over.

'Your card,' he demanded. 'Where is it? Hurry up, man, you ought to have it ready.'

'Ee yarr,' replied Twinny, and handed over his dole card.

The clerk shied it onto the table, 'Not that,' he barked out, 'Your little blue parish card? Where is it?'

'I've never had one,' replied Twinny. 'This is my first time here, I thought—'

'You never thought,' sneered the clerk. He looked up. 'Why didn't you tell—' He stopped short, blinked, and was finally convinced of what he saw. This new applicant was standing in front of him WITH HIS CAP ON. 'Haven't you forgot something?' he asked.

Twinny fumbled in his coat pocket and produced the rent book. 'Sorry,' he stumbled, 'I was not thinking. You'll find it is clear.'

'I don't mean that,' snapped the clerk.

'Well, I've got nothing else,' said Twinny, 'I understood you'd give me the other card in here. It's only for this week anyway.'

Other applicants knew quite well what the clerk was referring to, thought it wise not to interfere, from further along the opposite side of the table a stentorian voice barked out 'Hey! Take that cap off there.'

Twinny, rent book in hand, seemed unaware that the order was aimed at him. Some of the applicants standing near him surreptitiously tapped their heads to attract his attention and did a little lifting movement.

Twinny glanced from one to the other enquiringly, but his cap remained where it was. The stentorian voice bawled out louder: 'WILL YOU TAKE THAT CAP OFF WHEN YOU'RE TOLD?'

The clerk facing Twinny stared hard at him, 'You he means,' he shouted. 'Yes, you.'

Twinny's eyes widened in an imprudent challenge. 'What for?' he countered. 'I'm not a beggar. I wouldn't be here at all only my dole isn't through, and if I'd thought it was going to be like this, this place wouldn't have seen me. The Labour Exchange advised me to come here. Wait till I go back.'

The clerk stretched back in his chair. 'I don't care what the Labour Exchange advised,' he said. 'You'll get no attention here till you take that cap off.'

'Is this a church or something then,' asked Twinny, 'I thought we were in England.'

A fresh batch of applicants spread quietly into the room, some of them lining up two deep behind where Twinny was standing. His clerk straightened up immediately beckoned the first of the new arrivals to the front, and thumbed Twinny aside.

'Out of the way, you' he ordered, 'Stand back over here against the wall, or get outside altogether.'

'After being here for two hours' snorted Twinny, 'I'll watch it.'

Glancing belligerently around him, he did not budge. His two hands groped mischievously at his groin as he loosened his belt, and hung it around his neck. Suddenly lifting the bottom of his belly up, he dropped it with a dull bounce on the trestle-table. The long boards sagging under the jolting weight creaked as if they were about to break. Heaps of piled-up case-papers toppled over and spread forward, blocking some ink-bottles that had started a crablike twerk towards the lowest part of the table.

The startled clerk jumped angrily to his feet. 'You clumsy clot,' he burst out, 'What the hell are you playing at. Can't you stand up properly? Look at this mess. Now stand away from there quick.'

Twinny, his hands on his stomach, did not move. 'The weight of this thing's getting me down,' he complained, 'I've got to rest it somewhere. I think me old pair are giving away under the strain.' He turned to the applicants nearest him. 'It's terrible to be like this, isn't it,' he said. But none of them answered, only a couple risked a smile.

Towards him hurried the man with the stentorian voice. 'Stand right back against that wall, you,' he ordered. 'And take that cap off. We'll have no more of that dammed fooling.'

Twinny coolly patted his stomach. 'And what am I supposed to do with this,' he asked. 'Am I supposed to hold it up all day?'

'Perhaps you would like a chair,' came the sneering retort.

'It's a good idea, anyway,' replied Twinny, 'I could rest it on my knees then.'

The stentorian one was fuming. 'We'll soon render it down for you,' he boasted 'if you're here long enough.'

Twinny eyed him calmly, 'So that's how it is, eh?'

'Yes,' came the answer. 'That's exactly how it is. Now do as you're told. Stand right back out of the way and let these men in.'

Twinny's stomach was still on the table. 'So this is what they call Public Assistance,' he remarked.

'Never mind what they call it,' replied the stentorian one, 'now hurry up. Now stand back or I'll have you shifted. Go on. Stand back out of the way.'

'Stand back?' repeated Twinny, 'No fear, mate. I've done enough standing for one day. Out in the yard, then in that place there, and now in here. And you expect me to stand there. What do you think I am? A tailor's dummy?'

The stentorian one's jowls waggled as he glowered angrily up and down the room, but all the clerks were either busy at their work again or waiting for a new batch of applicants. He turned to Twinny's clerk who was restacking some of the case-papers.

'Where's his card' he barked.

'He has none,' answered the clerk. 'He's a fresh application.'

The stentorian one spun back to Twinny. 'What made you come in here without a card,' he snapped 'wasting our time this way?'

'How was I to know,' replied Twinny 'Nobody told me anything.'

'And you couldn't ask? Well, ask next time.'

He beckoned the case-paper clerk huddling in the doorway. 'Take this fellow outside with you and make him up a card. He had no right in here in the first place without one.' He turned to Twinny again. 'Got a rent-book?'

'Aye, Eee arr.'

'Where's your labour card?' The table-clerk passed it up. 'Alright, follow him.'

Twinny rebound his belt under his stomach. 'Do I have to come back in here again,' he asked.

'No,' snapped the stentorian one. 'This officer will deal with you out there.'

Twinny hunched himself up and fell in behind the case-paper clerk. Half-way across the room, he turned to give a parting smile to the stentorian one, impishly tapping his cap as he did so.

'Good morning, Sir' he shouted, 'Sorry to have caused all this bother, no ill feelings.'

'Go on. Hoppit [sic],' came the reply.

'Ah now, you don't mean that really,' smiled Twinny as he passed out, fastening the solitary button above his navel that held the wide sides of his coat together.

That was the last I saw of him. He was merely one of the thousands to discover that 'Public Assistance' was a sugary euphemism for the same old parish procedure, and that the newly titled adjudicating officers had not yet trimmed their bumbledum [sic] nail. It could not be otherwise in the same old building via the same old staff conditions by the same old workers.

During the twelve months I was going to this depot I was never booked for a routine committee, so large was the increase of young men applicants that came from the Labour Exchange. Mostly under thirty, these were the sawdust bread rearings [sic] of the war and the two shillings a week beneficiaries in the years that accompanied their slump. Though skinny-looking and ragged, they were livelier than older men in the queues submitting to bumbledom in the relief-room, but outside talkative and jolly.

They separated boorish clerks from the courteous ones, and when one came out bawling 'John Doe!' and 'John Doe' happened to be missing, covert cat-calls would burst from the queues.

The bore would glare past rows of faces, muttering threats about stopping relief, and on bawling again for 'John Doe' be greeted worse than before.

This would set him raving. 'I'll find out who that is,' he'd roar. 'You must take this place for the pictures; now stop all that fooling at once.' He would wait until there was some silence. 'I won't call that fellow again. So let him step out and answer his name. QUIET THERE! JOHN. DOE.'

From somewhere in the crowd a falsetto voice would squeal 'Not here, Miss.'

'WHO SAID THAT?' he'd ask charging down into the queue.

From somewhere else another voice would pipe: 'Little Jack Horner.'

'I will Jack Horner some of yer yet.' He'd growl and back he would push his way to the relief-room, followed by the young men's cat-calls.

Only once in the queues was there an objection to them. It came from a grouchy old capmaker [sic] who blamed the hatless ones for his own unemployment.

'You'll know about it, someday,' he moaned, 'swankin' around with nowt on. Wait 'till the rheumatics get in yer nut.'

A young wag turned to his mates. 'There you are,' he gesticulated. 'That's what I say too. Wear a warm cap and keep yer brains circulatin'.'

'It's boots we want most,' shouted another, 'to keep our feet circulatin'.'

The old man swung around on them. 'Damn whippersnappers,' he snorted, 'Bah!' He spat out, and was immediately mimicked the whole length of the queue. Back he swung again, scowling.

'If I had my way,' he declared, 'I'd stop all this parish and dole business. And damned quick.'

'And if we had our way, dad,' chimed in several, 'We'd stop it too. And damned quick.'

'Ahhh. Some of yers never worked in yer lives.'

Which was quite true. Most of them had grown up in a world that was slamming all the doors. The opportunities of stowing away, open years back to pre-war youths like myself had gone. Alien regulations had tightened up everywhere, and stowaways were imprisoned as soon as they stepped ashore.

Emigration too was finished. America, Canada, and Australia were all closed. Returned men from these places stood in the parish queues. They had sold up their homes to emigrate; had built new ones, and lost them. Jobs and savings were now gone; everything, except a few pleasant memories of the past. But they had once had homes, once had jobs, once had money to spend; and that was more than many young men in the queue could say.

They were the poorest off of all. They had spent little time in industry or none at all. Changing times had put their sisters there. The coming of the 'Means Test' had driven them away from home and on to the parish. No young man with dignity could sponge on his sister's pocket money or his brother's dole; nor could he allow his sister to leave home because of him. He walked out instead and found a separate address, preferably a room in a neighbour's. Common lodging-houses were supposed to lead to bad company and Borstal, and had made hundreds of mothers curse the 'Means Test'.

The 'Means Test' was the parish method of assessing income applied to the whole body of unemployed. Before the Government adopted it, the unemployed had been divided into two separate categories; the 'genuine respectable' of the Labour Exchange, and the 'unemployable workshies [sic]' of the parish.

For years, the 'workshies' had been squeezed and branded by the pressure of poor-law and public opinion, and from the commencement had faced a means test that many 'social reformers' had helped to enforce. Not until it struck the 'respectable unemployed' and dragged millions of them down to the parish level was there a national outcry.

After six months on the Labour Exchange, a 'respectable' had now to disclose all family earnings, war pensions, and any other income. For the purpose of assessment, lodgers were included in the family. This caused all-round reductions in benefit. The thrifty man with his scanty savings was told to live on them, but the worst sufferers were the single young men whose benefit was stopped altogether. They had to leave home, and formed the bulk of the demonstrators who marched through the streets in protest and were batoned down in the usual way.

They were soon joined by those reduced to five shillings weekly or less. The receipt of this small amount gave Government investigators the right to visit the wage-earner's firm and verify all statements of family earnings. The employer sent for the wage-earner. To be called into the office was frightening; to be openly connected with public assistance or the parish was humiliating. Girls felt it the worst. They went home crying. There was a family flare-up and a threat to leave. The brother left instead. There were thousands like him.

In the parish queues they revealed a wisdom of their own. They seemed to have absorbed the post-war disillusionment of soldier-parents and relatives. Yet war was a frequent topic. They would not join the Territorials in case the parish grabbed the bounty. To their minds, Government training camps were part of a stunt to condition them for the army. They felt they were the real scapegoats of peace, and were unwilling to be made the scapegoats of war. But if it did come, they were ready. All the fit men in work would be called up, and into their places would step the 'no-marks' of the parish. Meanwhile, they eked out a starvation existence on relief.

A couple of them would pal together in one room and pool the rest of their money to buy raw food, and coal to cook it with. This was preferable to just going home where detectives with search warrants for suspects invaded the dormitories at midnight to root them out for identification. Others paid the nominal rent of a room to sleep in, then sneaked home with the few shillings balance to eat their meals at the family table. Others, at variance with their families, and unable to afford coal, dawdled for hours over a penny cup of tea in one of the cheap eating-shops close to the main pay-station where all the windows were chalked: 'A cup of tea, slice of bread, and a cigarette, 2d.'

On paydays these shops were crowded. The new pay-station was a dull workhouse waiting-room inside a high gateway; and all that remained of a group of buildings that once formed the old paupers compound. The walled-in hospitals and churches had recently been demolished to make room for a £3,000,000 cathedral, in plans of which the 'down and out' had not been forgotten. In one of the twelve new chapels, a crypt was to be reserved where a dozen homeless men might shelter at night from the weather. The crumbly outer walls were already down. Hoardings were up instead. And queued against them four and five deep, stood thousands of ragged pale-faced men waiting for their relief, and the chance of adding a boiled egg to the tuppenny [sic] breakfast.

As the queue pressed slowly through the gateway into the yard, the men kept their own order, shouting back into place any latecomers dodging out of their turn. Four policemen controlled the pay-room by letting in batches of a hundred at a time. In the dash across the cobbled yard, some nipped into the payline [sic] ahead of their turn. The policeman nearest, bellowed across the room and waved them back. Occasionally one managed to sneak all the way round until he reached the cash-desk. The policeman there would quietly stop him.

'Here a minute,' he'd say. 'I want to show you something.' Back he would walk the sheepish queue-ite [*sic*] to his original place in the pay-line. 'There you are,' he'd tell him 'That's where you belong; between these two here. There's just thirty ahead of you. They've been standing out in the cold for the past hour or so. Now how would you like it?'

'All right. You win.'

'Bet your life I win. Get up a bit earlier in future if you want your money first.'

'Oke [*sic*].'

'Never mind. OKE! Come on you lads. Keep moving. Don't keep the pay-clerk waiting.'

Two clerks near the pay-box challenged each man for his identification card. This was to guard against abuses, and to make sure the cash-card was properly signed. 'I hereby declare,' it read, 'that the income of my household has not changed, nor has there been any alteration in my circumstances during the past week.' On presenting it, the man drew his money, and hurried straight out of the room.

The money passed into immediate circulation. The first charge was rent; that had to be paid. The remainder went for cheap food, and very little of that. One hot meal a day was the limit. There was nothing to spare for clothes. Boots were usually somebody else's cast-offs. Maybe once in two years it was possible to get a new pair from the parish. These were additional to relief, and only given to a man bold enough to ask for them. Before applying, his old boots had to be dropping off his feet, and be examined by a supervisor to make sure they were past repair. After particulars were entered in the case-paper, the man's name was placed on a waiting-list. Next a visitor came to the house and examined the boots again. Within a fortnight, the man received a note to take to the parish store. If the delay was longer, he could hurry delivery by buttonholing a sympathetic councillor at his private address or part rooms. A letter from him to the relieving officer soon produced the boots, and the man walked erect again for another few weeks at least.

The Labour Exchange 'respectables' [*sic*] had not that privilege. During the 'gift war' between rival cigarette firms, new boots, shirts and caps appeared for a while in the queues, but stopped when the firms reached an agreement. The boots given for empty cigarette packets never wore as long as the parish boots, and made some of the 'respectables' whine about the disadvantages of not being a pauper.

But what made them really jealous was the Christmas extras at the parish. On the pay-day before Christmas, the parish queue was a mass of smiling faces. Men who had been glum and tongue-tied all the year round broke out into jokes and laughter.

Playfully they flicked their pay-cards in each others faces. 'I'll swop yer.'

'I'll have yer for the most.'

'Now why can't it be like this every week. That's what I want to know.'

'Aw, hey. Chuck it, mate. You're expectin' too much.'

All were included in the big share-out. Single men drew half-a-crown more and in addition a coal allowance. Married men fared better because so much per head was included for the children. The total amount was sometimes ten, fifteen, and twenty shillings above the dead level of the starvation existence. But it put a temporary spring in a man's body again. There was still some good in the world. And the parish always remembered when everyone else had forgotten.

It was the one week the investigators never bothered a man's doorstep with a string of questions that had already been answered at the relief office; any army or navy pension? Are you sublet? Do you owe any arrears? Does your wife go out to work? Have any of the children started yet? How much burial club do you pay? Any clothing checks? Furniture on hire? Any other income? There was none of this. A man felt for once he was not being spied upon.

To the women fell the job of finding clothes for the children; pants for one, and a frock for another. They'd risk a check in the hope that the New Year would bring sufficient luck to pay it off quickly. A deposit, it swallowed part of the 'extras'. Then followed the dash around the crowded shops, the rush back home with parcels, and a last-hour squeeze through the threepenny and sixpenny stalls to rummage the 'damaged' counter for toys.

Meat-market bargains were scrambled for at the butcher's stalls practically at closing time, when the butchers auctioned off the left-overs sooner than 'fridge' them up over the holidays. 'We're giving it away,' they'd boast, 'absolutely giving it.' And very often they were near the truth. And very often Christmas morning arrived with fruit and potatoes in the tin dish, just enough coppers to pay for its cooking.

The lean weeks returned again; the parish queues, the counter probings [sic] and one meal a day, until after months of it a man's stomach contracted and he became incapable of eating a square meal. His body drew on its reserves until his face went bony and yellow, and fearing a collapse he was compelled to ask for the doctor.

To the doctors' parish offices hundreds of patients now came daily, the doctors having increased from one to six to meet the abnormal rush. A barn-like building filled with wooden forms served as a waiting-room, the top end being bearer-board partitioned from wall to wall. The back of the partition was subdivided into curtained-off sections where each doctor examined his patient under conditions discomforting to all.

The long wooden forms outside were now mostly packed by lantern-jawed young men, and anaemic girls with their new babies, sitting cheek by jowl with skull faced gaping open mouthed seniles [sic]. In the dull light, the room looked like a monster opium den minus its paraphernalia where greenish faces, shrivelled faces, gristly faces stuck up out of each pack of rags.

Huddled in between were genteel come-downs of the newly made poor, no longer able to afford a private doctor, and forced to wait for hours in this inescapable meeting-place of filth and disease. It was easy to pick them out as they sat with eyes closed in an effort to shut out the squalor surrounding them on all sides, but above the constant sepulchral whisperings, they could not for long close their ears to the sly digs at their own lingering respectability and their final disintegration came, they were squirming hopelessly in the parish rut.

Sometimes, due to the rush, two doctors had to use the same curtained off section together, making proper examinations impossible. Patients popped in and out as their turn came, hoping for extra nourishment notes valued at three shillings each, and exchangeable for eggs and milk. Who got them depended on the doctors they saw. The gruff ones were never asked twice.

Particularly dependent on these notes for post-natal nourishment were mothers in their thirties. Most of them dreaded the non-appearance of their menses, for unintentional pregnancy brought a dominant horror to the daily drag. Strained faces came until eventually someone turned up with free whispered advice on the kind of pills to take, the safest doses, and where they were obtainable. If these failed, there were other riskier methods which led to flooding haemorrhages or an early death. Survival necessitated an immediate visit to the parish doctor where extra nourishment notes for a few months inevitably merged itself into the family budget.

Where a patient had to be visited at home, bed-clothes where possible were usually borrowed from a neighbour to present a tidy face to the doctor when he called. He generally advised 'The Hospital'. The old people's dread of parish hospitals was not shared by the younger ones, for they had been transformed from 'butcher holes' where the poor, years back, were 'polished off' for dissection, to places of rest and services where first-rate medical skill was at hand.

But the fear of being buried as a pauper still persisted. Insurance payments could not always be met, and arrears mounted up until membership finally lapsed. Re-joining meant a higher premium and a harder struggle to pay. Boots wore out, food prices jumped, and the rent dare not be missed. So the burial club was let slide for a week, and the arrears quickly rose again.

It was difficult to re-enter a sick child or an aged person. The sudden death of one or the other threw a household into confusion. The nights off sitting up at the bedside, and the desperate scraping of fees for a private doctor were only the beginning of a bigger worry: who would bury the dead?

Sometimes a body lay in a house for a week. Neighbours soon learnt the reason, and women collectors went from door to door asking for threepences and sixpences towards the burial. The total was handed over to the deceased's relatives as a small advance to approach the undertaker with. If the undertaker had been let down by some other customer he demanded more money. This involved further running around from one neighbour to another. On such occasions, the street moneylender volunteered a loan, and the parish promised a small grant. The undertaker then proceeded with the funeral.

The bereaved family waited his arrival. On the house windows instead of bed-sheets for 'deathblinds' [sic], paper tablecovers [sic] hung instead. Crockery had to be borrowed, and knives and forks, for the laying out of the snack customarily given to the mourners on their return from the cemetery. Those unable to borrow tidy clothes rode out in their rags.

Conditions were little better where insurance money had been paid, excepting a family owed less to the neighbours and had no moneylender's bill to face. But there was no chance of a mourning suit or a black dress out of the club money, for once the undertaker had pocketed his share, the parish claimed the remainder.

It was the snatching of every cent that stopped a man taking a casual week's work because whatever wages he earned had to last him the following week too. No allowance was made for extra food and the buying of necessary work-tackle, so that he finished up owing more than if he had not worked at all.

Growing children were a similar problem, for regardless of appetites, the parish only allowed three shillings per head whether for a week-old babe or a youth in his teens. A boy or girl on leaving school with a reference came out keyed up for a job, and if they happened to find one, the parish took seventy-five per cent of their wages. That meant six shillings out of seven and sixpence, and seven-and-six out of ten, and very little was left after that to pay for the daily bread. Car-fares took another shilling at least, boots and clothes needed constant repair, and the mother as a concession had to give her wage-earner a few coppers to spend.

A boy son knew he was a drag on the house, and hoped his first year's work would slip over, then in the normal way he could ask for a rise in wages. If successful, he came home beaming, showed his mother three or four shillings more, and the next week was staggered to hear it had been deducted by the parish. Disheartened, he talked of running away, and this led to continual squabblings [sic]; it was hard for him to understand why he was penalised from the start.

It was harder still for a father to explain why the parish had power to do it, and how when a man was driven there, everything pushed him down. Employers ignored him, the public condemned him; he was a ragball [sic] for most politicians, and when newspapers 'screamed' about rates, they always blamed the man on the parish.

The newly-formed U.A.B. promised a way out, men looked to the 'appointed day', when according to queue rumours, the government would take them over. Repeated postponings caused plenty of mix-ups, thousands were chased to the Labour Exchange and back, while the local authorities and government officials were disputing who would pay.

The first transferred were single men mostly, who again drew seventeen shillings, and believing the parish could not touch it, went back home to their parents. The change of family income had to be reported, the parish took thirteen of the seventeen dole; straightaway, there were family rows over pocket money, and the young men cleared off from the home.

Married men fared better in the change-over; children's allowances were graded by age, until to-day with the new adjustments U.A.B. scales are much higher than the parish. Officials meet men on a different footing. Questions are not sapped in the Bumbledom way. That's a big step forward to make. But what of the men still left on the parish?

PROVINCETOWN PLAYHOUSE

133 MacDougal Street, New York

JAMES LIGHT, Director
EUGENE O'NEILL, Advisory Director
M. ELEANOR FITZGERALD, Manager
CLEON THROCKMORTON, Technical Director
HAROLD McGEE, Stage Director
PAULINE H. TURKEL, Business Manager
STELLA HANAU, Press Representative

Box Office, Spring 8363
Telephones: Business Office, Spring 7410

January 9, 1926

George Oswald James
238 East 42 Street
New York City

My dear Sir,

We are returning your manuscript, "Tombstones

and Grass".

Thankyou very much, but we cannot make use of

it.

Very sincerely,

PROVINCETOWN PLAYHOUSE

The Royal Mail Steam Packet Company.

(ROYAL CHARTER, DATED 26TH SEPTEMBER 1839.)

"TELEGRAMS"
AT HOME "OMARIUS, AVE, LONDON"
OR ABROAD "OMARIUS, LONDON"

TELEPHONE:
LONDON WALL.6460 (10 LINES)

All communications to be
addressed to the Company.

Your reference

18, Moorgate Street.

London, 9th April 1918.
E.C.2.

Reference Marine.

Mr. George Garrett,
    2, Sands Street Sth.,
    St. James Road,
        Liverpool.

Dear Sir,

In reply to your letter of the 8th instant, we find
on looking at our records that you were employed as Saloon Boy on
R.M.S.P. "POTARO" when that ship was captured by the enemy raider
"KRONPRINZ WILHELM" on the 10th January 1915. It is also true,
according to the Commander's report, that you were forced to sign
a declaration to the effect that you would not take arms against
Germany during the period of hostilities.

We hope this letter is what you require, and that it
will serve your purpose.

Yours faithfully,

THE ROYAL MAIL STEAM PACKET COMPANY.

FOR THE SECRETARY.

MERSEY DOCKS AND HARBOUR BOARD.

HET/MC/

Memorandum   25th July, 1928.

From H.E. Thompson.   **To** Mr. G. Garrett,
2 Windsor Street,
Liverpool.

Referring to letter applying for a position as fireman, I regret to say that there is no vacancy at present. A note has, however, been made of your name and you will be considered when a fireman is required.

3. 1928 letter from the Mersey Docks and Harbour Board informing Garrett there were no vacancies for Firemen

---

UNEMPLOYMENT ASSISTANCE BOARD

AREA OFFICE.

WALTON (1)

114/116, Anfield Road,

Liverpool, 4.

Determination of Allowance

1. With reference to your application for an allowance, the following determination has been made in accordance with the Unemployment Assistance Regulations approved by Parliament.

2. Payment will be made weekly at the Local Office of the Ministry of Labour so long as this determination remains in force and provided you satisfy all the conditions referred to in paragraph 2 overleaf. This determination, which cancels any previous determination, is subject to review at any time.

3. The determination does not take into account the needs of the following members of your household on the ground that they are not dependent on, or ordinarily supported by, you.

4. If you wish to have any explanation in regard to this determination you should either write to or call at this office between the hours of 10 a.m. and 4 p.m. (10 a.m. to 12 noon on Saturdays) bringing this form with you. By so doing you will in no way prejudice your rights of appeal.

Local Office L'POOL SEAMENS   Claim No. LLCE 94407

Applicant's Name GARRETT G   C.P. No. 10.12.13636

5. **Appeals**—If you are dissatisfied with this determination you may request that your case be placed before the Appeal Tribunal.

An appeal must be lodged within fourteen days of the date on which this notice is issued to you, after which period no appeal can be accepted.

A form of application for appeal together with an Explanatory Leaflet B.L.2 may be obtained from the Local Office of the Ministry of Labour or from this Office.

	PERIOD		Weekly Rate	
	Pay week which includes	Pay week which includes day following exhaustion of benefit	s.	d.
1.	22.9.38		32	-
2.	Following pay weeks		32	-
3.	Pay week which includes and each pay week thereafter.	20/10/38	29	6
4.	Each pay week thereafter.		29	6

6. The weekly rate shown above is subject to deductions in respect of earnings and unemployment benefit as explained overleaf. Earnings will be taken into account from

   (i) beginning of first pay week.

   (ii)

Signature A. L. PEACOCK   Date 22 SEP 1938   Date of issue to applicant
Area Officer.

B.3 (Revised)   **N.B.—Read carefully the directions printed overleaf.**

4. September 1938 Determination of Allowance form from the Unemployed Assistance Board

5. 'Marching On!' approx. 1922, Garrett's earliest known published work, printed on a flyer to be distributed on demonstrations organised by the Seamen's Vigilance Committee. The flyer was sold to raise funds for the First Hunger March in 1922

Marching On!

[By G. Garrett.]

(Tune : " Hold the Fort.")

Outcasts are we from factory,
From workshops, mine and sea,
Despised by those who used our blood
To save their property.

Chorus.
Scorn to take the crumbs they offer
To appease our wrath,
Forward to Emancipation,
'Tis the chosen path.

Onward, comrades, organise,
Burst the ruthless chain,
Solidarity shall prove
Our quest is not in vain.

Too long we've starved in silence grim
And watched the parasite
Waste in luxury the wealth
Produced by Labour's might.

Marching on with hearts undaunted,
Workers! sound the drum,
Let the tyrants hear our voices,
Victory will come.

this leaflet goes towards defraying the
ployed March to London.   Liverpool
October 29th, 1922.

SEAMEN'S VIGILANCE COMMITTEE.

SEAMEN AWAKE!

Arise ye toilers of the deep,
Who fight the waves while many sleep,
That they may this world's gifts devour,
They take the sweets, leave us the sour.

Too long we've languished in subjection,
But now we raise our stern objection,
Poverty, and starvation have been our dole
While wealth and riches the looters stole,

The race-horse in his master's stable,
Proves our liberty a lying fable,
Earth's lowliest slave ploughs the sea,
"Good Christ"! we pray "why should this be"?

Crowded together in dreary cells,
Listening to the sound of bells,
That do not laud our deeds of bravery,
But actually mock us in our slavery.

We brave the deep and prove we're strong,
Yet are too weak to right a wrong,
We've been contented in our chains,
While robbing masters used our gains.

This surely will not last for ever,
The chains that bind us, we must sever,
Only through powerful organization,
Can we decide our own salvation.

Stand together! Sons of Neptune,
Emancipation shall come very soon,
If one sea-slave trusts his brother
Liberty and justice, our cause will mother.

Let us prove to all the world,
The longing to be real free men,
Our battle cry shall urge us on,
Rise up in arms The Rebel Seamen!

GEORGE GARRETT.
Vig. Com.

ALLEN & SONS, Ltd., Hunter Street (late M'Call's) Liverpool.

6. 'Seamen Awake', another of Garrett's marching songs for the Seamen's Vigilance Committee

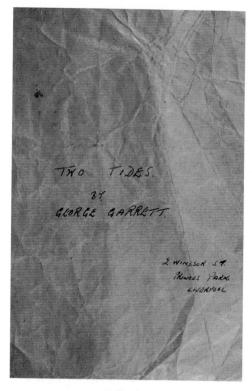

THE

ADELPHI

June 1934

A New Socialist Party
The Editor

Marx-Engels : Briefe an Dritte
reviewed by K. K.

Saving Madam and her Butler
Edmund Wilson

Pagan Virtue and Things
Rayner Heppenstall

William Morris
J. Middleton Murry

First-born
a story by Matt Low

6^D

7s. 6d. per annum, post free   58 BLOOMSBURY STREET, LONDON, W.C.1

TWO TIDES.
By
GEORGE GARRETT.

2 WINDSOR ST.
PRINCES PARK.
LIVERPOOL

1-2

"Flowers   and   Candles"

C H A R A C T E R S.

Mr. O'Prey
Mrs. O'Prey
Manuel
Mollie O'Prey
Pete O'Prey
Oscar Johnson
Mrs. Jeffries
Rita Muller
Ben O'Prey
Jerry Fitzgerald
Rose Brown
An Italian

ACT ONE

SCENE-----Takes place in the parlor of the O'Prey home.
TIME------A few days before Thanksgiving.

ACT TWO

SCENE-----The same as ACT ONE.
TIME------Fifteen minutes later.

ACT THREE

SCENE-----The same as ACT ONE AND TWO WITH A FEW MINOR CHANGES.
TIME------Four months later.

ACT FOUR

SCENE-----The same as ACT ONE, TWO AND THREE with a few changes.
TIME------Five months later.

7. The front cover of the *Adelphi* magazine, June 1934, featuring Garrett's first published story, 'First Born' written under the pseudonym Matt Low

8. *Two Tides*, Garrett's first play, set in Liverpool in 1918, written approx. 1922

9. Characters and scenes in *Flowers and Candles*, Garrett's second play, set in New York, written approx. 1923–1925

10. Flyer advertising Liverpool Trades Council's Centenary Celebrations in 1948, featuring *One Hundred Years Hard*, a play co-written by Garrett

11. Garrett's New York Visa and Identity Card, 1919. Note Garrett's dress, in the fashion of the day – baseball top and flat-cap

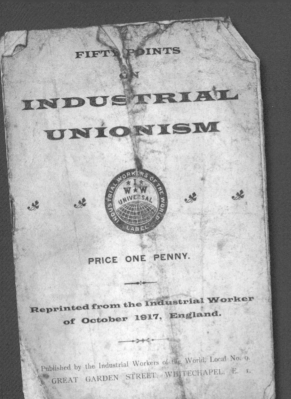

12. Garrett's copy of the Industrial Workers of the World *Fifty Points on Industrial Unionism* Manifesto

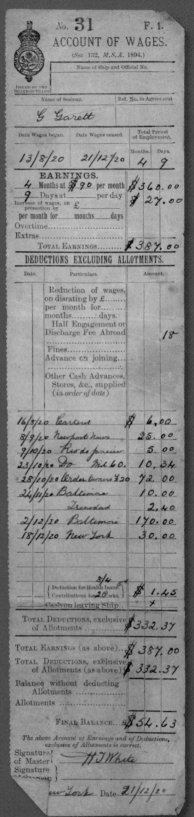

13. Garrett's Wage Slip from 1920, paid in US dollars, detailing deductions and the various ports he visited, including, Baltimore, Rio de Janeiro, Trinidad and New York

IN THE CITY OF LIVERPOOL,

TAKE NOTICE that you *George Garrett*

are bound in the sum of *Fifty* Pounds as Principal, and you

In the sum of Pounds each as Suret , that you,

the said Principal, appear at the next Court of Assize for the West Derby

Division of the County of Lancaster General or Quarter Sessions of the Peace

for the said City, to be held at St. George's Hall, Lime Street, in the said

City, to answer any Bill or Bills of Indictment which may then be preferred

against you, and not depart the said Court without leave : and unless you, the

said Principal, appear and plead and take your trial accordingly, the said

sums will forthwith be levied on you severally.

DATED the *23rd* day of *September* 192 *1*.

Charles Barton

Justice of the Peace for the City aforesaid.
Clerk to the Court of Summary Jurisdiction
for the City aforesaid.

51890 500.8/21(71602)214

14. Court Summons, September 1921, following Garrett's
arrest during the unemployed demonstrations

15. George Garrett's Discharge book stamped with
his last known sailing on the *Nagara* in 1940

Nombres de Vapores y fechas	
Names of Vessels and Dates	
"NAGARA."	27 JAN 1940
"NAGARA."	26 APR 1940

"NAGARA"
SOUTHAMPTON
O.N. 135709
NETT
TONNAGE 5571.

Firma del tripulante *George Garrett*
Signature of Seaman
Puesto que ocupa *FIREMAN*
Rank
Lugar y fecha *LIVERPOOL*
Place and Date
23 DEC 1939

16. Identity and Service Certificate showing sailings in 1918, 1919 and 1920

18. Garrett as The Stoker 'Yank' in *The Hairy Ape* by Eugene O'Neill, Merseyside Unity Theatre

19. Garrett in 1948 playing his young self on the 1922 Hunger March in the play *One Hundred Years Hard*

17. George Garrett, 3rd from left wearing a cap, setting off with the Liverpool contingent on the 1922 Hunger March

20. George, mid-1920s, living and working in New York under the pseudonym George Oswald James

21. Garrett, second from left unknown at an unknown location during the First Hunger March, October 1922

22. Dedication page of
Ten Years On The Parish

DEDICATED TO

" *The ageless voice, the voice both brave and resigned,*
which soothes comrades, scolds naughty brats, bullies the
bakers, argues with relentless tradesmen, beseeches bailiffs,
comforts the dying — the voice of the workingwoman
which goes on through time, probably never changing,
The voice which holds out against all the miseries of the "
world."

GEORGES BERNANOS. (*Diary of a Country Priest.*)

23. Circa 1936: English poet, writer and editor John Lehmann (1907–1987). He founded the periodical *New Writing* (1936–1941), was managing director of the Hogarth Press (1938–1946) with Leonard and Virginia Woolf and inaugurated and edited *The London Magazine* (1954–1961). (Photo by Gordon Anthony/Hulton Archive/Getty Images)

Vienna.) as from
Fieldhead, Bourne End, Bucks.

3.12.36.

George Garrett,
52a St.James Street, LIVERPOOL 1.

Dear Garrett,

     Sorry for the long delay, - but I was travelling
most of the time.

     I like your HUNGER MARCH I saw at first certain
difficulties in accepting it for NEW WRITING, chiefly that it
was too like an essay. But I now think that can be obviated by
one cut of nearly two pages, - from the third line 'Weeks of
preparatory work...' to the paragraph on page 2 ending '...bed
and breakfast.

     If you can consent to this cut being made, I would
be very glad to publish it, in No.3 or 4, - always provided that
a way is found out o the difficulties created by Lane's
bankruptcy.

     Yours ever

52ª ST JAMES ST
LIVERPOOL.1.
17.12.35

Dear Lehmann,

    The story or stories referred to by Wintringham
are still in his possession — if not, then Montagu
Slater has them. Anyway, I am writing by this post to
ask Slater to forward them on to you. If you should see
him in the meantime, worry him for them. You might get
quicker results seeing near at hand than I seem to get at
such a long distance. I've even threatened him.

    Thanks for the offer of consideration. Whether the
stories are acceptable to you or not I will welcome a peep
at the Bridge. Success to your effort.

      Yours Sincerely

      George Garrett.

Answered.
JL
23.12.35.

Dear Garrett:

An introduction to the Garrett–Lehmann Letters

The forty-eight letters exchanged between George Garrett and *New Writing* editor John Lehmann between January 1935 and July 1940 are a unique window into the relationship between a working-class writer and his editor, corresponding across boundaries of class and geography with the mutual aim of publishing *Ten Years On The Parish*.

George Garrett and John Lehmann's backgrounds could hardly have been more diverse. Garrett left his 'slum school' at the age of 14 and spent time 'sleeping out'[1] in a stable before jumping ship, bound for Argentina and the hard life of a stoker. Lehmann was Eton and Cambridge educated, could trace his ancestry back to 1296 and 'William de la Chambre, "Bailif e burgois de Peeble"'. Compare Garrett's early memories of mixing with children who went without shoes to that of Lehmann, who remembers being in his 'father's library at our old family home of Fieldhead, on the Thames' where 'James the butler has been in to draw the blinds and curtains, and my father is reading under a green-shaded lamp'.[2]

This introduction aims to put the letters between these two seemingly incompatible characters into context by exploring what brought them together, some of the issues highlighted within the letters themselves, and to try and reach some understanding of why Garrett left *Ten Years On The Parish* unfinished and, unbeknown to Lehmann at the time, moved on to new forms of writing and radical, social activities.

In 1926 the General Strike shook British society to its core. Its defeat, being called off by the Trades Union leadership after ten days, was a crushing blow to the working class. It is both symbolic and significant that Garrett's return from America should coincide with the end of the strike, when the colossal explosion of working class energy that had taken over the running of towns and cities across the country had dissipated into Garrett's lethargic description of 'police and workers playing football together'.

John Lucas, who has himself played a crucial role in recovering Garrett as well as many other lost voices, argues that 'the failure of the General Strike was of crucial importance to the development of radical thought and activity – including writing – and that it, rather than, say, the Wall Street Crash was decisive in shaping or conditioning attitudes both at the time and later'.[3]

Although Garrett was in America during the strike itself, there is little doubt where his allegiances lay. John Lehmann though, born in 1907 and almost ten years younger than Garrett, was still at Eton in 1926 where it 'caused hardly a ripple'. But when it did he and his school chums 'rather wished' they had been allowed to 'volunteer as engine-drivers or printers';[4] in other words, to take the place of the striking workers.

John Lehmann published two collections of poetry (*A Garden Revisited*, 1931 and *The Noise of History*, 1934) and two novels (*Evil Was Abroad*, 1938 and *In The Purely Pagan Sense*, 1976). He came from an artistic family; his father's family published *Chamber's Encyclopaedia*, his sister Beatrix became a celebrated actor, his other sister Rosalind a prolific novelist. Lehmann was well travelled, spending many years in Europe and living for six years in Austria where he witnessed the first stirrings of fascism. He had originally wanted to establish himself as a poet and was connected and often good friends with all the major literary names of the day; W.H. Auden, Christopher Isherwood, Stephen Spender, Julian Bell, to name only a few.

While working on his poetry he was offered a job at The Hogarth Press, owned and run by Leonard and Virginia Woolf, where the idea began to take hold of developing his own magazine; although it's possible the thought may have been sparked many years earlier through a prescient comment by his sister Rosalind in a letter she wrote to him in the late 1920s saying, 'What you'd do well would be to edit a paper'.[5]

After witnessing first-hand in Austria the growing tide of fascism, Lehmann took the decision to launch *New Writing*, a magazine he hoped could serve as 'a rallying point for the so rapidly growing anti-fascist and anti-war sympathies in my intellectual generation'.[6] It also aimed to break down barriers between writers who had a 'middle-class education and already moved to some extent in metropolitan intellectual circles' and working class writers who 'when they wrote of mines, seamen, factory workers or East End tailors' wrote from 'the inside, out of their own experiences'.[7]

Garrett had already published seven stories; four in the *Adelphi* magazine under the pseudonym Matt Low and three in *Left Review* before his work was recommended to Lehmann by Tom Wintringham, the editor of *Left Review*. This led to Garrett's story *Fishmeal*, and later his reportage piece *The First Hunger March* being published in *New Writing*, but it also resulted in Lehmann being asked to act on behalf of the Communist Party-owned publisher Lawrence and Wishart as their agent to contract and work with Garrett towards publishing *Ten Years On The Parish*.

Lehmann offered more than editorial support for Garrett; in many ways he became his patron, offering practical support – arranging for Garrett to travel to London to meet him and discuss his work, and even direct financial support by at one point sending Garrett money from his own pocket to replace a publisher's bounced cheque.

This relationship wasn't unusual. Andy Croft in *Red Letter days – British Fiction in the 1930s* makes the point that 'Few working class writers between the wars were able to secure publication for their work without this sort of encouragement, support and material help from at least one established writer'.[8]

The letters themselves contain a lively debate between Garrett and Lehmann about the editing of Garrett's work. Lehmann, perhaps conscious of his reputation for being an interventionist editor,[9] wrote to Garrett in June 1936, saying 'You'll dislike me for being so high-handed, but I really do believe the story will be all the better for them [the edits]', and hoping Garrett can 'stomach such vandalism'. Garrett replied that Lehmann can 'forget about me disliking you. Instead, I say "Thanks".' But Garrett was no pushover to Lehmann's authority. In response to Lehmann's suggestion of the use of 'rivulets' instead of 'stream' to describe the sweat coming from stokers in the stokehold, Garrett puts his foot down: 'stream is not an exaggeration ... I have known men not to wear laces so that as fast as their boots become full of sweat they would kick them off and empty them immediately. Rivulet would hardly describe the amount they empty out. <u>Stream</u> is best.'

So it was in a spirit of cooperation that Garrett made mention of writing the story of the 1922 Hunger March, describing himself as one of the 'pocket commissars at the time with Wally Hannington' (The leader of the National Unemployed Workers Movement). 'Oh for the good old days' writes Garrett', who felt he was 'still young enough to hope for that spirit to reassert itself'. In July 1936 Lehmann, sensing something special, replied, 'Well, why not write the story of that march?' and urged Garrett to 'make it racy'. Garrett obliged, and by late September had submitted 4500 words to Lehmann, who after proposing a cut of two pages said he would be 'glad to publish it in No 3 or 4'. (It was eventually published in *New Writing III* in the spring of 1937.)

George Orwell, whom Garrett had met in February 1936, encouraged him to write his autobiography, and in December of that year Garrett hinted to Lehmann he was considering doing so by saying he may want to work his Hunger March piece 'in with something bigger later on.' By the time he read George Orwell's *The Road To Wigan Pier,* which he regarded as a 'terrible hotchpotch from start to finish,' Garrett had started writing *Ten Years On The Parish,* to tell the 'true story of unemployment and repair the 'damage' he felt had been done by Orwell's book, and to 'give the average person a "feeling" of what it means' to be unemployed'.

But soon the difficulties began to mount up as the tasks associated with writing a much longer piece of work than the short stories that had been his main focus became apparent, and his problems, which at root were associated with extreme poverty and overcrowding, began to multiply and hinder his attempts to write.

During the five years covered by the letters, Lehmann moved freely between his family home at Fieldhead in Buckinghamshire and his flat at 5/10 Invalidenstrasse in Vienna; Garrett moved from the slum housing in Liverpool's Park Lane area to an overcrowded tenement in the Dingle and on to the then new housing estates of Speke.

In February 1937 Garrett, whom Alan O'Toole pointed out was enormously sensitive to noise,[10] briefly listed the problems he faced; living in a tenement; a wife and five boys, whom he has to 'terrify' into silence; physical exhaustion; having to deal with the troubles of other unemployed men; the 'cruel' P.A.C. (Public Assistance Committee) 'having him by the balls', who will 'drop him for desertion' if he tries to move away to write in a cottage out of town. In March 1937 he wrote of his week ahead: 'Monday – Parish. Wednesday – Parish. Thursday – Labour Exchange.' In between the parish visitors will come, and his wife Grace 'won't open the door to them' as she 'does not like the neighbours to know we are on the parish',[11] so he had to wait at home to meet them.

And yet, as well as deciding on the title *Ten Years On The Parish*, Garrett revealed he had 'already got down twenty-thousand words towards the book and was considering sending it in to the 'Left Book Club' Competition.' This was remarkable progress. It is doubtful that Lehmann, who was still working on the agreement for the book with Lawrence and Wishart, expected Garrett would have written twenty thousand words in just one month. As Garrett's progress continued, because of his financial situation and living conditions, his mood inversely worsened.

Around this time the founder of the Mass Observation Movement, Tom Harrisson, who Garrett met during a visit to London funded by John Lehmann, made an intervention. He urged Garrett to break with Lawrence and Wishart who, 'by their attitude have shown that they do not appreciate the true position', and wrote to Lehmann to suggest another offer for Garrett. Lehmann reminded Garrett that he had 'agreed by an exchange of letters to let Wishart have the book', and therefore didn't see how Harrisson could 'handle the script.'

Bearing the brunt of Garrett's anger were Lawrence and Wishart, the publisher he had hoped would offer him the financial security that would relieve him of the burden he was carrying. 'I have never been free – never felt free,' wrote Garrett in July '37, 'this book has become such a load on my mind that I cannot do anything else. I can't even read a book. My whole time is spent trying to catch a few minutes to write in.'

And so Garrett found himself, in his mind, trapped between a publisher who would not provide him with the wherewithal to be able to both provide for his family and find a private space to write, and his own people who didn't appear to know or understand Garrett as a writer, who he claimed would view him as an 'exhibit'.

'So as I say, just as I get my papers out to make a fresh start, a knock comes, and the papers have to be stuffed out of sight, because there is no separation in these places.

'Even in the old slum houses where I lived previously, I could stay upstairs and sometimes get a couple of consecutive hours. This is utterly impossible in a tenement.'

Even though by this point Garrett had had 13 stories published in national magazines, he was reticent, among his own class, and particularly those he lived and mixed with on a daily basis, about being identified as a writer. 'I have even tried a couple of rooms close at hand,' he told Lehmann, 'but there, conditions were almost as bad as at home. There was continual interference and I had to give up.' He tried to work in the library but had to give up 'because of chaps who come to me as a father-confessor and general-life guide. It is an advantage at times to be known, but at the moment I am paying a heavy price for being too well known.'

Garrett was searching for a place to write, for his 'room of one's own', and in August 1937 he told Lehmann he had finally managed to find an unfurnished cottage to write in, and had even paid the first quarter's rent, although, perhaps symbolically, he never managed to furnish it.

Garrett had found in Lehmann his own 'father-confessor', and he poured out his frustration and anger, opening up his creative soul in a way that he appears to have felt unable to with those closest to him. Lehmann time and again reiterated his belief in Garrett's ability; 'I fully appreciate the nature of the fix you find yourself in: but I don't intend to take no for an answer, because I believe in the future of your writing'; 'I know you have the foulest difficulties to struggle against; but I feel just as sure you'll get it done, and make something else of it no one else could'. And, as indicated earlier, Lehmann's support extended beyond the moral. After writing to Garrett almost pleading with him to 'tell me privately' what was to be done, he sent an extra £10 and negotiated a £10 increase on top of the £50 advance from Lawrence and Wishart.

Unfortunately it wasn't enough, and in truth it appears unlikely, possibly throughout the process but certainly by this stage, if anything would have been enough, for in his next letter Garrett revealed:

'It reached its climax just two weeks ago when I broke down and cried for an hour. My brain had snapped and I was a physical wreck

... if you would say you cannot imagine a fellow like me crying, well I could not imagine it myself until it happened.'

For Garrett, a man who took pride in his physical ability, who had stoked in the 'Subterranean Theatre' of the *Mauretania*, the 'huge Scouse boat' that retained the *Blue Riband* as the fastest ship to cross the Atlantic Ocean for twenty years, his breakdown must have been a terrible experience. Far greater then was the stigma, far less the understanding and far fewer the services to support people suffering mental health issues. Garrett's short story, 'The Pianist', based on true events related in *Ten Years On The Parish*, indicates just how much he was aware of this.

Lehmann's shock in receiving this letter was understandable, and he took some time to reply. But although he implored Garrett not to 'hesitate to ask' if he needed more money, he opened the letter with the words 'I felt there was really nothing more for us to say, as you had used the £10 in getting hold of the cottage as I hoped'. All he could offer in response to Garrett's candid admission of his breakdown was to say, 'As I can't write myself if there is a radio two rooms off, I think I can imagine what conditions ten times worse mean as obstacles'. In this reply the distance between Lehmann's world and Garrett's was revealed to be as far apart as perhaps they ever were.

It was almost a year later until, after two further letters from Lehmann begging Garrett for news about the book, although not about his health, Garrett replied, revealing the full extent of his breakdown:

> The strain was too much for me. I could feel my mind going. When a man tightens his fingers around his baby's throat, he has reached a pretty dangerous condition. Everything snapped. I broke down and landed myself in hospital. Oh yes, I was knocked out alright, and feelings towards Lawrence and Wishart who had driven me into that position were not too pleasant. They had killed the chance I had of getting out of the hole I was in. I became a wreck.[12]

Garrett then revealed that two major American publishers, Simon and Schuster of New York (in the Garrett Archive there are two envelopes, one addressed to George Garrett and one to George Anders, dated 1938) and Secker and Warburg, were both looking to publish his work. According to Garrett 'Simon and Schuster wanted a sea novel'. Tragically, at the very moment when the major publishers were knocking and he was on the verge of potentially life-changing opportunities, Garrett, 'half-lunatic', 'could not sit down to fill a post card'.

And then silence. Until almost exactly two years later, when Lehmann wrote again, his sympathy for Garrett's plight and his inability to be able to respond in any meaningful way no doubt still playing on his mind. 'I have always felt that the fees which contributors to *New Writing* used to get in the old days were far too small', wrote Lehmann, and 'had hoped that one day I should be able to pay them some more'. He offered three guineas to Garrett for him to be able to publish *The First Hunger March* in a new series publishing 'select volumes from the past' under the imprint of *Penguin New Writing*.

However, perhaps reflecting the distance that had grown between them, the tone of Lehmann's letter had changed. The familiar 'Dear Garrett' was replaced by the more formal, Mr. George Garrett. This was the last of their correspondence.

In *The Whispering Gallery*, the first volume of his memoirs written in 1955, Lehmann recalled the bitter 'disappointment when the writer one was trying to keep going had to throw his hand in' and 'sometimes, totally defeated and discouraged, he vanished altogether from my ken'. He went on to single out Garrett for praise, and made a remarkable plea for 'him to tell me what happened to him', and wrote what appeared to be his last word on Garrett and a relationship that clearly meant a lot to him:

> If George Garrett, Liverpool seamen and heroic battler against impossible odds, should by any chance read these words, I should like him to know how much I have always regretted that he found it impossible to go with what he had so vigorously begun.[13]

But Garrett did 'go on'. He never completed *Ten Years On The Parish* but he did continue to write and was active in Merseyside Left Theatre, late to become Unity Theatre, set up by Jerry Dawson to support the struggle of the Spanish working class during the Spanish Civil War. Here Garrett found a way to again combine grassroots activity with his love of drama and theatre. He took on leading parts, co-authored a series of plays and was active up until the mid-1950s in the Unity Theatre and until the early 1960s in the worker's movement generally.

These letters paint a complex picture of a working class writer simultaneously drowning amidst the poverty of his conditions and struggling to keep his head above water to maintain and be faithful to his creative urges, instincts and talents. In these circumstances it is surprising, as noted by Alan O'Toole, 'not that George wrote so little' but in the circumstances of his life, 'that he wrote so much'.[14]

Notes

1 George Garrett, *Ten Years On The Parish*, original manuscript.

2 John Lehmann, *The Whispering Gallery* (London: Longman, Greens and Co., 1955), p. 3.

3 John Lucas, *The Radical Twenties: Writing, Politics, and Culture* (New Brunswick, NJ: Rutgers University Press, 1999), p. 217.

4 Lehmann, *The Whispering Gallery*, p. 120.

5 Ibid., p. 132.

6 Ibid., p. 232.

7 Ibid., p. 257.

8 Andy Croft, *Red Letter Days: British Fiction in the 1930s* (London: Lawrence & Wishart Limited, 1990), p. 178.

9 In *Red Letter Days: British Fiction in the 1930s*, Andy Croft refers to Jack Hilton refusing to 'allow his work to appear in *New Writing* since he objected to changes suggested by John Lehmann'. Ibid., p. 253.

10 Alan O'Toole, 'George Garrett: Seaman, Syndicalist and Writer', unpublished monograph, p. 19. Available in the George Garrett Archive, Central Records Office, Liverpool.

11 George Garrett, Letter to John Lehmann, 10 February 1937.

12 George Garrett, Letter to John Lehmann, 12 July 1938.

13 Lehmann, *The Whispering Gallery*, p. 259.

14 Alan O'Toole, 'George Garrett: Seaman, Syndicalist and Writer', unpublished monograph, p. 19. Available in the George Garrett Archive, Central Records Office, Liverpool.

Letters between
George Garrett and John Lehmann

14.12.35.

Dear Mr. Garrett,

I'm sending you, at Tom Wintringham's suggestion, a copy of
the 'manifesto' for a new periodical, in which I think you might
be interested. Tom mentioned that you had one or two stories
(particularly one which he had seen) which would be well worth our
consideration. If you therefore care to send these stories (to the above
address), we would be very glad to have a look at them.

The sooner you answer the more grateful I shall be.

Yours sincerely,

John Lehmann.

52a St James St
Liverpool. 1.

17.12.35

Dear Lehman

The story or stories referred to by Wintringham are still in his possession – if not, then Montagu Slater has them. Anyway, I am writing by this post to ask Slater to forward them to you. If you should see him in the meantime, worry him for them. You might get quicker results being near at hand than I seem to get at such a long distance. I've even threatened him.

Thanks for the offer of consideration. Whether the stories are acceptable to you or not I will welcome a peep at The Bridge. Success to your effort.

Yours sincerely

George Garrett.

(Answered. JL. 23.12.35.)

Dear Garrett,

Your stories have been rescued, and I have now read them. I think
The Ghost, the long one, is easily the best, and I should very much
like to publish it. Unfortunately, owing to its length and lateness in
emerging, it can't go into Number 1, but might well do for No. 2.

May I make a suggestion? First of all, that if possible you cut it a
little. Secondly, that you think over altering the end? The descriptions
of life on the boat, the sea and the rescues seemed to be admirable,
almost epic, but the end unworthy of them, almost irrelevant. It's
difficult to be very interested in the boxer after all the action has
passed him over, and anyway why should he choose to hang about in
a sheet? The triumph of the sailor over him seems to have very little
to do with the essence of the story, to make smaller something that is
very finely told and human. I may be quite wrong, but I'd like you to
think it over a bit, and if you see your way to doing a little alteration,
let me know <u>as soon as possible</u>, and I will send the story back to
you.

Many thanks.

Your sincerely

John Lehmann

George Garrett Esq.,
52a St. James Street, Liverpool 1.

52a St James St
Liverpool. 1

16/1/36

Dear Lehman

Thanks for your trouble and interest. Suggested alteration of The
Ghost places me in a quandary. Domestic conditions make it almost
impossible for the writing of a postcard. Anyway, I do agree that
The Ghost can be improved. But it will be a hell of a job cutting the
boxer out and altering the end. Mind you I am willing. Perhaps you
might run over the story again, and then if you still think alteration
is necessary, send the M.S.S. back, maybe with some suggestions. I
understand from Slater that the other stories are in your hands. If
they are of use to you, will you return them to me. You will have to
pay the postage – but it won't become a habit.

Sincerely yours

George Garrett

P.S. 'The Ghost' is not exaggerated. That 148 degrees is the stoke hold
might sound a bit high. I have worked in higher.

GG.

(Between you and me, what do you think of 'Shot After Dawn')

52a St James St
Liverpool. 1
30 May 1936

Dear Lehmann

I see that 'New Writing' is reviewed in the June 'left Review'. This means I can now write to you and expect an answer.

What do you intend to do about 'The Ghost' which you promised to publish in No 2.

The sooner you return the M.S.S. the sooner I can make the alterations which to meet your wishes would also improve the story. So will you say when?

I have just finished something that may interest 'New Writing'. It is called 'That Four-Flusher Prospero.' It is an original analysis of 'The Tempest'. I mean to say that I have not gone elsewhere to find material against Prospero. I understand that Renan once wrote on the same theme, but I have not read his opinion and don't know what he had to say. It was only on reading a recent book on SHAKESPEARE that I had to get down something that will I hope explode all those conceptions of the 'gentle Prospero'. The article is too long for the 'Left Review' otherwise I would have sent it to Rickwood.

Anyway, will you drop me a line at your earliest and let me know whether I should send it on. And most particularly, don't forget to answer my query about 'The Ghost'. I can shorten it by almost 1500 words.

Fraternally Yours

George Garrett

Fieldhead, Bourne End.

1.6.36.

George Garrett.

Dear Garrett,
Sorry to have kept you waiting so long. I hadn't forgotten, and wasn't just being lazy, but wanted to wait until I was in England again before writing. I only got back two days ago.

Now about THE GHOST. As you know, I am keen to publish it, but I never actually promised No.2. I can, however, now definitely promise No.2 or 3, – if you will accept some cuts I propose. You'll dislike me for being so high-handed, but I really believe the story will benefit by them. You asked me to indicate what I wanted: I propose therefore, (as I think my letter of May 30th.foreshadowed,) to cut out simply everything to do with the boxer, reducing the story from 12,000 to 9,500 words, a length which seems to me to suit it better. And the boxer, I think, really disturbs the essence of the story, which is very fine. If you can stomach such vandalism, please send the story back to me at once, and I'm 90% certain I can get it into No.2. I've indicated in pencil what I want out. I'm quite prepared to add a note at the end to say it's been shortened. You may want to smooth over the joins a bit now, – but please do it as soon as possible, and if you're keeping the M.S a little longer, please write to me in the meantime. The title will also have to be altered, – something like THE SICK MAN now, perhaps?

That notice in LEFT REVIEW which you saw seemed to me about as measly as one could hope for, and as misunderstanding. The notices in general have been remarkably good. Surprisingly enough even the TIMES LIT. SUPP. gave it a first-class notice, and saw its point (and its unity) as literature and left literature too. So I think there's no doubt NEW WRITING will carry on.

THAT FOUR-FLUSHER PROSPERO would interest me enormously personally, but I'm afraid it's barred for NEW WRITING, as it's criticism. Why not INTERNATIONAL LITERATURE? If you want me to read it, and send it on, if it seems suitable, to Dinamov myself, send it along sometime.

Yours fraternally

John Lehmann

52a St James St
Liverpool 1
4 June 1936

Dear Lehmann

I hope the story meets your approval. Before your letter reached me I had decided to pencil out parts you left untouched. I have re-written other parts. Let me know if this is to the good.

Now, the compromise. There is just one part you had struck out that I particularly want leaving in. It is the first paragraph on <u>page</u> 3. The forecastles of British ships, are, as perhaps you know, the worst afloat. The experience of seamen is confirmed by published reports of the medical Officers of Health belonging to Bristol, Liverpool, Manchester, and other ports.

No provision is made for a sick man. He's not supposed to fall sick. He does not like to appear sick. That paragraph is an explanation. Duffy's comment at the funeral service justifies it. It reasons itself out this way: "He's dead. He must have <u>been</u> sick." But the man must die first. That's the only way of proving he was sick.

The story is not exaggerated. The temperature in the stokehold – , well I've sweated in worse than that.
Believe me.

Sincerely Yours.

George Garrett.

Fieldhead
Burne End, Bucks.

5.6.36.

George Garrett, Liverpool.

Dear Garrett,
Many thanks for the returned Ms. Fishmeal. It's very much improved, and I shall put it into No.2 unless anything unforeseen occurs. I can certainly give you thee guineas for it; whether more depends on how the allotment of what Lane provides for each number turns out when everything has come in.

I didn't cut that passage about there being no room because I disbelieved it, but as part of the surgical operation of eliminating the boxer. I'm very glad you've got it back in again.

I'd like a few autobiographical notes to be used, as in No.1, at the beginning of the book. Please send them as soon as you can.

Yours sincerely

John Lehmann

52a St James St
Liverpool 1
7 June 1936

Dear Lehmann

Glad the M.S.S reached you and you like it. I don't know what exactly
you mean by autobiographical notes. I am not particularly keen about
splashing myself all over the page. It isn't a question of shame or
pride. I only agreed for my name to be printed in the "Left Review"
because Slater pointed out it was the only way to justify myself for
the noise I had kicked off at the conference. The Left Review just
described me as "a seaman from the North of England."

Whether that is enough for your purpose is hard for me to say.
Quite frankly, I know less about literature than I do about shovelling
coal. They don't allow me to do that now. Unemployment is a bar to
me obtaining a council house on the outskirts where I might have
a better chance of doing some writing. Under slum conditions it is
absolute murder. I just mention this in confidence so that you will
appreciate the handicap, one only of many. I would suggest then that
you let me see your "biographical note" before publication.

All the Best
Sincerely yours
George Garrett

Dear Lehmann

The M.S.S. arrived an hour ago. I accept the cuts. In some respects
I was ahead of you; in others, we can perhaps compromise. But
whatever happens, the story is now much better. So forget about me
disliking you. Instead, I say "Thanks". I was thinking of FISHMEAL
as the new title. Let me know how it appeals to you. I will return the
script within 2 days. I hope this will be suitable for you.

Re "THAT FOUR-FLUSHER PROSPERO". I will get someone to
type it first. I would certainly like it to go into INTERNTAIONAL
LITERATURE, that is, if they would be willing to publish. Anyway,
I will put it on to you first for your opinion. Many thanks for your
kindly interest.

Sincerely Yours

George Garrett

Fieldhead, Bourne, Bucks.

26.6.36

George Garrett Esq.,

Dear Garrett

A distressing thing has occurred. James Hanley, who has for some time promised to send a contribution for NEW WRITING, and whom we definitely want for No.2, has sent a story: it is excellent, but unfortunately it is about a stoker. Now I fear that it is impossible to put two stories, rather of the same length, and treating of the same subject, in No.2. And I must therefore ask you not to be enraged if I put you off to No.3. (This is a promise, No.3.) I feel sure your story will come off better that way. But I'm really sorry; if Hanley had written about anything else I would have kept you in. Meanwhile I am sending you a fee as advance on account of eventual royalties for your story, – £3.3.0.

'Seaman from the North of England' will do, if you won't give me more. I only want three or four lines, as you'll see from No.1. For instance, what age are you ? How did you start life ? (Worse than the means test, isn't it ?)

Yours very sincerely

John F. Lehmann

Dear Lehmann

Sorry for the delay in sending on receipt. Likewise, a bit disappointed over being put back to No.3. I suppose it can't be helped.

I would like to dash off some good stuff for you, but at the moment – no chance.

Regarding description of me. Best leave it as "Seaman from the North of England".

For your private information, the enclosed receipt is out of the book used on the first unemployed march of 1922. I am still young enough to hope for that spirit to re-assert itself. Was one of the pocket commissars at the time with Wally Hannington. If I ever wrote the story of that march (I'd like to), you'd piss your sides laughing.

Then the atmosphere was hectic: the marchers weren't windy; the government were. The press referred to us as the "Red Army". The Red Army to us was an ideal force that lived on at least four meals per day. So did we. Oh for the good old days.

Sincerely yours

George Garrett

52a St James St
Liverpool. 1
3 July 1936

Dear Lehmann

Enclosed find article "That Four-Flusher Prospero". I had to wait until I could pay for it to be typed. You will see it is too long for the "Left Review".

Maybe it is suitable for INTERNATIONAL Literature. You promised to send it to DINAMOV. Perhaps you can suggest an alternative. Anyway whatever you do, I will welcome your opinion on its content matter. Thanks for your kindly interest.

Sincerely Yours

George Garrett.

Fieldhead, Bourne End, Bucks.

4.7.36.

George Garrett
52a St James Street, Liverpool 1.

Dear Garrett,
I expect you'll think I'm crazy, but this is to tell you that FISHMEAL
is going to be in No. 2 after all. There was a bad last minute hitch
over Hanley, and we've had to cut his story out. You'll get proofs in
due course.

Any thanks for the MS. of THAT FOUR-FLUSHER PROSPERO. I'll
read it as soon as I can, then advise you.

Well, why not write the story of that march? Can you make it
between 3000 and 6000? Or two, of about 4,500? Let me know. This
is <u>not</u> a commission (I'm afraid I have to say that now, owing to a
recent misunderstanding with an author,) but an urgent instigation
if you like. Make it racy – but an eye on the libel, obscenity, sedition
and other mumbo-jumbo laws.

Your sincerely,

John Lehmann

52a St James St
Liverpool. 1.
24 July 1936

Dear Lehmann

This script has been fairly well corrected by yourself. I have got down
to The First Hunger March for you. I think it will be best to have it in
two parts of 4500 words each.

When you can will you let me know about "THAT FOUR-FLUSHER
PROSPERO"

And Obliged

Yours Truly

George Garrett.

P.S. I don't know whether you intend to change MORNING to
small type in the first sentence. As it is in capitals, it arrests you
immediately. If it makes no difference to you I prefer to have it stay
that way.

GG

VIENNA III
Invalidenstrasse 5/10

3.8.36.

George Garrett
52a St James Street, Liverpool 1.

Dear Garrett,
It is very interesting to hear you are at work on THE FIRST
HUNGER MARCH. I can never give promises about publishing, but I
can assure you I shall read it with the greatest pleasure and attention.

I have now heard from International Literature, They thank us for
sending THAT FOUR-FLUSHER PROSPERO, but say they don't feel
it's quite what they're looking for. I'm sorry. I'm keeping the MS., in
case you would like me eventually to try it somewhere else. Please let
me know.

Before sending your proofs back for page-proofs I took the liberty
of making one or two alterations with the aim of simplifying your
English in a few cases where it seemed to me a little involved, or
cliché, or repetitive. I hope you won't mind. I now send you another
copy with these corrections incorporated. Please let me have it
back, and at the same time let me know whether you find any of the
corrections intolerable; they can always be corrected in page-proof.

Yours ever

John Lehmann

52a St James St
Liverpool 1
England
7 August 1936

Dear Lehmann

Thanks for your note on THAT FOUR-FLUSHER PROSPERO. If you can find a place for it, I will be glad. I was expecting you to pass an opinion on it –, <u>anyway</u>, I can wait.

Re FISHMEAL. Some of your alterations are acceptable, but not all. I have placed a pencil X against those I prefer to be read as suggested below.

Page 7 4. Strike out "vaguely". "To grope on the floor etc" reads all right.

7 4. As insertion: Rivulets of perspiration ran down their faces etc

<u>75.</u> Rivulet does not read or sound right here. <u>Stream</u> is the better word. The only alternative I can think of is "quantity", but that sounds a bit vague. "Stream" is not an exaggeration; though to anyone unaware of stokehole conditions it may sound so. In the tropics, particularly, I have known men not to wear laces so that as fast as their boots become full of sweat they would kick them off and empty them immediately. Rivulet would hardly describe the amount they empty out. <u>Stream</u> is best.

78. I think "part huddled" should remain. In a crowded boat, men bend over and inward, except the oarsmen whose bodies are in constant motion. If Maxwell lay huddled in the bottom of the boat, the other men would easily recognise that something unusual had happened. But being slumped forward against a seat or another man's back would not arouse suspicion under such circumstances. I hope this is clear. Read first sentence, page 79.

All the Best

George Garrett.

52a St James Street
Liverpool
22 Sept 1936

Dear Lehmann

Just a feeler to find whether you are at home, so that I may send on the FIRST HUNGER MARCH for a reading. Will you let me know, when? Also, if anything has happened to that Prospero article of mine you promised to try and place. I hope you are well.

Sincerely Yours

George Garrett.

52a St James St
Liverpool 1.
3 October 1936

Dear L

I don't know whether the enclosed can really be called a story. It is, as the title suggest, an attempt to recapture the spirit of the First Hunger March.

As you advised, no names are mentioned. Whether the result is in keeping with your requirements is up to you to say. Anyhow, I hope you find it interesting as a piece of working-class history.

Sincerely Yours

George Garrett.

P.S The bully-beef "funeral" got a short notice in "Reynold's". The cutting is somewhere in the house. But where, is a problem. GG.

64a Dingle Lane

Liverpool. 8.

23 November 1936

Dear Lehmann

This seems a belated acknowledgement of your services on my behalf. I hope its value is not lost on that account. I have been in a hell of a soup lately and consequently have lots of things still undone. "Life and Letters" sent a cheque for £5. <u>My thanks to you</u>. John Lane sent me three guineas in a settlement of 'FISHMEAL'. I have not yet posted receipt but will do so before the end of the week.

I am enclosing cutting of "corned beef funeral" which I found last night. I don't know who was responsible for this report as printed. If I remember rightly it is taken from Reynold's. You may find it of interest. Wasn't it peculiar that the very week I sent you the script of "FIRST UNEMPLOYED MARCH" the national newspapers should ballyhoo the Jarrow march (sic). It read more like a conducted tour than a march. In its own way it has a value so why worry.

Sincerely Yours.

George Garrett.

P.S. Note change of address.

Vienna.) as from
Fieldhead, Bourne End, Bucks.

3.12.36.

George Garrett
52a St James Street, Liverpool 1.

Dear Garrett,
Sorry for the long delay, – but I was travelling most of the time.

I like your HUNGER MARCH I saw at first certain difficulties in accepting it for NEW WRITING, chiefly that it was too like an essay. But I now think that can be obviated by one cut of nearly two pages, from the first line 'Weeks of preparatory work...' to the paragraph on page 2 ending '...bed and breakfast.

If you can consent to this cut being made, I would be very glad to publish it, in No.3 or 4, – always provided that a way is found out of the difficulties created by lane's bankruptcy.

Yours ever

John Lehmann

64a Dingle Lane
Liverpool. 8.
15 December 1936

Dear Lehmann

I trust to your judgement for the HUNGER MARCH effort. So it is
not likely to lose force by delaying publication too long. I may want
to work it in with something bigger later on. Must I have permission
for this? Will you let me know.

There is something more pressing that perhaps you would look
into for me. Lane's sent me a cheque for £3-3-0 in settlement for
"FISHMEAL". As I have no banking account, a friend of mine cashed
the cheque to oblige me. It has been returned to him marked "Refer
to drawer. Receiver appointed". This business has placed me in a
rotten predicament. I owe this chap £3-3-0 and see no possibility
of paying it unless Lane's send me word of some description. I have
written them but so far had no reply. Perhaps you may be able to
advise me what to do in a case of this kind.
Thanks for your trouble

Sincerely Yours

George Garrett.

P.S.

P.S. Just received letter from the receiver for John Lane. I have
been listed with unsecured creditors. Will let you know of further
developments.

Fieldhead, Bourne End, Bucks.

16.12.36.

George Garrett, 64a Dingle Lane,
Liverpool 8.

Dear Garrett,

I'm most terribly sorry to hear about the Lane cheque. I can only
assume that your friend delayed some time before paying, as the rest
of the cheques, including my own, seem to have got through just in
time.

I'm sending you a cheque now for £3.3.0. Pay it to your friend, and
let me have it back when (if ever) you get your money from Lane's
receivers.

I'm so glad about LIFE AND LETTERS. I found the correspondence
waiting for me here when I got back a couple of days ago.

I'm glad you'll let me make that cut in the HUNGER MARCH. I
think I can get it into No. 3. But first of all I've got to find a new
publisher anyway.

Yours ever

John Lehmann

Fieldhead, Bourne End.

23.1.37.

George Garrett
64a Dingle Lane, Liverpool 8.

Dear Garrett,

Many thanks for your last letter.

I'm not a publisher, you know; only a badly paid Editor. At least I was, but I think Lawrence and Wishart, who are taking N.W. over, are going to give us a better deal.

They are, by the way, very interested in the book you mention. They've asked me to deal with you about it. Is it a sort of biography? Or a novel? Or are you writing two books – I feel you could write a first class book about your experience as an unemployed, but also a very fine novel about your sea experiences. Please let me have another letter, with more details when you can, – when you've thought it over.

I'm sure Wishart, who want a bigger fiction list of the right sort would give you a decent contract; and even a lump sum advance once you've defined the project and could show some part of it to us.

All the best.

John Lehmann.

Dear Lehmann

Sorry about not replying earlier had no opportunity. Though I
appreciate your offer I in such a jam I cannot take advantage of it.
I have started under a lot of outside pressure to write a book on
"Unemployment" (I mean the flesh and blood experiences). It is a
terribly hard job placed as I am. I have the material, also a little
capacity, but rotten facilities. A chap offered me the use of a cottage
out of town; I could not accept because the cruel PA.C. have me
by the balls. If I move, they drop me for desertion. From the stand
point of a job here, the bar is definitely against me.

Yet I am keen on this "Unemployment" book, not as my own
particular bellyache but to give the average person a "feeling" idea
of what it means. It seems so difficult to get it across. I had an
experience a few weeks ago with the B.B.C. I got an audition, passed
the test, then said I would speak on "unemployment" from the
standpoint of the man in the queue. Nothing doing! The Ministry
of labour would object. I could speak on say, drama, or became an
interested listening – correspondent – but no unemployment – at
least, not from a man in the queue.

That's why a book I thought was the only other way left of
getting under their skins. But my domestic circumstances are really
too hard. First, I live in a tenement which is about as away (?) by
Euston Station. Secondly I have a wife and five boys (including
a baby) now I must terrify them into silence or 'wait' until they
go to bed. This is generally near midnight. By that time I am too
physically exhausted to do much writing. There is the problem too
of extra light and coal – so you can imagine my handicap. During
the day most of my time is used by others in distress who forget or
don't seem to understand I have my own load of troubles. So you
will see that my only chance of doing anything would be to get out
of town altogether. And as conditions are at present I have as many

lashes to (?) me as a ship in dry dock. All this is to show you how difficult it is for me to send you anything at the moment. I wish I could.

Sincerely Yours

George Garrett

P.S. None of this is for inclusion in New Writing. It is just a confidential explanation of the why's.

Fieldhead, Bourne End, Bucks.

28.2.37

George Garrett,
64a Dingle Lane,
Liverpool 8.

Dear Garrett,
Thanks for your letter of the tenth. I didn't answer it before because I was abroad.

I fully appreciate the bloody nature of the fix you find yourself in: but I don't intend to take no for an answer, because I believe in the future of your writing.

And I think you've got a social duty to do something about it too.

So please let me know as soon as you can how I can help, practically. You know best what plans are feasible, so I won't make any proposals myself. NEW WRITING is perfectly prepared to spend money on this.

An if you want to talk it over first N.W. will pay your fare to London and back any tie in the next fortnight or three weeks.

Yours Ever

John Lehmann

64a Dingle Lane
Liverpool. 8
9 March 1937

Dear Lehmann

Sorry again for the delay, but was unable to say anything definite. I had intended to write to you and arrange a meeting in London for next Friday. It would happen that today at the parish I received a form to hand to the Labour Exchange on Friday. So this is how I am fixed this week. Monday – parish. Wednesday – Parish. Thursday – Labour Exchange. Friday – Labour Exchange. In the days between, wait for the parish visitors. My missus won't open the door for them, which means me being on hand. I have no trouble with them, being too old a customer. But my missus is sick, and tired, and does not like the neighbours to know we are on the "parish". That's really rot?, because the dogs in the street know it. Anyway, that is the title of a book I had started "Ten years on the Parish". I got down twenty-thousand words – but it is murder under these circumstances. It was my intention to send it to Gollanz, but I don't see how I can do it for the closing date of the "Left Book" competition.

I see by to-day's news-chronicle that Orwell's "Road to Wigan pier" is out. Actually there is a Wigan Pier. I left Orwell (Eric Blair, now in Spain) there, after showing him around Liverpool. So you can understand that I do recognise my social duties. To-day's blurb says that "The Road to Wigan Pier" is the most vivid description of the means test yet written. But, this is what I meant by shocking some of the know alls and strutting politicians – THE MEN ON THE PARISH HAVE NEVER BEEN OFF THE MEANS TEST. I am not saying it was my intention to screech that down a reader's ear, but I was bent on whispering it if you like, just to let him know what these things are – and how.

I had hoped to explain verbally to you this weekend, but for receiving that note today. Anyway, I may have the opportunity of seeing you (perhaps you can make a suggestion) when I would be able to talk the matter over easier than I am trying to write it. I have broken my spectacles. This will account for my zigzagging all over the page and why I am ending this note here.

Sincerely Yours

George Garrett.

12 March 1937.

Telegram appears to be to Lehmann from Garrett.

Yes Friday morning

Garrett

Note on it written by Lehmann (signed JL): £2. 14 3 37

(The following letter suggests the copy of the telegram may have been in the letter to Garrett)

64a Dingle Lane
Liverpool. 8
15 March 1937

Dear Lehmann

Your letter arrived with enclosure. I am not quite clear where I have to go, whether to Parton Street, or, the place where the meeting is being held. Perhaps you can drop me a line.

It was my intention to stay down in "The Smoke" for the week-end, and I am trying to figure where I can park my body. There are a number of people I could drop in on – the difficulty is, the lack of time to give warning. I would like to make a few calls. Perhaps by Friday I will have a better idea of what to do. The first thing to settle is, where am I to meet you, and when; drop me a line by return.

Yours

George Garrett.

P.S. That "Road to Wigan Pier" is a terrible hotch-potch [*sic*]. From beginning to end it is one long sneer; this includes the first part. The only decent material is the visit to the mine, and the photographs. I wish I had been given the job of reviewing it. A book of that type can do a lot of damage. That it should appear as a "Left Book" gives it an added danger.

GG

64a Dingle lane
Liverpool. 8
23 March 1937

Dear Lehmann

Circumstances kept me in London until Monday night. If I'd know this was likely to happen we might have managed another talk. Anyway, I had a few minutes to spare, and called in on Richard yesterday (Monday) afternoon. He said he had not seen Parton (?) or Wishart and that only Garmen was there in the office. This was at three in the afternoon which Slater told me was the most suitable time to call. Having little time to share I could not wait around. Richard suggested I write and let him know what I intended to do. He was not offering much in the sense that you are. Maybe that is because he is outwardly phlegmatic. It so happened that later in the afternoon I made a few contacts that suggested I forget about Wishart. But that seemed so terribly unfair to you. Your P.C mentioning Knopf is another indication of your kindness. I would like us to agree to something as soon as possible. Again, let me list one of the difficulties. It is utterly impossible for me to write at home. I happen to have five boys. We are all crowded in on each other. I cannot terrorise the kids into going to bed early or leave them too afraid to open their mouths in ordinary conversation, nor can I chase them out into the streets. This life is hard enough. As I have to try and write at the same table that they eat and play around, you can imagine how difficult it is for all of us. Quite definitely I would have to leave home and rent a room. I would then have a sense of freedom that would be almost impossible in the homes of my friends. If I went to their houses to write – it would be as an exhibit. I would have to tell them what I was doing and they would want to tell others, so my position then would be worse than what it is now. This secrecy would not be necessary if I was clear of the P.A.C. I am to be transferred to the U.A.B. Enclosed is a note that arrived from them after I had left for London. I don't know yet what I will do about this. It will mean another fight that is bound to have them watching me more than they do at present. And yet, the discussed offer of £2 per week will not be sufficient for me to get clear of them. If I were a single man none of these problems would arise. As it is, I cannot accept a peculiar kind of job where in working my family's condition will be worse than if I was not working. Out of the £2, I would need at least 10/- per week for a room, a few bob for food, coal and light. Then I would like to put something aside to meet an emergency like typing and pretages(?). There is also the question of Harrison's £8. So you reckon there will be very little to spare out of £2 per week, and I would still have to risk drawing the other. I do wish it had been possible to go right ahead with the script without all this "trading". I still feel we have a slight advantage in having a script under way. I don't want to lose that. I am quite sure you don't. Unless Wishart's let me know quickly what they intend to do, I will take advantage of the other suggestions that were made to me on Monday afternoon. There is still a sense in which I think I could manage along on the £50 (plus the other). I will do the whole script in six months or less. I do want to get down to it NOW. Suppose then they let me have £16 immediately (£8 to settle with Harrison), and pay me in further instalments of £8 monthly until the £50 is exhausted. Would that be reasonable? If any other outgoings arose I could let you know. Let's hope it doesn't. Perhaps you will acquaint Richard as soon as possible. I will write him later.

All the Best
George Garrett.

P.S. Send cheque. Don't send registered letter and in future no P.C. Will you talk this matter over with Wishart. It saves me sending another long letter.

31.3.37

George Garrett
64a Dingle Lane, Liverpool 8.

Dear Garrett,
I thought I told you I had to come out here almost directly after our meeting, for my work? That anyway, added to Easter, is the reason why your letter is only getting an answer now. I'm sorry, but it couldn't be helped.

I was very glad to have your letter indeed, and fully appreciate all the points you make. The difficulty with Wishart is that decisions seem to need the approval of all the directors, and they manage all to get together about once in a blue moon – ! But they are fundamentally decent people, very sound too for the sort of stuff I'm after, and can be pushed: and in your case I intend to push them quite hard.

I am writing to Rickword (who is undoubtedly a person of ultra-reserved manner) by the same post as I send this, and hope very much he will get in touch with you straight away. I am transmitting to him the concrete proposition you make at the end of your letter, – it seems very sound to me. That is: £16 straight away, and further instalments of £8 monthly until the advance they are willing to make (minimum £50) is exhausted.

As soon as you tell me this is fixed up, and you're going to sign an agreement with Wishart, I'll write off to Knopf.

Looking forward enormously to seeing more of the book when I get back home.

Yours Ever

John Lehmann.

64a dingle lane
Liverpool
England
8 April 1937

Dear Lehmann

After a chance rereading of your letters, I find I am to reply to you.
On the first reading I thought you were to depend on Rickwood for
details of proposed book. We did come to an arrangement. I would
have preferred it to have been sufficient to allow me to leave home
and take a room somewhere. As it is I have to blackmail my wife
into taking the baby to the cinema or the park (D.V and the weather
willing and the state of her mind(?)). I must stay in the house to
meet the U.A.B officials. My wife is dead scared of them. So you
will appreciate that the domestic difficulties are still present, except
that now a better chance exists for a little extra food, coal and light.
Anyway, I must keep on pegging away. I have the advantage of
knowing you will be patient with me.

Rickwood suggests I collect my short stories into a volume.
Altogether, there so few. Fishmeal is the longest. Others are
published in the Adelphi. Middleton Murry want new one of them.
Perhaps I will have more to tell you about them next time I write.
Until then, Cheerio.

Yours sincerely

George Garrett

George Garrett, 64a Dingle Lane,
Liverpool.

Dear Garrett

Awfully glad to hear you fixed up finally about the book. This is a great relief and a pleasure to me.

I know you have the foulest difficulties to struggle against; but I feel just as sure you'll get it done, and make something else of it no one else could.

About the short stories: not a bad idea at all, but I think, purely as a matter of publishing tactics, the long book should come first. And then also you may have some newer stories to add. But I'll discuss this with E.R.

I look forward to seeing you again.

All the best –

John Lehmann

64a Dingle Lane
Liverpool. 8
27 April 1937

Dear Lehmann

I am not moving as quick as I would like to. This damned arrangement of having to wait until the kids or missus make themselves scarce seems harder now than it has been before. I struggle on, on account of you.

As you know, I am a 'Little Eric' over publication rights etc. You said you were writing to KNOPF, NW YORK. Will you let me know what happens as somebody else seems keen on doing this.

Yours Sincerely
George Garrett

3rd. July 1937.

George Garrett.
64a Dingle Lane,
Liverpool.

Dear Garrett,
I am very anxious to hear how you are getting on with your book.

Please let me have word as soon as you can.

I hope you have received your copy of No. 3. by now. How did you like it?

Yours Sincerely,

John Lehmann

Dear Lehmann

I am glad to hear from you. Frankly, I am very disappointed over
the book. I mean by that, that had the arrangement been nearer to
normal I would have been able to report more done that I can at the
moment.

I have completed 40,000 words. This is very disappointing to me.
I have tried every damn way to hurry the thing along. It does not
matter which, I am continually beset by difficulties. In case these
might sound like an excuse, I will give you some of the factual
conditions. I live as you know in a tenement. Although they are
cleaner and certain amenities like bath and hot & cold water, they
are another form of overcrowding. More people are squeezed into
a smaller floor space than they occupied in their old slum dwelling.
It was my hard luck to be placed in the noisiest part of the block.
I have heard music hall jokes about jerry-built houses, but when I
tell you that I can hear the people next-door and upstairs pissing, it
is no exaggeration. When I say noisiest, I mean it. Next door to me
are eight children, four of them are under five years of age. Above
there is nine children. Above there is also roller skates, marbles,
coal-breaking, firewood-chopping, and daily cobbling [*sic*]. You will
say that this will stop at night. Well the usual sleeping hours for
school-children in these parts is 10.30 to midnight. The worst of all
the nuisances is the piano. It is knocked about all day by the younger
children, then from midnight until 1.30, the older girls, three of
them, get in their finger practice.

Even if these outside difficulties were non-existent, my internal
arrangements are a hindrance. We have five kids, all boys. The whole
bunch of us are crowded in together. There is no separation. All that
these tenements are, is one room sub-divided, like a hen-coop. It is
impossible to have privacy or peace. I have tried sitting up until two
in the morning to work, but by then I am physically exhausted. And

handicapped as I am by the means test business, I cannot take a snooze during the day.

Although I fore-saw some trouble when I undertook to write this book, I never imagined they would pile up the way they have done. The less I get done, the more irritable I become in the house. Everyday there is constant unavoidable fighting. There is no one to blame.

A lot of this disagreeableness could have been avoided had Wishart's arrangements been a little different. I was practically condemned to write under conditions which were not helpful. The only way out was to leave home. But the arrangement did not allow of me doing that. I could not walk out and leave my wife financially worse of than she is under the means test. The least I needed was £3 a week; that is, £1 for myself, and £2 for her. I am not saying I could not have pressed for these terms, but I was so eager to do a good job that I thought the £50 spread out at £3 per week would not last me long enough to the job I wanted. So I remained on the Labour Exchange. Consequently, I have never been free – never felt free. And this book has become such a load on my mind that I cannot do anything else. I can't even read a book. My whole time is spent trying to catch a few minutes to write in.

And now, if you know anything more annoying than this let me know. Besides my own family, there are the canvassers, peddlars [*sic*], hawkers, rag and bone men, coal men, old gold buyers. The concentration of so many families in a small area is a godsend to them. They are banging at the door by the minutes.

The intimate callers must be admitted. I can't say "get out, I want to write" or "Stay away altogether". You must remember that the psychology of these people is entirely different to the psychology of your friends who appreciate there are times you should be let alone.

So that to tell people under my circumstances that I was writing or wanted to write would produce a crop of questions that would worsen matters. There would be a whole series of "What are you doing", "Why are you doing", "How are you doing", "What will you get", Etc, etc.

So as I say, just as I get my papers out to make a fresh start, a knock comes, and the papers have to be whipped out of sight, because there is no separation in these places.

Even in the old slum houses where I lived previously, I could stay upstairs and sometimes get a couple of consecutive hours. This is utterly impossible in a tenement.

This letter now is being written because the my kids are on holiday and the eldest has taken the baby out. Otherwise I would have had no chance to get this much down. I hope you will understand now why I am disappointed and feel unhappy about the whole business.

I have even tried a couple of rooms close at hand. 'I can't move on a account of The means Test Man', But there conditions were almost as bad as at home. There was continual interference and I had to give up. In the environment I live in, a fellow sitting down to write is considered as a freak. I suppose it works out all right if one is normally a private person, but I have lived a fairly active life, and people will not leave me alone. I cannot go into the library because of chaps who come to me as a father-confessor and general-life guide. It is an advantage at times to be known, but at the moment I am paying a heavy price for being too well known. Still, I'll persevere. The thing I will do for you is not the thing I would like to do. I don't offer these conditions as an excuse, but I do say, "here they are". And believe me they are damned awkward.

Yours Very Sincerely

George Garrett

Dear Lehmann

I felt sure I had already acknowledged your letter and cheque for
£3-3-0. Forgive me if this is not so. I have heard nothing further from
Lane's. When I do, I will write you. Regarding the signing away of
'future worth', I have not been asked to do so. But I have mentioned
THE FIRST HUNGER MARCH to a chap who is interested and he
said that if I wanted to include it in a book on Unemployed, it would
be wise to retain some right in it. Quite frankly, I don't the first thing
about this writing business. I understand there are plenty of rogues
in it. But there are also people who are capable of decent gestures –
yourself for one, and this chap I mention is another. If I can make
any headway on a book about unemployed you will hear about it. But
with all my inconveniences – ITS MURDER.

Yours Sincerely

George Garrett.

Fieldhead,
Bourne End.
Bucks.

July 16th 1937.

George Garrett
64a, Dingle Lane,
Liverpool. 8.

Dear Garrett,
Than you very much for your letter. I have read it and re-read it,
and feel very distressed about the whole thing. I can't imagine more
difficult conditions in which to produce decent work.
I am afraid I don't know my way about all the regulations which
hem you in, but I had hoped you had found some way out in your
negotiations with Wishart that would really mean you had a chance
to write properly. If that is not so, what is the thing that needs to
be done? If you would write and tell me, privately, as concretely as
possible I would see at once whether any additional help could be
given to you. I want to help, because I want that book to be finished,
but I don't know how to help. So please just write as soon as you can,
and make a suggestion. I would like to get your answer within the
next few days, as by the end of the month I may be wandering about
again.

Yours sincerely

I hope you saw that Wishart's have now made a useful arrangement
with the left Book Club about all their books. This may be developed
to give even greater facilities to NEW WRITING novels. I am
negotiating this at the moment.

64a Dingle Lane
Liverpool 8.
24 July 1937

Dear Lehmann

I would have written sooner, only there was nothing helpful I could say. What I need most is to get away from these conditions, and do the book as I feel it might be done. Living as I am, I have never had a chance to be book. The whole time has been one long period of intense irritation, constant interference, and daily fights. It cannot be otherwise. I am not saying anyone is to blame. In the old dive I lived in before, there was a chance of escaping upstairs for a couple of hours and getting something done. That is impossible here. I dare not go out to any of the libraries, the lads pester me with their troubles. They forget I have my own.

There is only one way out of this difficulty. I must get away from Liverpool. Tom Harrisson has written offering me a place outside Bolton, but he talks in terms of handling the script, not for the sake of financial gain. He is concerned about seeing the book in print as soon as possible. You are; I am. I have advised him to write to you.

Being so much behind has added a lot of burdens to those already wearing me down. I now face an extra one. Within a week I will be sent to some holiday relief work, and unless otherwise occupied, must accept. It will be put me at least three weeks further behind, if not six.

It is a miserable prospect, and I miserable enough as it is. It is damned dissatisfying that our arrangements have become balled up this way. I did try to point out to you and Rickword at the beginning how awkward conditions were. Now perhaps, you can see how awkward.

I want to get that book done, and well done. Harrisson's offer points the way out. But I don't wish to break with you. Can you understand my predicament. Neither you, or Harrisson, or myself, think primarily in terms of cash. But you say I must write this book; Harrisson says the same. And I WANT TO. Because of a lousy set of circumstances that have tied me up, the book is delayed, and none of us are satisfied. And worst of all, I am bearing the whole weight of the material, and so fed up I could tear to pieces what so far has been written. I would never attempt anything again under like conditions. And I would not think much of anyone who tried to force me into them.

Sincerely Yours

George Garrett.

Enclosure.

Fieldhead,
Bourne End.
Bucks.
26th, July 1937.

George Garrett,
64a Dingle Lane,
Liverpool 8.

Dear Garrett,

Thanks very much for your letter. I was beginning to fret, as I have to go away again in a very few days.

How difficult it all is, with all of us scattered in different places, and not quite understanding one another. Rickword isn't in England either, which complicates matters. However, I have some news for you, and I think I can help now that I have read your letter.

I am very glad to hear that Tom Harrisson is taking such an interest in the book. If he is not thinking of financial gain, nor am I, but I do definitely want the book to come out in the NEW WRITING LIBRARY which is now a fact. And that's my news: within the next eight months we shall be publishing the first three or four volumes, and I don't see why yours shouldn't be among them. You have in any case agreed by an exchange of letters to let Wishart have the book, but as it was I who encouraged you to tackle it properly, and got you down to London, and shoved them into making some arrangement with you, I want it not merely to appear under their imprint but also in this new Library.

Tom Harrisson's offer of a cottage is very generous, and I want you to be able to take advantage of it. I don't see how Harrisson can 'handle the script' as you have already agreed with Wishart to take the book, but perhaps I misunderstood your letter on that point. I want you to take advantage of the offer, or go somewhere else at any rate where you can write in peace for a few weeks. I gather from your previous letter that it is a question of raising the amount that Wishart send you by about £1 a week, and leaving you a pound or two in hand. I am therefore sending you a cheque at once for £10, and will fix it up with Wishart that your advance be raised to £60. I hope that will really do the trick now. I rang up Wishart this morning, and learned that you had already had £32. The money will continue to come as before, until the £50 is exhausted, but you will now also have this £10 to oil the wheels. I hope they will revolve with much greater rapidity. I send you a cheque, because I seem to remember you said you could deal with cheques. I also found out from Wishart that the exchange of letters had never been followed up by a proper contract. I told them to deal with this at once.

Please write me by return. And please <u>do</u> something at once about getting away.

All the best

John Lehmann.

Fieldhead,
Bourne End. Bucks.
28th July 1937.

George Garrett,
64a, Dingle Lane.
Liverpool 8.

Dear Garrett,

This is just to tell you that I have heard from Tom Harrisson, and I have also written to him fully explaining the position. I think he was rather confused about your exact relation to Lawrence and Wishart, and did not know you had agreed to give them the book by an exchange of letters. That the contract did not follow, is, of course a scandal of slackness or forgetfulness, – with which I can assure you I had nothing to do. I think they will be writing to you now.

I do hope the £10 will do the trick for you. But you must let me know if you are in further difficulties. I can't risk a great deal of money, but I will do what I can, and I know that you on your side will do what you can to get the book finished in good time. I think it would be a disaster if your book was not among the first to appear in the New Writing library. I don't get any extra money for this (on the contrary I risk more) as my new Writing fees, though they are not unreasonable, only manage at the moment just to cover my expenses.

Yours very sincerely

John Lehmann.

64a Dingle Lane
Liverpool. 8.
8 August 1937

Dear Lehmann

I could not write before as there was nothing definite for me to say. In fact, I did not know whether to return your cheque. My problem all along has been one of conditions. Yet Wishart's arrangements chained me to the very place I wanted to escape from before I could write. I stressed it at the beginning, and have repeated it ever since. It was not so much a question of me expecting a lot of money. I have already explained to you that I could not walk out of the house leaving my wife worse off than she was under the U.A.B.

That's why Harrisson's offer was so much better. It gave me the chance of going away. He understood my difficulty. Why Wishart's or yourself could not see it the same way mystifies me. Either I have failed to get it over, or, for some reason you suspect me of trying to cross you. Rickword said that Lewis Jones wrote "Cwymardy" while drawing the U.A.B. That may be so, I don't dispute it. But Lewis Jones nor nobody else ever tried to write under the conditions I am doing now. They are unique and abnormal, and I have failed to convince you of that, it is so futile me trying any further. Since just before your cheque came, I have written NOTHING. I kept waiting day by day for a whole fortnight for a chance to get something done. I hope you appreciate that I have to wait. There is no separate place for me. Seven of us are packed in together, carrying out every domestic function from six in the morning until midnight. The outside racket varies, the inside racket is continuous, but there is worse. I don't know how you would feel if you turned you back for a second, and found the baby had tore up a fortnight's work, and was scattering it around like confetti.

My wife is justified in defending the kids against my shouting. I am torn to shreds. For months I have been living in this atmosphere of daily warfare. And the relationship between myself and my kids has become so unnatural that it is doing me a lot of harm.

It reached its climax just two weeks ago when I broke down and cried for an hour. My brain snapped, and in a moment I was a physical wreck. I did not know whether I had had a paralyse stroke or not. If you would say you cannot imagine a fellow like me crying, well I could not imagine it myself until it happened.

Two people near at hand offered me the use of their sitting room. But in each instance I was exhibited to their friends like a new circus act. And this was by people who ought to know better.

There is some excuse for children. Our kids see are stuck, continually in the house. They know I sign on at the Labour Exchange. <u>Therefore I am not working</u>. If I sit down at the table to write, they can't understand that I am working. Working to them is going out daily, and coming home at the week-end with wages. So they play their games and squabble as all boys must do, while I am forced to become a physical brute or else a surly bastard who makes their life unbearable. And my missus is caught in between the whole gang of us.

I have tried all ways to escape from it, even to searching around for an office where I could stay late on in the evening, but without success. I could not go into lodgings; first, because I had not enough money, and secondly, because it would place the whole family relationship in a false light. Had I been living in an ordinary four-roomed house, most of the problems would not have arisen; or had I been a single man, able to choose lodgings, Wishart's £50 would have been ample. As I have stated before, it has not been a question of money so much, as it has been of awkward conditions. If someone down at your end could have offered me hospitality for a few months, I wouldn't have give a damn what old room they pushed me into so long as I had peace, and could leave my missus £2 a week. That's not a hell of a lot. It's just a bare minimum. But it would have eased my mind a great deal. Tom Harrisson could see this, and his offer to me was a way out.

Yet here I am caught between the pair of you, liking both of you, respecting both of you, but unable to meet the requirements of either. It's a hell of a position and one that gives more troubles on to me than I ought to have.

I did not know whether to return your cheque or not, because handicapped as I was, there was no way I could justify its use. It was in my possession for a week before I changed it. The I spotted an advert for an unfurnished cottage in North Wales, so I took a chance, prefer a quarter's rent on, and secured the tenancy. Very definitely I must leave home, and very definitely I can't mess about with the U.A.B. Wishart's arrangement worked out in a way that drawing the U.A.B. became more important than writing the book. It should never have been like this. I tried hard to prevent it but nobody would take any notice of me.

I have still to furnish the cottage, and am trying to get some stuff on hire-purchase, With Wishart's balance of £18 I reckon I can scrape on for about six weeks. I am not guaranteeing it complete in six weeks. I've got to pick myself together again first. But I am doing at last what ought to have been done at the commencement. All this friction and arguing could have been obviated by the use of a little imagination at your end. Wishart's supposed to have a wide knowledge of worker's conditions. "Ten years on the parish", suggested the worst possible kind. Yet instead of Wishart's helping me escape from them for a while so I could write the book, their cheapening arrangement condemned me to the opposite. As a consequence, nobody is satisfied. You probably have a distorted opinion of me, and my enthusiasm has become smothered in bitterness. But for the fact of being concerned over this book, and feeling under an obligation to you, Wishart's could go to buggery. It seems we are all caught a net, and it is disgusting that it should be like this. I could wish (?) it would have been otherwise.

Sincerely Yours

George Garrett.

Vienna) as from
Fieldhead, Bourne End, Bucks.

9.9.37.

George Garrett,
64a Dingle Lane, Liverpool 8.

Dear Garrett,

I haven't answered your letter before, because for one thing I felt there was really nothing more for us to say, as you had used the £10 in getting hold of the cottage as I hoped.

If you need any more money, please let me know. No, really, don't hesitate to ask. I needn't repeat again how anxious I am see to see the book finished, and worthily of you.

Both you and Harrisson seem to think I haven't a notion how hard it is for you to write under your Liverpool conditions. As I can't write myself if there's a radio two rooms off, I think I can imagine what conditions ten times worse mean as obstacles.
Let me know how things are faring.

Yours

John Lehmann

12.12.37.

George Garrett,
Dingle Lane, Liverpool.

Dear Garrett,
I have been away, and do not know at all how you are and how your book is faring. It is finished? I am also very anxious to see something of yours for NEW WRITING No.5, which I am now preparing. Do please let me know as soon as you can.

Yours Sincerely

John Lehmann

Fieldhead, Bourne End, Bucks.

27.6.38.

George Garrett,
64a Dingle Lane
Liverpool 8.

Dear George Garrett,
I am rather distressed not to have heard anything from you for such
a long time. It seems to me a very great pity that your name should
drop out of our writers' movement like this, particularly when I
know that you have a large proportion of that book already written
from which extracts might be made. Garmen tells me that he has
heard nothing from you at all. New Writing is now going over to the
Hogarth press but there will be no change at all in editorial policy. So
please let me hear from you as soon as possible, and send something
if you can.

Yours ever,

John Lehmann

45 Worsely Crescent
Liverpool 9
30 June 1938

Dear Lehmann
Could not reply to your letter any sooner. At the moment this can
only serve as an acknowledgment. Will do my best to write to you
over the weekend. Sorry it has to be like this, but it is unavoidable.

Yours Sincerely

George Garrett.

45 Worsely Crescent

Liverpool. 9

12 July 1938.

Dear Lehmann

You will have to forgive my delay in replying to you. I have been waiting all week for the chance and can only do it when and as best I can. You said in your letter: "I had dropped out of the writer's movement." I haven't dropped out. I've been <u>Knocked out. It's no use</u> me covering the old ground telling you the vile conditions under which I was trying to write. I sent a detailed letter to Garmen hoping that would be sufficiently convincing it itself. That letter contained only half the story. There was the other half I didn't think it was necessary to include as I considered there was enough imagination amongst a group professedly interested in workers' conditions to understand my handicap. I had to write in the same room where others had to eat and play.

Now Lehmann, in your own circle when you sit down to write it is understood immediately that you are working. People will be thoughtful enough to respect what you are trying to do, and if a knock comes at the door you haven't got to sweep your material up and hide it out of sight until the caller has gone. You will probably have a room of your own to write in, not a crowded place where each member of the family is treading on the other's heels.

I was not so lucky. There are seven of us; five growing boys. I could not sit down and write without barking at them; they could not talk, sing, whistle, or more without shattering me. There was a maddening domestic friction and quarrelling. The worst feature was that, when I sat down to write, I was not working. I was just sitting down. Can you appreciate the psychology of such an atmosphere! It was no use of blaming anybody, but this is the viewpoint. WORK is something you go out of the house to do and bring wages home for. It isn't anything that's done inside the house at all, particularly when it is something that causes discomfort to everybody around. If I had been coming home each evening covered in cow dung and bringing in as pay a handful of buttons, I would have been WORKING. Most of my time was spent trying to tell my own family, wife and children, that when I sat down to write I was doing hard work. They could not see that. All they could see was me sitting down demanding peace, while they were too terrified to breathe. There you have the situation. Outside and inside I was trapped. Harrisson could grasp it and offered me a release. If I had gone to his place, I would have been sending home weekly money. I would have been WORKING and could have written without interfering with anyone or being interfered with. But you and Lawrence and Wishart decreed otherwise. In a place where I was continually telling you it was impossible to write, you condemned me to stay to be a torture to others and myself. I persevered, and persevered, and persevered. Daytimes I cut out altogether. I usually had to wait until 2am in the morning for a chance to write. (Don't forget, there was 9 children living overhead, and 8 alongside) By the time 2 o'clock arrived I was physically exhausted. I could not sleep in the day on account of the U.A.B. and other callers. Rest and sleep of any kind passed out of my experience. The strain was too much for me. I could feel my mind going. When a man tightens his fingers around his baby's throat, he has reached a pretty dangerous condition.

Everything snapped. I broke down and landed myself in hospital. Oh yes, I was knocked out all right, and feelings towards Lawrence and Wishart who had driven me into that position (?) were not too pleasant. They had killed the chance I had of getting out of the hole I was in. I became a wreck.

Postgate asked me to do a fact. Simon and Schuster of New York wanted a sea novel. Secker and Warburg, and others were asking me to write; me, that had reached a plight where I could not sit down to fill a postcard.

Half-lunatic that I had become, a change of some sort was necessary. My only way of getting it was through an unemployment camp. After four weeks I was sent home to hospital for an operation. Two weeks of the four I was on my back – completely buggered. I am coming around a bit now, but don't know when I will be able to write. But I am not prepared to go through the terrifying experience again that I have just come out of. I could not do so. Not could anyone else. The first week out of hospital, I picked up a book called "Sentences".

Rickword's name attracted me. There was an essay in it by Garmen. The essay was written in 1928. Garmen writing since then should surely know the difference between feasible conditions and impossible ones. When his letter arrived a day or two later, I was too sick and disgusted to answer. But it set me thinking that most of the disagreeable things I have heard of L&W's are correct.

I am sorry if all this is a terrible let down for you. It has not been done wilfully. Perhaps later on, I can collect my scattered mind a bit to write a piece, but under the present conditions it is impossible. I dare not risk it, believe me.

Yours Sincerely

George Garrett.

The Hogarth Press
John Lehmann   Leonard Woolf
37, Mecklenburgh Square
London
W.C.1.
Telephone: Terminus 7545 Cables: Hogarth London.

4th, July 1940.

Mr. George Garrett.
64a Dingle Lane
Liverpool. 8.

Dear George Garrett,
I have always felt that the fees which contributors to New Writing
used to get in the old days were far too small, and hoped that
one day I should be able to pay them something more. The
chance comes now, as I have just concluded arrangements with
the Penguins for a series of selections from past volumes to be
published as The Penguin New Writing. In one of the first two
volumes, I want to include your The First Hunger March and
suggest £3 guineas, as an extra fee for those second serial rights.
I would be grateful if you could let me know as soon as possible
if that is all right.

Yours Sincerely,

John Lehmann.

Additional information

1926 general strike (3–13 May 1926). The 1926 general strike involved millions of workers and shook the foundations of British society, with many areas falling under control of workers and trades unionists. It was called off by the leadership of the Trades Union Council (TUC) after ten days, without any of the aims of the strike being achieved.

Adelphi (or *New Adelphi*). The *Adelphi* was an English literary journal founded by John Middleton Murry and published between 1923 and 1955. George Garrett's first published short story 'First-Born' appeared in the June 1934 issue alongside articles by the celebrated critic Edmund Wilson and a review by *Adelphi* Editor John Middleton Murry.

W.H. Auden (Wystan Hugh Auden, 1907–1973). Regarded as one of England's greatest poets and best known for 'The Age of Anxiety' which won him the Pulitzer Prize. Auden, similar to many of his generation, was radicalised by the Spanish Civil War, writing poems such as *Spain*, although he later moved away from his previous radical positions.

Louis Mbarick Fall, aka 'Battling Siki' (1897–1925) and briefly World Light Heavyweight Boxing Champion.

Mary Hardie Bamber (née Little) (Linlithgow, West Lothian, 18 January 1874–4 June 1938 in Liverpool). Often known as Ma Bamber, she was a socialist, trade unionist, social worker and suffragist. Her daughter Bessie Braddock was a prominent Labour Member of Parliament (MP). Bamber was active in Liverpool and nationally for the best part of fifty years, present at key moments in Merseyside labour history, at the forefront of several prominent disputes. As a Labour councillor and a Justice of the Peace she promoted the dissemination of contraceptive advice as a mechanism to empower women.

William Bendix. Bendix was an American film, radio and television actor, who typically played rough, blue-collar characters. He is best remembered in films for the title role in *The Babe Ruth Story* and *Lifeboat*. A native New Yorker, he was a radical and a Democrat.

George Bernanos. French author and a soldier from the First World War. Of catholic and monarchist leanings, he was nevertheless critical of bourgeois thought. Garrett read him because of his quotations, namely: 'a poor man with nothing in his belly needs hope and illusion more than bread'.

Aneurin Bevin. A miner from a mining background, Nye Bevan was a Welsh Labour Party politician who was the Minister for Health in the post-war Attlee government from 1945 to 1951. He is credited with the founding of the NHS.

Beyond the Horizon, Eugene O'Neill. Pulitzer Prize winning play premiered 1920.

The Blue Riband. This is an unofficial accolade given to the passenger liner crossing the Atlantic Ocean westbound in regular service at the highest speed. Traditionally, a ship is considered a 'record breaker' if it wins the eastbound speed record, but is not credited with the Blue Riband unless it wins the more difficult westbound record against the Gulf Stream.

Board of Guardians. Boards of Guardians were ad-hoc authorities that administered Poor Law in the UK from 1835 to 1930. See page 98 and below for The Poor Law.

Boce (possibly from Bosun). Master, or person of authority (US).

Boer War (1889–1902). Rebellion by the South African Republic and the Orange Free State against Great Britain. Britain eventually won the conflict primarily using Empire troops from Africa, Canada, New Zealand and Australia. Both republics were incorporated into the Union of South Africa in 1910.

Jack Braddock met his future wife and campaigning Liverpool Labour MP, Bessie Braddock, at a Labour Party meeting in 1922. He became the leader of the Labour Party in Liverpool from 1948 until his death in 1963. Braddock also held the position of leader of Liverpool City

Council from 1955 till 1961 and again in 1963. Although radical in his younger days and a member of the Communist Party, he later, along with his wife Bessie Braddock moved to the right of the Labour Party.

Elizabeth Margaret Braddock (née Bamber; 24 September 1899–13 November 1970). Better known as 'Bessie', she was a British Labour Party politician who served as Member of Parliament (MP) for the Liverpool Exchange division from 1945 to 1970. Although, like her husband Jack, Bessie was originally a member of the Communist Party, she moved steadily to the right and became a bitter opponent of the left wing of the Labour Party.

Bully beef. Low-grade corned beef. Staple of First World War British troop rations.

Michael Collins (1890–1922). Irish politician and soldier in the struggle for Irish independence. He was killed in an ambush in the Irish Civil War in 1922.

Colonel Bogey. The 'Colonel Bogey March' is a popular march that was composed in 1914 by Lieutenant F.J. Ricketts (1881–1945). It was played here as a humorous retort to the town of Rugby's poor treatment of the Hunger Marchers. Described as a national anthem to rudeness when the tune was put to the lyrics of the war time song 'Hitler Has Only Got One Ball', it's clear it was already seen as a rude song at the time Garrett refers to it in 1922.

Congress of Industrial Organisations (CIO). A direct link to the pre-war Wobbly movement in that its aim was to organise the margin-alised and unskilled workers. In contrast to the earlier movement it became a broad-based mass movement particularly within the automobile industry. It broke previously racial and gender lines and was a dominant force for the unskilled between 1935 and 1955.

Jerry Dawson. The Unity Theatre in Liverpool was formed by directors Jerry Dawson and Edgar Criddle as the Merseyside Left Theatre in 1936. George Garrett walked in off the street and offered his services. In 1944 it became Merseyside Unity Theatre. The company was radical and experimentalist, staging classics alongside contemporary left-wing theatre and its aim was to make theatre accessible to everyone. Jerry Dawson remained a lifelong friend and supporter of Garrett.

Dixie. A large iron pot used for cooking.

Doxology. A short hymn of praise in various forms of Christian worship.

Robert Edwards (16 January 1905–4 June 1990). Usually known as Bob Edwards, he was a British trade unionist and an Independent Labour Party (ILP) and Labour Co-operative politician. Edwards was a Member of Parliament (MP) from 1955 to 1987.

Ralph Ellison. This quote is from the prologue to Ralph Ellison's novel *Invisible Man* (first published in 1952). Ellison's novel examines the nature of being a black man in America in the first half of the twentieth century, exploring the social and psychological effects of being treated as a 'non-being' by a racist society.

The Emperor Jones, Eugene O'Neill. Play premiered 1920. Adapted for film in 1933 starring Paul Robeson.

William Empson (1906–1984). Literary critic and Shakespearean authority.

The Fellowship of Reconciliation. The first body to use the name 'The Fellowship of Reconciliation' was formed as a result of a peace pact made in August 1914 at the outbreak of the First World War. In Britain, its founders were Quakers committed to non-violent progress between opposing groups within or between countries. In Liverpool, it worked to improve relations between Catholics and Protestants.

Barry Fitzgerald (William Joseph Shields, 1888–1961). Irish film and theatre character actor.

Francisco Franco (1892–1975). General and dictator of Spain following the Nationalist victory over the republic in the Spanish Civil War (1936–1939).

Douglas Garman (1903–1969), poet, radical and publisher.

Mahatma Ghandi (Mohandas K. Gandhi, 1869–1948). Often referred to with the title 'Mahatma' (Great Soul), he was a key figure in the Indian freedom struggle. At the time Garrett was speaking, Gandhi was already well known for his anti-racist and civil rights campaigning in South Africa, before returning to India in 1915 to lead the struggle for India's independence.

The Ghetto Pastoral. Michael Gold was one of the first writers to suggest that great literature could be produced in the tenements of the lower East side of New York and other areas of high immigration. This included the street vernacular later associated with Damon Runyand and Eugene O'Neil. Gold set up a number of writing groups and magazines in New York.

James Gleason (1882–1959). American actor, playwright and screen-writer. Typically played fast-talking cop or reporter.

Michael Gold (Itzok Isaac Granich, 1894–1967). New York born poet, essayist and activist.

Maxim Gorky. Russian and Soviet writer and founder of the social realist literary method. His great autobiographical work, *My Universities*, begins with his early working life on the docks of Odessa.

Antonio Gramsci (Italian Marxist, 1891–1937). Best known for his theory of cultural hegemony, which describes how the state and ruling capitalist class – the bourgeoisie – use cultural institutions to maintain power in capitalist societies.

The Great Crash or Wall Street Crash (1929). Marked the end of the 'Roaring Twenties', and followed overproduction in the US agricultural sector and excessive speculation on stock and shares. The crash marked the beginning of the Great Depression that would come to epitomise the 1930s.

The Hairy Ape, Eugene O'Neill. Classic, dramatic production of life depicted below decks of a transatlantic liner and how the stokers were portrayed by polite society. First produced by the Provincetown Players in 1922 and later transferred to New York.

Wally Hannington. Hannington was a founding member of the Communist Party of Great Britain in 1920 and National Organiser of the Unemployed Workers' Movement, from its formation in 1921 to the last hunger march in 1935.

James Hanley. 'Great neglected genius of the British Novel' (*The Times* obituary 1985). Always maintained he was born in Dublin in 1901 but in reality, born in dockside Liverpool in 1897 and like Garrett went to sea. Maintained a furious pace of production from the 1930s until his death. Buried in Wales.

The Hogarth Press. Founded by the Woolfs in 1917 at their home in Richmond. Expanding in the interwar years, after 1938 the Press was run by Leonard Woolf and John Lehmann. Today it is an imprint of Random House.

Henrik Ibsen (1828–1906). Major Norwegian playwright, dramatist and poet.

International Brigades. The International Brigades were a number of volunteer paramilitary units which fought on the side of the Spanish Republic during the 1936–1939 Civil War. Often, but not always, linked to the Communist International, the Brigadiers were leftists who, as the name implies, travelled from abroad to fight in Spain, with over 30,000 men and women from upwards of 20 countries eventually being involved with the Brigades at one point or another during the war.

Irish Patriotic Strike – see Dr Daniel Maddix below.

Christopher William Bradshaw Isherwood (1904–1986). English-American novelist. His best-known works include *The Berlin Stories* (1935–1939), two semi-autobiographical novellas which were adapted into the acclaimed film *Cabaret* (1972).

Lewis Jones (1897–1939). Writer and political activist of the left, Jones was born in Clydach Vale in industrialised South Wales. He occupies an honourable place in the history of left-wing politics in Britain, and in the ranks of socialist writers. Like many young activists of his generation Jones attended the Central Labour College in London from 1923–1925, where he joined the Communist Party of Great Britain. During the 1926 General Strike he was imprisoned for three months in Swansea Prison for his trade union activities in the Nottinghamshire coalfield.

Bonar Law (1858–1923). Andrew Bonar Law was a prominent Conservative politician and prime minister 1922–1923. He was an opponent of Irish Home Rule and advocate of tariff reform.

David Herbert Richards 'D.H.' Lawrence (1885–1930). English novelist, poet, playwright, essayist, literary critic and painter.

Lawrence and Wishart. Founded in 1936 by the merger of a number of radical publishers, Lawrence and Wishart continues to be a leading publisher of communist, radical and libertarian/anarchist literature.

The Left Book Club. Founded by Victor Gollancz, the Left Book Club was a publishing group that exerted a strong far-left influence in the UK from 1936 to 1948. It offered a monthly book choice, for sale to members only, as well as a newsletter that acquired the status of a major political magazine. It also held an annual rally. Membership peaked at 57,000, but after the Soviet-Nazi non-aggression pact of 1939, it disowned its large Communist element, and years of paper-rationing led to further decline. It ceased publishing in 1948.

Beatrix Lehmann (1903–1979). Beatrix Alice Lehmann was a British actor, theatre director, writer and novelist.

Rosamond Lehmann (1901–1990). Author of *Dusty Answer* and member of the Bloomsbury group of writers.

Little Red Songbook. Compilation of songs used by I.W.W. (Wobblies). Published 1909.

Liverpool race riots (1919). The 1919 race riots affected a number of port cities in the UK, including Liverpool, Glasgow, Cardiff and South Shields. The riots took place in a context of post-war demobilisation, but were caused in large part by racist attitudes across British society to black and other colonial men and women who had arrived in the UK during the war. Tensions caused by these attitudes led to a prolonged period of rioting during 1919. In Liverpool, Charles Wotton, a 24-year-old sailor from Bermuda, was chased by a mob from his lodgings to the docks, where he was either thrown or jumped in to the River Mersey, and then pelted with objects until he drowned. It was in this context that Garrett was speaking.

John Lucas (born 1937). Poet, critic, biographer, anthologist, literary historian and Professor Emeritus at the Universities of Loughborough and Nottingham Trent, John also founded Shoestring Press and has played a major role in the rediscovery of many lost or excluded voices.

It was through John Lucas that Michael Murphy came to edit *The Collected George Garrett* at Nottingham Trent University.

Alderman Terence McSwiney, Mayor of Cork. An Irish playwright, author and politician, he was elected as Sinn Fein Mayor of the City during the Irish War of Independence. He was arrested by the British on charges of sedition and imprisoned in Brixton Prison. His death (at the prison) in October 1920 after 74 days on hunger strike brought him and the Irish struggle to international attention. He became one of the heroes of the independence movement.

Victor Maclaglen (1886–1959). Anglo American Academy Award winning actor. Often played pugnacious Irishman.

Dr Daniel Maddix, Roman Catholic Archbishop of Sydney and passionate supporter of Irish independence. It was reported that a crowd of 200,000 waved him off from Circular Quay on his proposed journey to New York, Liverpool and Dublin in 1920. It was the White Star Owners' refusal to carry him across the Atlantic that led to the revolt by the Liverpool stokers that precipitated the Irish Patriotic Strike.

Karl Marx (1818–1883). Communist philosopher, revolutionary writer, political economist and lead theorist of communism.

The Mass Observation Movement. Launched by Tom Harrisson (an anthropologist), along with Humphrey Jennings (a painter and film-maker) and Charles Madge (a poet and journalist), the movement was an attempt to create an 'anthropology of ourselves' documenting the everyday lives of 'ordinary' people in Britain by combining academic anthropological fieldwork by investigators with diaries and records collected from people across the UK.

RMS *Mauretania* (1906–1939). A transatlantic passenger liner of the Cunard Line. Held the Blue Riband (award for fastest trans-Atlantic crossing) for twenty years. Garrett served on the *Mauretania*, which he referred to as 'one of the big-scouse boats' between February and May 1918. His short story *The 'Maurie'* is based on his experiences in the ship's engine room, which he described as 'like a subterranean theatre'.

Mask of Anarchy (or, alternatively, *Masque of Anarchy*) was written by the poet Percy Bysshe Shelley in 1819 as a response to the Peterloo massacre in Manchester. Army cavalry were charged into a crowd of protestors, who were demanding Parliamentary reform, in St Peter's Field, resulting in the deaths of 15 people and injuries to hundreds of others.

Means Test. A means of determining whether an individual or family is eligible for state support, dependent upon circumstance. Garrett fought against the demeaning application of this system, one of the main grievances which led to the creation of the National Unemployed Workers Movement.

Merseyside Left Theatre. Established in the 1930s in response to the Spanish Civil War, the company was radical and experimentalist, and staged contemporary left-wing theatre plays across the Merseyside region to raise awareness and support for the Spanish people in their fight against international fascism. George Garrett was one of its founding members.

Michael Murphy (1965–2009). A Liverpool-born poet and academic who brought together for the first time Garrett's short stories in *The Collected George Garrett* (Trent Editions, 1999). In 2001 he won the Geoffrey Dearmer Prize, awarded by *The Poetry Review* to the New Poet of the Year. He has published three collections of poetry, edited *Kenneth Allott: Collected Poems* (Salt, 2008) and with Deryn Rees-Jones, edited *Writing Liverpool: Essays and Interviews* (Liverpool University Press, 2007).

Benito Mussolini (1883–1945). Fascist dictator of Italy from 1922–1943.

The National Unemployed Workers' Movement. Set up in 1921 by members of the recently formed Communist Party, its purpose was to draw attention to the plight of unemployed workers during the post-First World War slump, the aftermath of the 1926 general strike and Means Test, and the Great Depression of the 1930s.

New Masses. The magazine was produced by the Communist party in 1926. It echoed many of the changes in America from its predecessor, *The Masses*, in the transition from Anarchism and Syndicalism, and support of the Wobblies to a more formal Communist party position. It was strong during the Roosevelt administrations of 1932–1944, designed to encourage working-class voices. Its first editors had come from the Ghetto Pastoral movement.

New Writing (published from 1936–1950). This was a series of periodical publications established by Lehmann for Penguin. Anti-fascist in inclination, the series featured a number of writers, including Orwell and Tom Harrisson.

Clifford Odets (1906–1963). American playwright born in Philadelphia in 1906. A protégé of Eugene O'Neill, his works were also influenced by Sean O'Casey. His most famous work is *Waiting for Lefty*.

Eugene O'Neill, Provincetown Playhouse Theatre. The Provincetown Playhouse is a historic theatre at 133 Macdougal Street in Greenwich Village, Lower Manhattan, named for the Provincetown players who converted the former bottling plant into a theatre in 1918 after their early plays had been produced in a warehouse on a fishing wharf in Provincetown, Massachusetts. The original players were Eugene O'Neill, Edna St Vincent Millay and Djuna Barnes. The theatre gave an opportunity for O'Neill to turn his one-act radical plays about dockside culture into fully fledged productions that later transferred to Broadway.

Brian O'Nolan / Flann O'Brien / Myles na gCopaleen – Brian O'Nolan (1911–1966). Irish novelist, playwright and satirist, considered a major figure in twentieth-century Irish literature.

Alan O'Toole. O'Toole was a great but sadly unrecognised literary historian from Liverpool who first placed Garrett's, Hanley's and Phelan's work in the context of Liverpool Irish Seamen Writers.

George Orwell, *The Road to Wigan Pier* (published 1937). Seminal work on poverty and the bleak living conditions among the working class in Lancashire and Yorkshire before World War II. The second half explores Orwell's middle-class upbringing, the development of his political conscience, questioning British attitudes towards socialism and socialists in particular. It was particularly this latter part that Garrett regarded as 'one long sneer'.

Thomas Paine (1737–1809). English revolutionary and author of *Rights of Man*.

The Palmer immigration raids (November 1919–January 1920). Led by the Department of Justice and the US Attorney General, A. Mitchell Palmer, the raids were attempts to deport suspected left-wing radicals to their country of origin. They were part of the wider 'Red Scare' which took place in post-war America.

Jim Phelan (1895–1966). Irish 'tramp' writer and contemporary of both Hanley and Garrett. Started to publish in 1937 after a lengthy prison sentence and continued to write and wander until he died in 1966.

'Pie in the Sky', 'Dump the bosses off your back' and 'There is power, there is power in a band of working men'. Songs associated with the Industrial Workers of the World (The 'Wobblies') and included in the *Little Red Songbook* published March 1916.

The Poop Deck. Commonly referred to as 'the poop', this was a deck that forms the roof of a cabin built into the rear, or 'aft' part of a ship.

The 1834 Poor Law Amendment Act. In 1834 the Poor Law Amendment Act, widely known as The Poor Law, was designed to reduce the cost of looking after the poor by dividing people into the 'deserving' and 'undeserving' poor. It resulted in many people being forced into workhouses to get support from the government.

The Quiet Man. 1952 film directed by John Ford featuring Wayne, Barry Fitzgerald, Victor Mclaglen and Maureen O'Hara.

Red International of Labour Unions. Running from 1921 to 1937, the RILU was the Communist International's body dedicated to promoting Communism in trade unions.

'Red Scares' (1919). Given the context of events in Soviet Russia and elsewhere in Europe after the 1917 revolution, the period 1919–1920 was marked by heightened fears of left-wing radicalism in the US, particularly Bolshevism and anarchism. The Palmer raids (see above) were one consequence of this, but the era was marked by heightened struggles between organised labour and capital, as well as restrictions on freedom of expression.

John Edgell Rickword, MC (1898–1982). Rickword was an English poet, critic, journalist and literary editor. He became one of the leading communist intellectuals active in the 1930s. He was born in Colchester, Essex and served as an officer in the British Army in the First World War, having joined the Artists' Rifles in 1916, being awarded a Military Cross. He was a published war poet, and collected his early verse in *Behind the Eyes* (1921).

Alexei Sayle. Liverpool-born writer, comedian and actor born 1952. His parents were committed Communists. Provided the voiceover for the George Garrett Archive video.

Molly (Malka) Sayle (1915–2013). Lifelong radical activist, mother of comedian Alexei Sayle.

F. Scott Fitzgerald. *Tales of the Jazz Age* (1922) is a collection of eleven short stories divided into three separate parts according to subject matter. It includes one of his better-known stories, 'The Curious Case of Benjamin Button' but it was his novels, *This Side of Paradise* and *The Beautiful and Damned* published also in the early 1920s that characterised him as the writer of the jazz age and most associated with the American post-First World War boom, particularly in New York and Chicago.

Secker and Warburg. Formed in 1935, the company was both anti-fascist and anti-communist in its publishing ethos. Today it is known as Harvill Secker following a merger in 2005 with the Harvill Press.

Seven-league boots (from European folklore). They allow the person wearing them to take strides of seven leagues per step, giving them great speed.

Percy Bysshe Shelley (1792–1822). Romantic poet.

Simon and Schuster. Founded in New York in 1924, it continues today as a subsidiary of CBS Corporation.

Charles Montagu Slater (1902–1956). Slater was an English poet, novelist, playwright and librettist. He joined the Communist Party in about 1927. In 1934 he founded the *Left Review*, becoming its editor while publishing literary criticism, plays, poems, short stories and film scripts, often using the pseudonym 'Ajax'.

Sir Stephen Harold Spender CBE (1909–1995). English poet, novelist and essayist who concentrated on themes of social injustice and the class struggle in his work.

Sprayport's large Hall plateau. Liverpool's St George's Hall and Plateau, a popular gathering place for demonstrations and rallies, and where the unemployed demonstrations Garrett refers to took place in 1921–1922. Also, referred to are Liverpool's Central Library, Walker Art Gallery and Sessions Courts on William Brown Street.

Johan August Strindberg (1849–1912). Major Swedish playwright, novelist, poet and essayist.

'That Four-Flusher Prospero'. A 'Four-Flusher' is a US military colloquialism for a braggart, a cheat, a pretender, a humbug. Garrett's essay appeared alongside essays on *Othello* and *Timon of Athens* by Shakespeare expert, William Empson (note taken from original in *The Collected George Garrett* by Michael Murphy).

Tickler and Macconachie. According to David Tuffley's *Battlefield Colloquialisms of World War I (1914–1918)* the term 'Tickler' refers to TICKLER'S, which was a jam from the brand name of a company in Hull, Yorkshire, although it became synonymous with other jams, the tins of which were used to make improvised hand grenades packed with nails, glass and explosives. A maconachie was a tinned vegetable stew ration, named after the manufacturer. Michael Murphy, in his notes to *The Collected George Garrett* writes that 'A "tickler" is a rolled cigarette, or the tobacco for making a cigarette'.

Millie Toole. A biographer whose publishing career began when she published *Our Old Man*, a biography of her father Joseph Toole, radical mayor of Salford in the 1930s. Her most well-known work was the biography of Bessie Braddock in Liverpool in the late 1950s. She received a great deal of help from Garrett about the stormy years of early communism in the city.

Transport Workers' Strike, Liverpool (1911). The boiling hot summer of 1911 brought a series of strikes across the Liverpool waterfront amongst seamen, dockers and railwaymen, and brought the city to a different sense of order. Eric Taplin, historian of the early Dockworkers Unions, deals with these events in detail in his book

Near to Revolution: the Liverpool General Transport Strike of 1911. The outcome was the radical mass unionisation of the casual workers of Liverpool.

Tribune **magazine.** Founded in 1937 as a democratic socialist newspaper, it was an attempt to create a united anti-fascist front between the Labour party and other socialist parties/movements in the UK, and remains in circulation.

Waiting for Lefty. Highly influential one-act play by Clifford Odets, first performed at the Civic Repertory Theatre in New York in 1935. The play focuses on members of the Taxi Drivers Union during a strike and how they deal with personal, political and economic pressures.

Auberon Alexander Waugh (1939–2001). English journalist, whose eldest son was the writer Evelyn Waugh. He was commonly known by his nickname Bron.

John Wayne (Marion Mitchell Morrison, 1907–1979). Star American actor. Mainstay of John Ford rep company with Fitzgerald and Maclaglen.

White Star Line. Major transatlantic shipping line, based in Liverpool 1845–1950 (merged with Cunard in 1934).

Thomas Henry (Tom) Wintringham (1898–1949). Wintringham was a British soldier, military historian, journalist, poet, Marxist, politician and author. He was an important figure in the formation of the Home Guard during the Second World War and was one of the founders of the Common Wealth Party.

Index